Intelligent Au
Rules, Relationships and Robots

Foreword by
Keith Swenson

Published in association with

Workflow Management Coalition

25 Years of Thought-Process Leadership

Edited by
Layna Fischer

Future Strategies Inc., Book Division

Lighthouse Point, Florida

Intelligent Automation
Rules, Relationships and Robots

Copyright © 2020 by Future Strategies Inc.

ISBN-13: 978-0-9863214-7-4

Published by Future Strategies Inc., Book Division

Lighthouse Point FL 33064 USA
1.954.482.0693 fax 1.954.719.3746
www.FutStrat.com; www.BPM-Books.com; books@FutStrat.com

Publisher's Cataloging-in-Publication Data

© ISBN-13: 978-0-9863214-7-4

Intelligent Automation

/Fischer, Layna (editor)

/Swenson, Keith; Palmer, Nathaniel; Manuel, Alberto; Khoshafian, Dr Setrag; Altman, Roy; Kowalkowski, Frank; Winkler, Kay; Keirstead, Karl Walter *et al* (authors)

p. cm.

Includes bibliographical references, glossary, appendices and index.

1. Adaptive Case Management, 2. Intelligent Systems, 3. Knowledge Work, 4. Business Intelligence, 5. Business Process Technology, 6. Business Process Management, 7. Big Data, 8. Predictive Analytics, 9. Business Process Innovation, 10. Internet of Things

Table of Contents

FOREWORD: 5
Keith Swenson, Senior VP, Fujitsu America and WfMC Chair

INTRODUCTION AND OVERVIEW   11
Layna Fischer, Future Strategies Inc., USA

Part 1: Intelligent Automation

INTELLIGENT AUTOMATION   19
Nathaniel Palmer, WfMC, USA

MANAGING THE TRANSITION TO IA   25
Karl Walter Keirstead, Civerex, Canada

USING INTELLIGENT AUTOMATION TO PROMOTE ORGANIZATIONAL AGILITY   37
Roy Altman, Peopleserv, USA

THE ROLE OF DATA FOR INTELLIGENT BUSINESS PROCESSES   51
Kay Winkler, NSI Soluciones, Panama

INTELLIGENT AUTOMATION AND INTELLIGENT ANALYTICS   67
Frank Kowalkowski, Knowledge Consultants, Inc, USA

OPERATIONAL EXCELLENCE WITH DIGITAL PROCESS AUTOMATION   85
**Dr. Setrag Khoshafian, Gerry McCool, Carolyn Rostetter,
Pegasystems Inc., USA**

THE MAN AND THE MACHINE AND THE FUTURE OF WORK   97
Alberto Manuel, Microsoft, Singapore

Part 2: Award-Winning Case Studies

ALQUERÍA, COLOMBIA PROCESS INTELLIGENCE / INTELLIGENT BUSINESS OPERATIONS   107
Nominated by AuraPortal, Spain

CALIFORNIA RESOURCES CORPORATION, UNITED STATES   113
Nominated by ProcessMaker, USA

CITY OF FORT WORTH, TEXAS USA   119
Nominated by BP Logix, Inc. USA

DISCOVERY BENEFITS INC., USA   133
Hyland, USA

HOME HEALTH CARE MANAGEMENT, USA   145
Nominated by i-Sight, Canada

IBM GLOBAL SALES INCENTIVES   151
Nominated by IBM Corporation, US

IIC TECHNOLOGIES, CANADA/ INDIA/UK/US   157
Nominated by Bonitasoft, France

PALMAS CITY HALL, BRAZIL   169
SINAX Integração e Gestão de Processos, Brazil

POWERHEALTH, AUSTRALIA   177
Nominated by IDIOM Limited, New Zealand

SICOOB COOPERCREDI, BRAZIL   193
Nominated by Lecom Technology, Brazil

VINNITSA EMD CENTER (VEMC)   201
Nominated by Eccentex

Appendices

WFMC STRUCTURE AND STANDARDS INFORMATION   211
AUTHOR APPENDIX   215
INDEX   219
FURTHER READING AND RESOURCES   223

Foreword

The emergence of *intelligent automation* could not be timelier. Step back and take an overview of our world; you will see a dramatic increase in the automation of handling information in every part of society. Big data is the term of art and it goes without question that these immense data collections cannot be processed manually.

Increasing amounts of Twitter traffic, Facebook posts, and blog comments are submitted by bots instead of humans. Posts by celebrities go viral purely from the automated forwarding by bots following simple rules.

The thing you notice most about automation is that it is very powerful. Whether it is successful or good depends on how we value the results, but there is no doubt that the effect is quite influential. It gets more interesting when you apply automation to the creation of bots.

Process automation has traditionally been started by a manual activity. A business architect would use a process design tool to directly draw the process definition and that would become the core of the application that supports that process. This is changing.

1. Process Modeling is still Programming

The attraction of modeling was that a model is not a program. Programming is difficult. Programming requires highly-trained individuals. Programs have to be debugged. The dream was that a model would allow you to escape having to program things. The irony is that a model is still a program.

It is a program that is far easier to read and easier for a new person to understand, but it's still a program. The point I'm trying to make here is that the process model does not free you from most of the tasks that a programmer is engaged in while automating work at the office. Modeling is still programming and like any programming, the result must be carefully tested, it must be debugged, it must be carefully introduced into production use, and it must be maintained.

2. Office Workplaces are not Static like a Model

We understand the jobs that people do. It seems like those jobs are quite straightforward and could be programmed readily. But automation of the office tasks ignores the significant, subtle interactions going on among people who are doing the work. Office workers are often unaware of these factors because they seem so natural. When you actually automate what office workers do, then you find that it is not as straightforward as you might expect.

A business office is not as rigorously controlled as a factory. A *factory* is an environment where all aspects of the work can be controlled. The walls of the factory keep the chaos from the rest of the world out of the workplace. The controlled environment allows you to set up an assembly line where every step along the way is designed in advance. Every item that comes off the assembly line is expected to be identical. If there are variations in the items being produced, those variations are usually relatively minor. The process of putting the items together can be strictly controlled and it can happen in exactly the same order and amount of time each time.

But *office* work is not this way.

Even processes that are entirely internal to the organization need to change because the organization itself is constantly changing. New teams are organized. People take on new roles, new job assignments, and new positions. Some people leave the organization to pursue other opportunities. New products are defined that need to be handled differently and sometimes bring about new divisions in the organization. Even if your organizational structure remains the same, the people playing the roles will be constantly changing over time.

3. MODELING NOTATION IS NOT THE BEST FIT TO OFFICE WORK

BPMN[1] brought to the business process community a standard set of shapes and styles. An activity would always be a rounded rectangle. A solid line represented the control flow from activity to activity. If there was a branch in the control flow, then a diamond-shaped gateway would represent clearly that the flow might go in one or in a number of different directions. Processes would state and end with a circle shape.

We have a BPMN standard which is designed adequately for controlling a large number of servers but cannot reasonably reflect the work of people in a real organization. People designing processes with BPMN are often forced to treat human beings as if they are program units to which will be submitted jobs and from which results will be returned. Very many aspects of what people actually do in an organization cannot be described in these terms. People accept tasks without knowing in advance how they will meet those goals exactly. People advise each other on how to complete tasks and to do work. An expert is often called in for consultation. These are all things that are very hard to draw in a business process diagram in BPMN.

4. CMMN IS NOT ANY BETTER

CMMN[2] was a move to provide a more declarative style of modeling of the business process. CMMN offers some innovative capabilities to reduce constraints on the order of activities, but they still don't meet the needs of a dynamic organization for a completely different reason that we'll see in the next section.

5. PROCESSES DO NOT LEND THEMSELVES NATURALLY TO A CENTRAL CONSISTENT VIEW.

A process model, like any program, requires an omniscient view of the work being done. Let me explain what I mean by this. The model explicitly represents everything that anyone anywhere can know about the process. The process model contains a set of variables and those variables are expected to be a representation of the complete state of the process. The state of the process exists in one software system in one place in the computer system. The designer of the business process model is expecting to be able to look at a business process and have immediate access to all parts of the business process. This represents a kind of idealized process, the kind that you would express for a set of factory machines that were designed for the purpose. But humans aren't machines, and human organizations are not factories. In reality, as work is passed from department to department, it is handled and treated with differing terminology and mental maps. The vocabulary necessarily overlaps at the points of hand-off, but the detailed handling in the depth

---

[1] Business Process Model and Notation is a graphical representation for specifying business processes in a business process model.

[2] Case Management Model and Notation (CMMN) is a graphical representation for graphically expressing a Case[j], as well as an interchange format for exchanging Case models among different tools.

of the process might be impossible for someone from outside that group to understand.

The normal argument made is that all parts of the process should be uniform and should use the same terminology at every point, but again, that is not the natural way that human organizations work. To help accomplish this, a tremendous effort is spent on 'process discovery' which is where all the stakeholders get together and hammer out a common vocabulary and process to the necessarily level of depth to automate. However unnatural, it can be done by discussing the complete model with all stakeholders and getting agreement. The problems with an omniscient process model does not end when process discovery is complete.

6. MAINTAINING AGREEMENT IS A BURDEN

The problem with requiring a single agreed-upon model appears anytime anything changes. Imagine that Department X has a reorganization which affects their part of the bigger process. The stakeholder from department X will propose changes in the overall process to all the other stakeholders. If the business analyst changes the process, the only way to know the new process doesn't violate some assumptions from other stakeholders to ask them to review and approve it again. It can be a significant effort for the other stakeholders to review the changes, consider their internal constraints, and determine whether the change is acceptable. Stakeholders have other jobs, have their own fires to put out, and rarely have the free time to review the business process models again. They already did the process review and approval which took months; now you are asking them to do it again? They can't afford to do this every time any department changes. This push-back can be so significant that it can delay the change of a model for many months, in some cases years.

Don't think for a moment that the inability to change an update in processes is a technical limitation. Modern BPM systems can edit the process model and to put it into use almost instantly; often in only a few seconds. The barrier to change is an organizational one. Because the process model is shared across a number of stakeholders, it is necessary for all the stakeholders to approve any change. This requirement prevents many changes which would otherwise be easy to do.

7. AN ALTERNATIVE APPROACH

If you review all of the limitations listed above for business process models, they all add to one thing; *business process models are not agile.* They constrain the human activity to last month's or last year's process.

It seems that the solution involves avoiding a single omniscient process model for the entire process and fixing that in place by getting agreement. A possible approach is to allow different departments or different service providers to design their own parts of the models. How one department handles a job within their team is their business alone, and nobody else's business. Instead of designing an overall model, define only the hand-off points. This can be done with *service descriptions* instead of *process descriptions*.

Given a set of all the service descriptions, the software can generate the necessary process model on the fly. Given that the people doing that specific part of the process agree on that part of a process, there is no need to get agreement from the other stakeholders. Instead of defining the business process model as a single monolithic block that all stakeholders need to buy into, it federates the process into a collection of smaller pieces which can be assembled in a just-in-time way.

We are starting to see the appearance of systems that do this. It many ways it is simply applying machine learning to business processes. In exactly the way that Google does not have people organizing web pages into predefined categories, but rather has automation to consume, sort and organize your search results, this new approach does not have people make process models. Instead, it looks at behaviors of people, and 'service descriptions' that define a person's commitments, and lets the server do the work.

We are on the cusp of truly agile enterprises which are both optimized to do the most with the limited resources they have, and also able to change and adapt on a moment's notice This is the true promise of *intelligent automation*; automation that is not manually performed by humans, but automation that is constructed by the algorithms themselves from the behavioral surplus which workers generate in performing their regular daily duties.

This is not so far-fetched as you might think. If you look carefully at the chapters in this book and elsewhere, you will see the beginning of these concepts in work today.

-Keith Swenson

Excerpted from "Beyond the Business Process Model", Purple Hills Books, 2019

Introduction and Overview

Layna Fischer, Future Strategies Inc.

DESIGNING STRATEGIES AND PRACTICAL IMPLEMENTATION

Intelligent automation is about real business change and long-term value. If you're serious about transforming the nature of work in your organization through automation, you need to think beyond robotic process automation (RPA) and point solutions. A truly intelligent automation strategy utilizes a combination of powerful technologies like AI, RPA, and data access alongside established processes to work holistically, resulting in smarter systems and actionable data insights.

How Robots and AI Redefine the Rules

Robots and AI are redefining the rules for business execution and organizational agility. Investment in new technology is driven foremost by the goals increasing execution capacity (scalability) and organizational agility. Seeking more, faster, and most often with fewer personnel, enterprises prioritize technology investments which can speed time to market, to empower workers to make better-informed decisions, as well as to reduce the overhead otherwise required with delivering products and services to market.

FOREWORD

Keith Swenson, Senior VP of R&D, Fujitsu America and Chair WfMC

Intelligent automation could not be timelier. Step back and take an overview of our world; you will see a dramatic increase in the automation of handling information in every part of society. Big data is the term of art and it goes without question that these immense data collections cannot be processed manually.

Increasing amounts of Twitter traffic, Facebook posts, and blog comments are submitted by bots instead of humans. Posts by celebrities go viral purely from the automated forwarding by bots following simple rules.

The thing you notice most about automation is that it is very powerful. Whether it is successful or good depends on how we value the results, but there is no doubt that the effect is quite influential. It gets more interesting when you apply automation to the creation of bots.

Process automation has traditionally been started by a manual activity. A business architect would use a process design tool to directly draw the process definition and that would become the core of the application that supports that process. This is changing. This book explains how, why and what of Intelligent Automation.

Part 1: Rules, Relationships and Robots

INTELLIGENT AUTOMATION OVERVIEW

Nathaniel Palmer, WfMC, USA

In this opening chapter, Nathaniel Palmer explores how *Intelligent Automation* has come to the fore as a new discipline for business transformation. Over the past decade, even as we championed the need for organizational agility and adaptability, we simultaneously promoted Adaptive Case Management (ACM) from the generations of process automation which came before it. In this context, we have most often contrasted "automation" as being both limited and antiquated in the context of modern knowledge work and the inherent benefits of ACM.

Palmer describes how Intelligent Automation has emerged as a new discipline for business transformation, combining the traditional capabilities of ACM and Business Process Management (BPM) while extending these beyond what had previously been thought to be the limitations of automation.

MANAGING THE TRANSITION TO IA

Karl Walter Keirstead, Civerex, Canada

Intelligent Automation is a set of methods and technologies that allow organizations to increase operational efficiency and effectiveness.

IA integrates background orchestration provided by a method called Business Process Management [BPM], output from software applications generally described as Robotic Process Automation [RPA] and decision support assists from Artificial Intelligence [AI] to workflow/workload management platforms.

There are two ways for organizations to transition to IA. The easy way and the not-so-easy way. The purpose of this chapter is to outline a protocol for an easy transition to IA.

USING INTELLIGENT AUTOMATION TO PROMOTE ORGANIZATIONAL AGILITY

Roy Altman, Founder & CEO, Peopleserv

This paper explores why it is advantageous to move to a dynamic team-based approach, and how to overcome the obstacles to become the agile organization. Key to this approach is the introduction of a new metric; The Agility Quotient (AQ), which is intended to let companies know when they are adhering to agile principles, in order to encourage agile methods.

Roy Altman addresses the challenges organizations face and the solutions available to help companies pivot from purely hierarchical structures. But to fully understand the scope of the opportunities of moving to dynamic teams, it is necessary to understand the current challenges.

THE ROLE OF DATA FOR INTELLIGENT BUSINESS PROCESSES

Kay Winkler, Negocios y Soluciones Informáticas S.A., Panama

New technologies have assured an intuitive, non-programmatic approach for getting the most insights of all your data, intuitively. That, naturally, extends also into the realm of BPM and RPA. The ease-of-use of related platforms, in fact, has grown to such a degree that it has not only become a viable option for C-Level executive to delve into data science but rather a necessity. Here the author shed lights on what the different data components are that Business Process Management Professionals hold at their disposal and how the enterprise can gain a maximum benefit from these. The chapter also looks at the typical scenarios when it comes to harnessing the insights, stemming from process data and to all the new tendencies as well as technologies in that area, specifically data mining and process mining.

INTELLIGENT AUTOMATION AND INTELLIGENT ANALYTICS

Frank Kowalkowski, President, Knowledge Consultants, Inc.

The level of activity around the topic of intelligent automation (IA) indicates a high level of interest by management in improving the performance of their organizations. Like all waves of ideas and technologies, this one has a history as well as a mix of value and hype. Intelligent automation and intelligent analytics are in the middle of a wave and are a maturing discipline.

There is plenty of material in this book about IA so the focus of this chapter is on the analytics and how you position them to take advantage of the smarts in the automation. Automation especially automation of operational processes has become ubiquitous in most organizations. Intelligent automation involves applying analytics, and especially 'smart' analytics, to processes, mostly *operational* processes. The goal is more efficient and effective control of the process.

OPERATIONAL EXCELLENCE WITH DIGITAL PROCESS AUTOMATION (DPA)

Dr Setrag Khoshafian, Gerry McCool, Carolyn Rostetter
Pegasystems, Inc., USA

This chapter delves into the pragmatic aspects of operations improvements through the various Digital Process Automation capabilities including dynamic case management, robotic automation and artificial intelligence. It will also illustrate how digital enablers such as digital channels, cloud, and connected devices can be leveraged in DPA-enabled operational excellence best practices.

It delves even deeper into a DPA-enabled continuous improvement approach that aligns digital capabilities to lean methodology best practices: an approach that is much-needed and long overdue. It also covers the full excellence cycle from innovative ideation to dynamic execution with intelligent processes coupled with performance monitoring and best practice governance. The authors also discuss various personas in Digital Enterprises that will benefit from this pragmatic *operational excellence* approach; powered through DPA.

THE MAN AND THE MACHINE AND THE FUTURE OF WORK

Alberto Manuel, Microsoft, Singapore

Cognitive functions that fundamentally fall on creativity like scenario creation, reasoning and problem solving are tasks for which humans are, and most likely, will always be better. Machines might mimic these functions, but are not likely to duplicate them, and they will need to lean on human beings for that creative spark. Artificial Intelligence paradigms such as agent systems, evolutionary programming, reinforcement learning, automated theorem-proving, and probabilistic reasoning are looming in different industry sectors, which confronts the challenge if we are moving toward creating a new kind of digital mind that is enhancing the ability of humans to execute their work.

Alberto Manuel's ground-breaking chapter provides new horizons for what the future of work can look like by combining and blending the man and machine interface with a new set of emerging technologies.

Part 2: Award Winning Case Studies

ALQUERÍA, COLOMBIA

Nominated by AuraPortal, Spain

For 59 years, Alquería has specialized in the processing and commercialization of long-life dairy products and is now positioned in the Top 3 companies in the Colombian Dairy industry. Alquería has always sought constant evolution for business processes in its value chain, especially in critical processes such as supply and the optimization of fresh milk collection.

To stay ahead of the market, Alquería made the decision to digitally transform the company, using a Digital Business Platform to achieve real-time control of their daily processing of 1.2 million litres of fresh milk, integrating many processes including purchasing, collection, farm visits and supply to production for the entire company, consisting of 11 collection centers, 3 plants and over 1800 farms.

The competitive advantage gained is the ability to control relevant information for price calculations, including the certifications of each farm, analyzing volumes and centralized information of all the processing to analyze efficiency, pinpoint issues and calculate the probability of obtaining greater margins.

CALIFORNIA RESOURCES CORPORATION, USA

Nominated by Process Maker, USA

California Resource Corporation is a publicly traded oil and gas exploration and production company and the largest oil and natural gas producer in California on a gross-operated basis. CRC operates a world class resource base exclusively within the state of California, applying complementary and integrated infrastructure to gather, process and market production. Using advanced technology, CRCs workforce of approximately 5,000 employees and contractors focuses on safely and responsibly supplying affordable energy for California by Californians.

CITY OF FORT WORTH, USA

Nominated by BP Logix, Inc., USA

The City of Fort Worth is ranked 15th largest in the U.S. and is home to 800,000+ residents. Implementing a BPM initiative was spearheaded by the Kevin Gunn, CTO, and the City, whose vision it was to make Fort Worth the most livable and best managed city in the country. While gaining necessary support within the organization to embark on a business transformation project that involves both its residents and City employees, the City set out to digitally transform its business processes—a citywide implementation that involves almost 7000 users—and ensure that its vision becomes a reality. The effort was focused on making all City processes easier to initiate, leverage existing data, and extend it to where and how the customer needed to participate. The effort evaluated current business practices and re-engineered them to streamline the processes while integrating with other systems. Fort Worth is now rolling out its Citizens Forms Portal and looking to extend the City's previous years' achievements to citizens and those who do business with the City of Fort Worth, thereby favorably positioning the City as it vies for residents and businesses.

DISCOVERY BENEFITS, USA

Nominated by Hyland Software, USA

Since 1987, Discovery Benefits Inc. (DBI), one of the fastest-growing employee-benefits administrators in the industry, has simplified its process so its employers, participants and consultants can focus on the things that matter most. They do this by offering cutting-edge technology, instant access to information and expertise, and superior customer service. One component of that cutting-edge technology is its effective use of case management capabilities.

Most of DBI's 800+ employees interact with its case management solution on a daily basis. Its clients do as well through an online portal that allows customers to launch their own cases by submitting service requests.

HOME HEALTH CARE MANAGEMENT, USA

Nominated by i-Sight, Canada

Case management software is used by Home Health Care Management's visiting qaseworkers in eight counties. Users are nurses, physiotherapists, occupational therapists, speech therapists, social workers, dieticians and other mobile healthcare workers to report incidents, accidents, complaints and health and safety issues affecting themselves, their co-workers and their patients.

Implementation of a case management software solution improved customer service through the improved reporting of incidents, accidents, complaints and health and safety issues. It also improved operations by facilitating incident reporting from the field, saving hours of travel time and increasing the accuracy of reports. It also improved compliance with Department of Health reporting requirements and Joint Commission standards. Since implementing case management software, Home Health Care Management has saved $50,000 per year in salaries and boosted their billable hours while increasing compliance and reducing the risk of fines.

IBM GLOBAL SALES INCENTIVES

Nominated by IBM, USA

Using Robotics Process Automation (RPA) software, IBM has created an automated process to have a robot work as a delegate for sales managers. This robot, named Nano Second, can create Incentive Plan Letters (IPL) for sellers on a specific type of sales incentive plan known as a Pool Plan. The IPL is the formal agreement between IBM and each person who is eligible to be on an incentive plan.

By inventing a robot to follow a specific set of business rules and create the IPLs for 2H 2017 Pool Plans, sales managers are freed from manually entering data from other systems into the system where the IPLs are created and tracked. This has provided them with more time for other more productive engagements with their sellers and clients. In the past, managers would typically spend about 10 minutes per IPL creation. With the creation of Nano, IPLs for thousands of sellers worldwide, are created in an average of 18 seconds per letter. In total, during each cycle, sales managers who have benefited from this new process, have saved on average, about 70 minutes each.

IIC TECHNOLOGIES, CANADA /INDIA/UK/US

Nominated by Bonitasoft, France

Safer sailing in national waters with up-to-date information in Notices to Mariners.

Government Hydrographic Offices are responsible for providing up to date information necessary for safe navigation in national waters, and they issue Notices to Mariners (NtMs) to advise mariners of matters affecting navigational safety at sea.

NtMs have to be released on time and ensure that the information is accurate, clearly described, and easy for the mariner to follow. The previous nautical publications production process at one such national Hydrographic Office was a manual, Excel-spreadsheet based, desktop publishing exercise with a very complex workflow and many operational challenges.

After a lengthy, carefully-phased digital transformation implementation project with IIC Technologies, this Hydrographic Office is now using a fully integrated Workflow Management System (WfMS) on a BPM platform, integrated with the CARIS Publications Module (PM) software as their publication authoring platform.

PALMAS CITY HALL, BRAZIL

Nominated by SINAX Integração e Gestão de Processos, Brazil

Palmas is the capital and the largest city in the state of Tocantins. It is the newest state capital in Brazil, and it has the best quality of life among all municipalities in Northern Brazil. In 2017, a new project was initiated to modernize the city's public administration and citizen services with the objective of improving processes and reducing paper use. In the first year, the project has already shown several financial and productivity improvements. The Palmas City Hall initiative reflects a growing trend of Digital Transformation in the public sector in Brazil.

POWERHEALTH, AUSTRALIA

Nominated by IDIOM Limited, New Zealand

PowerHealth Solutions (Australia) provides its "Patient Billing and Revenue Collection" application [PBRC] to health organizations worldwide.

The billing rules that are used to convert patient encounter data into invoice line items are managed with the IDIOM Decision Manager, supplied by IDIOM Ltd (New Zealand). The separation of billing rules from the underlying application allows PBRC to provide bespoke billing behavior from a standard application.

SICOOB COOPERCREDI, BRAZIL

Nominated by Lecom Technology, Brazil

Founded in 1995, Sicoob Coopercredi is a Cooperative of Economy and Mutual Credit of Municipal Servers, with participation by public servants, entrepreneurs and professionals of the Western Metropolitan Region of the Capital of São Paulo State. It is duly registered and supervised by the Central Bank of Brazil. Its purpose is to unite the savings of its members, accumulating the capital of the cooperative, which becomes a fund to be loaned among the participants of this society, offered at lower interest rates. It operates within the concept of shared economy, with many exchanges and mutual gains.

By becoming an associate, the saver is encouraged to save by depositing a monthly capital share. Currently, there are more than eight thousand members participating in the decisions and enjoying the results, which have personalized services as Credit, Current Account; Debit and Credit Card; Special Check; Private Pension; Savings; Application in DRC; Consortiums; and Insurance, among others.

VINNITSA EMD CENTER (VEMC)

Nominated by Eccentex

Vinnitsa EMD Center is the full-service emergency service and major public safety agency in the Vinnitsa region of the Ukraine. There are 1,763 people in the emergency medical care system, including 248 doctors, 803 paramedics and other employees. Ambulance fleet is up to 210 cars. The agency services more than 1,460,000 citizens.

The Eccentex solution provides two major case types - incidents and service requests (transportation, blood delivery and non-emergency care.). It provides the ability to configure and implement changes in case procedures, business rules and forms on the fly as soon as possible.

The ERIM Solution implemented by Eccentex Corporation reduces response time and time to treatment by a factor of two, significantly improving chances for patient survival. Survival rates for out-of-hospital critical care treatments are now more than 23% (compared with 0.8% previously).

Section 1

Rules, Robots –
and *Relationships*

Intelligent Automation

Nathaniel Palmer, WfMC, USA

ABSTRACT

Over the past decade, even as we championed the need for organizational agility and adaptability, we simultaneously promoted Adaptive Case Management (ACM) from the generations of process automation which came before it. In this context, we have most often contrasted "automation" as being both limited and antiquated in the context of modern knowledge work and the inherent benefits of ACM.

In this chapter, we explore how "Intelligent Automation" has emerged as a new discipline for business transformation, combining the traditional capabilities of ACM and Business Process Management (BPM) while extending these beyond what had previously been thought to be the limitations of automation.

DIGITAL TRANSFORMATION AND THE NEW AUTOMATION IMPERATIVE

According to a recent survey by advisory firm Deloitte & Touche LLP, 95 percent of CEOs and 97 percent of corporate board members cited "serious threats and disruptions to their growth prospects in the next two to three years." The specific threat most frequently cited is the disruptive effect of digital technologies deployed by competitors, and their internal challenge of keeping pace via new technology investments. To put it in trendier parlance, what they fear most is *digital disruption*. What is the remedy to digital disruption? *Digital Transformation* – one of the most frequently cited phrases in current business circles. But what does it mean? In the most basic meaning, Digital Transformation is the transformation or "digitizing" of existing processes and operations into a software realization. It is not simply an "app" nor becoming a "dot-com" enterprise, but leveraging digital media (mobile apps, the Internet, smart appliances, *et al*) to connect with customers, partners, and even employers.

The *push* for digital transformation and looming *threat* of digital transformation are old news. We have all seen stories of once-dominant businesses who were run out town by digital disruption. Examples include (most famously) Blockbuster being displaced by Netflix. We see around us countless new and innovative digital natives rapidly outpacing erstwhile market leaders. We see firms such as Uber, Facebook, Airbnb, Postmates, and other success stories who ascended from ideas virtually unthinkable a decade ago to multibillion-dollar enterprises today.

While many a CEO may lay awake at night worrying about being "Uberized," a more pressing issue is how to align digital transformation with corporate governance. How do you avoid the risk of losing control of governance processes, and avoid the risks of security breaches, while ensuring digital access to your products and services by customers? Or enabling partners and employees to engage via digital media? The answer, from a technology investment standpoint is *Intelligent Automation*, the engine of digital transformation.

Intelligent Automation is the evolutionary step for Business Process Management (BPM) and workflow automation, complementing the use of business rules and process management technology with software robots and artificial intelligence (AI). The critical path to successful digital transformation (with managed risk) is combining information governance with Intelligent Automation.

DIGITIZING BUSINESS PROCESSES

Intelligent automation technologies support interactions with humans, as well as perform work as humans would do. A relatively simple example is an AI-powered "chatbot" able to interact with customers (and increasingly partners and employees) in a way which would otherwise require a human Customer Service Representative. These interactions blur the lines between human and machine. Interaction via digital media (mobile app or website) can be difficult or impossible to distinguish whether the entity on the other end of the interaction is living or virtual. They easily pass the infamous "Turing Test" (the test developed by Alan Turing in 1950 to assess machine's ability to exhibit intelligent behavior indistinguishable from that of a human.) Yet chatbots are just the thin veneer of Intelligent Automation. Rather, the processes which happen behind the scenes ultimately define digital transformation.

Specifically, a successful digital transformation strategy is one that ties together discrete moments of automation within a more comprehensive, end-to-end process, adhering to rules of corporate and information governance. Supporting this requires a clear model for the separation of concern between the rules of how work is completed and the systems that support it.

In most enterprises, the control points for enforcing the rules and policies of corporate governance focus on human beings. They are part of user interface of core business applications. Humans are part of the reporting systems for ensuring compliance with established policies and procedures. Firms focus on the actions of workers (human beings) who apply their knowhow and subjective judgment to perform work.

A chatbot may be able to check the status of an order, or an insurance claim, or even initiate one. But traditionally, the high-value work to process that claim, or fulfill that order, is left to skilled human workers. This work is often assumed to be "un-automatable" requiring logging in and out of different systems to complete the process (or even a single task). This work typically involves third-party systems or otherwise environments which cannot be integrated through a programmatic interface. Instead, people do it from swivel chairs using sticky notes, and as a result, the design of the related rules and workflows are based on how the applications were built, rather than the actual objectives of the end-to-end process which span them.

Intelligent Automation allows these existing user interfaces remain intact, enabling software robots perform the same functions as a human user. This allows the existing control points and reporting to remain intact. The work is indistinguishable between human and robot, as the same systems are used. Yet, who tells the robot what to do? This is critical role of information governance, ultimately the serving as the lifeblood of digital transformation, by enforcing the same rules that are applied to human workers and ensuring the same level of transparency (including audit trails, records management, and other means for capturing the chain of custody for how sensitive information is handled).

WHEN AUTOMATION IS INTELLIGENT AND WHEN IT ISN'T

Investment in new technology is driven foremost by the goals of increasing execution capacity (scalability) and organizational agility. Seeking to "more, faster, and most often" with fewer personal, enterprises prioritize technology investments which can speed time to market, that empower workers to make better informed decisions, as well as to reduce the overhead otherwise required with delivering products and services to market. The ability to adapt and respond according to both new events and consistent with existing rules and policies is critical to organizational agility. Yet this goal is often at odds with automation focused on scalability and repeatability. Current process automation looks a lot the picture below, with a complex set of conveyor belts designed for optimal efficiency and consistency. Industrial engineers designed the ideal routes to move packages in the most efficient way possible, and these pathways are fixed. They do not change or adapt their paths based on what is in the package.

Figure 1: Process automation currently looks a lot like these conveyors, with fixed pathways and process flows designed by architects and engineers, not adaptable to the context of work and business events

The majority of process automation systems currently deployed were designed and built in the same manner as broader business automation initiatives have been for the last few decades. This presented a model of automation rigidly following fixed pathways which are not consistent with the way we work. We do care about what's in the package. We cannot fully script out in advance the sequence of steps and end-to-end processes without knowing the exact context of any given task we will be performing. For this reason, process automation to date has been limited to repetitive and relatively simplistic process areas. When we combine case management and data-driven intelligence with process automation, we can expand the range of what can be automated or otherwise managed. This combination of capabilities enables Intelligent Automation.

What does Intelligent Automation look like? Using the same metaphor as before, see figure 2 showing one of Amazon's fulfillment centers where its Kiva robots have replaced the fixed conveyor belts. Just as we do in our own work, the robots do care and in fact know what is in the package. Using this awareness of context (what's in the package and where it's going) the robots determine the best pathways and placement of products to enable the fastest possible fulfillment process. The robots leverage process, rules and data to define pathways which adapt to the context of work at that moment, just as we need to adapt on successfully complete our work.

Figure 2: Intelligent Automation leverages the efficiency of automated actors with data-driven intelligence that leverage rules and analytics to enable goal-seeking optimization and decision making.

The combination of workflow automation and data-driven machine intelligence supports our ability to manage work while dynamically adapting the steps of a process according to an awareness and understanding of content, data, and business events that unfold. This is the basis of Intelligent Automation, enabling data-driven processes adapting dynamically to the context of the work, delivering the efficiency of automation while leveraging rules and policies to steer the pathway toward the optimal outcome. The process of the case is defined by the underlying policy and rules combined with the information that we gather along the way.

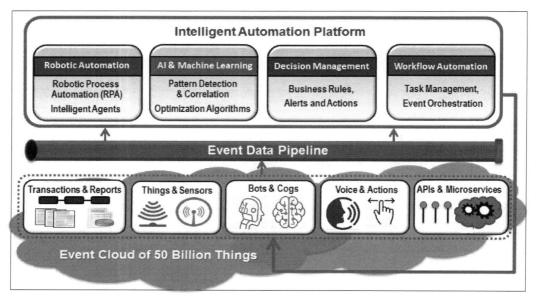

Figure 3: Intelligent Automation as an Integrated Digital Platform

ROBOTS ENTER THE WORKFORCE

Robotic Process Automation (RPA) is one of the fastest growing sectors of business technology, yet one which is often misunderstood. Some refer to RPA as, "It's just screen-scraping on steroids!" No, it is far more powerful than that. Indeed, it is merely a pillar, albeit a critical one, of Intelligent Automation. RPA itself is geared for scale and repetition. It replaces the subjective decision making applied by human beings and lacks the data-driven optimization offered through AI.

Yet while RPA correlates more closely to "Automation" than "Intelligent," its benefits can be compelling. Leveraging RPA as part of a broad Intelligent Automation approach offers the same opportunity for execution advantage, as well as an equivalent potential for business disruption, as adding physical robots into the enterprise workforce. Unlike solutions whose function is to coordinate and sequence tasks for humans to perform, RPA specifically acts on behalf of humans to perform work – e.g., RPA automates human tasks (manual work) rather than simply machine tasks, as with traditional software automation. Existing user interfaces remain intact, and the software robots perform the same functions just as a human user would do, in passing security credentials as well as entering and/or accessing data from the application it has logged into.

Intelligent Automation bridges the "islands of automation" where humans are the integration points among systems that otherwise cannot communicate. This is work which cannot be automated any other way. By definition, it requires logging in and out of different systems to complete the process (or even a single task) and these often third-party systems or otherwise environments cannot be integrated through a programmatic interface, and so they aren't. Instead humans do it, with swivel chairs and sticky notes and, as a result, the design of the related rules and workflows is based on how the applications are built, rather than the actual objectives of the end-to-end process which span them.

In Figure 3, the Intelligent Automation Platform is presented as a set of core capabilities. This visualization is intended to present the inherent synergy and interplay among sets of capabilities and does not suggest that these are modules within a tightly coupled monolithic architecture. Rather, Intelligent Automation exists as a layered architecture of best-of-breed components which work together yet most often run within their own environments. There is a necessary separation of concern between each layer, allowing for the leverage of best-of-breed components, and increasingly cloud-based services.

RPA by itself most often has no interface. It acts on behalf of the knowledge worker, rather than serving as a core system with which they interact. This underscores the fact that Intelligent Automation is not a category of software but rather a design pattern for leveraging best of breed components for delivering a powerful set of capabilities. At the foundation of any solution for either Intelligent Automation or case management in general is a data layer. This includes an Operational Data Store (ODS) for driving the actions and operations with which the knowledge work is engaged. In addition, there are necessarily one or more Systems of Record (SoR) which stores the data which comprises each case record and its supporting context.

Above the data services record are three distinct but synergistic components which provide the "brains" of Intelligent Automation. These three are RPA combined with a BPM System (BPMS) and Decision Automation package for defining and managing decision logic. On the latter, Decision Automation (or Decision Management) should be understood as more than Business Rules Engine (BRE). The engine is merely the execution, but Decision Management is a relatively new category of software which facilitates the definition and on-going management of rules and policies as distinct artifacts and business assets.

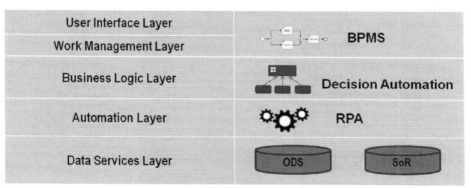

Figure 4: The Intelligent Automation Platform is derived as a layered stack of best-of-breed cots components

THE THREE R'S OF INTELLIGENT AUTOMATION

So far, we have discussed in quite detail about the role of Rules and Robots in Intelligent Automation. In many discussions "robots" and "AI" are treated as interchangeable when the reality is that with AI, we typically mean is learning systems; Machine Learning and neural networks (part of the domain of "Probabilistic AI"). In the context of robots, we're talking about something that is very prescriptive. In this context we can think of RPA as example of "Deterministic AI" which driven entirely by instruction sets. RPA doesn't make independent decisions other than that which is driven by business rules. Rules are by necessity unambiguous. There's no room for nuance or ambiguity with business rules or robotic automation.

The "Three R's" of Intelligent Automation are Rules, Robots – and *Relationships*.

The third R for Relationships related to how Intelligent Automation shifts the focus toward providing intelligence is understanding how to *get* data as opposed to having to *replicate* and *store* that data locally. Think about how many sources of data are used to present the complete view of a given customer. It is no longer the case that you can expect a single customer data repository. Rather, we may have single meta-model capturing the dimensions of that customer, yet the data required to complete an end-to-end process with that customer will inevitably exist on a multitude of systems. Often, the majority of required data may be within systems that are outside of the span of our control.

Consider this contradiction – robots and rules require data, which increasingly lays outside of our span of control, and requires specific formatting or transformation to be usable. This is the role of the third R – Relationships. If we know where to look (i.e., if we relationship between events, rules, and data sources), we can use Robots to find data. We can also use AI to validate real-time event and predict the most likely answer when the story is otherwise incomplete. This is where Intelligent Automation may apply as "probabilistic AI" (as distinct from deterministic) to bridge the gap where data is incomplete and thus insufficient to satisfy the requirement for rules and robots.

By knowing meaningful context about data, then applying Machine Learning and other packaged AI capabilities is required for predictive capabilities. Certainly, it isn't magic, and requires that both business rules and training data are thoroughly validated and unambiguous. Yet both (rules and data) are clearest in hindsight – we see the complete picture once a process is complete. Thus, we can leverage Machine Learning to read and learn from historic data, then evaluate in live scenario what the most likely answer is. In this scenario, we would typically apply confidence thresholds to determine with the "guessed" data is acceptable or not.

For example, if transactional step as part of an automated process requires a customer's Social Security Number, which happens to be missing and not otherwise queryable, can use AI to provide likely alternative sources of information. There will likely be various potential candidates and the Intelligent Automation platform can use AI to both find options and evaluate them; selecting the option with the highest level of confidence (e.g., probability) and only allow to path through if it makes a minimum threshold, such as 90 percent confidence. To the rules or the robot, it is simply the answer they are looking for, yet the *intelligence* in Intelligent Automation is able to close the gap where there would otherwise be an error or break in the process.

WHERE TO BEGIN WITH INTELLIGENT AUTOMATION

What is the best starting point for leveraging Intelligent Automation? One strategy is to look first at repetitive human tasks, where users are bogged down performing tedious work, repetitive steps, or otherwise where users are shifting back and forth among different application interfaces as part of the task or process step. These scenarios offer low hanging fruit, yet plans shouldn't be limited to the easy targets. Rather, your strategy should lay the groundwork for horizontal scale, tying together discrete moments of automation within a more comprehensive, end-to-end process. To support this, develop a clear model for the separation of concern between the layers of Intelligent Automation (as illustrated in Figure 4) and specifically that between the capabilities traditionally associated with BPM and RPA. It is worth noting that BPM was never designed to fully replace the work done by human beings, but rather to facilitate that work by assigning tasks, sequencing steps, enforcing rules, and other means of work management. In contrast, RPA in fact is purpose-built specifically to replace work delivered less efficiently and effectively when performed by humans.

Intelligent Automation enables BPM and RPA work in concert for far more efficient and effect coordination of both knowledge work and automated tasks. While the synergy of this combination offers great potential, realizing this value does not happen by default. There is not today an established standard or methodology which prescribes the ideal interplay between BPM and RPA, and indeed some of the greatest pitfalls lie in the poorly defined separation of concern between the two. For example, one of the common mistakes is to create rules within the RPA definition which are complex, and thus miss the opportunity for separately managing decision logic (business policies and rules) from the procedural logic necessary to the automated task. No RPA platform is designed for decision management, yet a well-architected approach can and should leverage best-of-breed capabilities. As part of a broader digital transformation strategy, we use decision management to ensure consistency of business rules, as well as enable workers to make better informed, data-driven decisions.

Leveraging Decision Automation to Drive Greater Value

Consider this in the context of a use case where process automation (and increasing RPA specifically) is most frequently applied today; the replacement of (typically offshore) manual transaction processing. In this context, it is assumed that workers perform relatively repetitive tasks related to matters such as application processing or adjudication. One of the greatest challenges in these scenarios is to ensure workers follow the rules and policy guidelines for how work should be performed, which are enforced via training, work instructions and SOPs, combined with surveillance-based Quality Assurance (QA).

Imagine an alternative scenario where users are relieved of subjective decision making (i.e., having to rely on their own interpretation of policies and rules) and instead their work flows through a library of business logic where 100s or 1000s of rules are applied to validate data accuracy, to ensure consistency with policy, and to present a data-driven recommendation for the best action to take next. This provides an objective measure (actual reportable data and analytics) to demonstrate that work is performed according to established policy. It also lowers the training burden, by removing the need to understand exactly what to do at each, while ensuring greater accuracy and consistency, as each and every transaction, process step, and data element is checked automatically (rather than applying QA to only a small sample).

Tackling the End-to-End Process

Expand the aperture on this scenario and imagine BPM doing what it does best by coordinating the end-to-end process, managing the sequencing of steps and state of process as it advances the span of control from one step to the next. Now with the much finer grain definition of how work must be performed, consider that many of the steps which had previously required human intervention can now be performed by software robots, coordinated by the master process, with the instructions provided not by an automation script, but a complete set of rules and policies able to scale to the complexity of your business. There is an immensely powerful set of "digital benefits" to be realized through leveraging automation in a way which enables not only improved work management practices, but also increasing the accuracy, efficiency and quality of work performed by using standard rules, and less reliance subjective judgement, improving data quality and more accurate analytics, while delivering the ability to understand the impact rule and policy changes *before* they are implemented.

CONCLUSIONS

Imagine, for instance, transforming the 1,000s of policy pages and multiple days of training required to support your current knowledge work into a manageable and measurable set of decision models owned and controlled by business stakeholders. How about gaining a rich new source of analytics and audit data based on actual decisions made and actions taken, rather than actual surveillance-based Quality Assurance? Intelligent automation offers the ability to integrate processes, rather than systems and applications, to deliver closer to holistic or comprehensive automation of work rather requiring (far more expensive) humans to perform this work manually. This provides objective measure (actual reportable data and analytics) to demonstrate that work performed according to established policy. It also lowers the training burden by removing the need to understand exactly what to do at each step, while ensuring greater accuracy and consistency. Rather than a "black box" of backend automation, each transaction, process step, and data element is checked automatically against business rules.

Expand further the aperture on this scenario; consider the role of traditional BPM coordinating the end-to-end process, managing the sequencing of steps and state of process as it advances the span of control from one step to the next. Now with the much finer grain definition of how work must be performed, leveraging the policies and rules defined as part of business logic, many of the steps which had previously required human intervention can now be performed by "intelligent" robots. Yet these robots aren't smart, per se.

This is not AI run amok.

Rather the software robots are held to the same compliance rules and reporting standards otherwise defined for human workers but digitized as part of a transformation strategy. Over time, the scope of this automation can grow to encompass an increasing number of erstwhile human tasks, as performance data are captured, and more is understood about how the work should be performed.

This is the promise of Intelligence Automation; expanding the efficiency of automation while delivering greater transparency and policy compliance. This is why the value proposition of Intelligent Automation can be so compelling. It is the ability to integrate process, rather than systems and applications, to deliver closer to holistic or comprehensive automation of work rather requiring (far more expensive) humans to perform this work manually.

Managing the Transition to IA

Karl Walter Keirstead, Civerex, Canada

ABSTRACT

Intelligent Automation (IA) is a set of methods and technologies that allow organizations to increase operational efficiency and effectiveness.

IA integrates background orchestration provided by a method called Business Process Management [BPM], output from software applications generally described as Robotic Process Automation [RPA] and decision support assists from Artificial Intelligence [AI] to workflow/workload management platforms.

There are two ways for organizations to transition to IA. The easy way and the not-so-easy way.

The purpose of this chapter is to outline a protocol for an easy transition to IA.

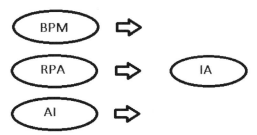

Figure 3-1: IA Integration Diagram

BACKGROUND

Industrial organizations have been using automated processes since the 11th century (i.e. mining industry).

Business-to-Business (B2B) organizations have been using workflow management methods such as BPM for around 20 years to auto-post tasks to knowledge worker InTrays, on the basis of *ability* (i.e. skill) to perform specific tasks.

Critical Path Management (CPM), the probable antecedent of BPM, goes back to the mid-1950s.

Given the early spotty history of Artificial Intelligence (AI), many IA enthusiasts recommend a go-easy approach to IA. The question therefore becomes how does/should an organization carry out an orderly transition to IA?

PRACTICAL IA

The logical starting position is a workflow/workload management platform, commonly referred to as a BPMs. Many BPMs address **operational efficiency** by providing orchestration of tasks along "best practice" workflows. Tasks post automatically to the attention of staff who have the qualifications to perform these, as tasks become "current" along workflow templates.

Unfortunately, few BPMs address **operational effectiveness**, even fewer provide supervisors with tools that accommodate periodic **non-subjective assessment of progress** toward goals/objectives.

Organizations need operational efficiency, operational effectiveness and a means of non-subjective assessment of progress toward goals/objectives.

Issues with BPMs are resolved by a transition from a traditional BPMs platform to an ACM/BPM platform. Many practitioners abbreviate ACM/BPM to "ACM" (Adaptive Case Management).

The most difficult part of the transition requires a change in mindset from "end-to-end processes", featuring plan-side goals/objectives, to "process fragments" where goals/objectives are, by necessity, parked at Cases, run-time-side. The degenerate of "process fragments" yields "processes of one-step each", leaving users to thread steps together or leaving IA to thread steps together at Cases.

ACM is a workflow/workload management platform. Add a method called F.O.M.M. (Figure of Merit Matrices [Rand Corporation]) plus a second method called R.A.L.B. (Resource Allocation, Leveling and Balancing [Civerex]) and you have the wherewithal to focus on both efficiency and effectiveness *at* Cases and *across* Cases.

Case Core Concepts

We need to pause here to define "Case": Case, not to be confused with "use Case", is a "container" that accommodates all manner of data relating to a topic of focus i.e. a patient, an insurance claim, a law enforcement investigation. The range of data needed at Cases goes from unstructured data, structured data, images, video recordings to .pdf, .docx, .pptx, etc. files.

Technically, a "Case" is nothing more than a cursor position at a Relational Database Management System (RDBMS).

- If your Case Management platform does not automatically build a Case History, complete with session dates/times and user "signatures", plus data, as it was, at the time it was input, on the data display/data collection Form versions that were in service at the time, you have a problem.

- If your platform builds Case Histories but allows editing of session recordings, you have a problem.

- If your platform does not accommodate reachout/data import from/to Cases, you have a problem.

A generic data exchanger accommodates custom mapping of data elements, custom data encryption and push/pull data transport, resulting in strict need-to-know data exchange.

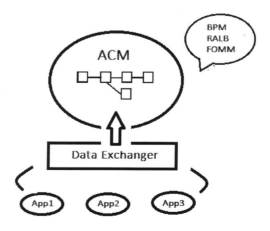

Figure 3-2: Case Essentials

Don't try to transition to IA without ACM/BPM/FOMM/RALB and data exchange facilities.

Here's why ...

The ACM\BPM\FOMM\RALB combo overcomes the rigidity of traditional BPM, by allowing users to micro-schedule their tasks at their InTrays, allowing Case Managers to dynamically prioritize/re-prioritize tasks across users and allowing Case Managers to make periodic non-subjective assessments of progress toward meeting Case goals/objectives.

Users like to micro-schedule their own tasks. Organizations don't want Case Managers making arbitrary assessments of progress toward meeting Case goals/objectives.

Users of ACM in the healthcare sector immediately bond with "Patient Cases". Users in the insurance sector, where a Case is an insurance claim, similarly have no problem with the term Case. Same for Law Enforcement. If your focus, on the other hand, is providing MRO (Maintenance, Repair, Overhaul) for Blackhawk helicopters, references to Cases can cause eyebrows to raise. Looks like we are stuck with "Case".

Some tasks at Cases can readily be automated by software, so the easy way to automate such tasks requires nothing more than setting up an ACM platform and letting the software auto-post these tasks to the virtual InTray of a user called "System".

User System is a user in the usual sense of the word – except that it does not physically need to log into the platform. Any process fragment step that has an encoded skill designation of System "posts" to the "attention" of user System as and when the step becomes current along a workflow. The posted step becomes a task.

In order for a task to be capable of being performed by System, a rule set must be present at the task. The rule set must be capable of progressing the state of a task from "pending" to "completed", with no user involvement.

Here are two examples of BPM task automation:

   a) A *'gatekeeper'* process **step** (Step #2) along a process or process fragment, waiting for data to become available, automatically impeding/allowing the workflow to move forward based on data available at the step. The data comes from Forms at tasks upstream from the gatekeeper step or the data comes from the Case itself, typically as a result of imported data sourced by local or remote systems and applications;

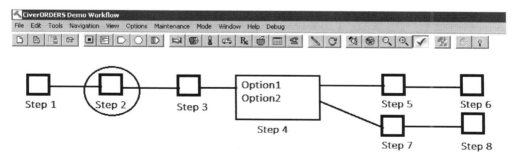

Figure 3-3: Gatekeeper Workflow Step

b) **Auto-branching** along a process fragment workflow to one or more sub-paths at **'branching decision boxes'** (Step 4), based on data values. A rule set is required at each branching decision box option. The data "fires" the option if the master variable at the option's rule set evaluates to TRUE.

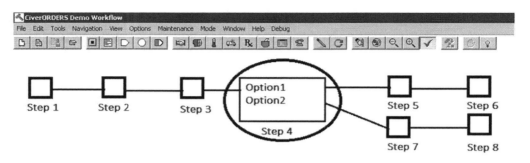

Figure 3-4: Branching Decision Box Workflow Step

We will revisit these two examples, upgrading their rule set automation by adding IA (Intelligent Automation).

We will find that it is not easy to distinguish between a rule set that gives the user the impression of providing behavior adaptation at a Case and IA, which provides behavior adaptation.

It probably is not worth it to try too hard to comply with IA eligibility.

What counts is to onboard staff (across the organization) to a mindset that retains a focus on increasing operational efficiency and effectiveness.

Enter RPA

RPA can provide automation *across* local and remote systems and applications that are not able to seamlessly communicate with each other.

An RPA application is a stand-alone software application. It does not perform interventions across local and remote applications above and beyond what a user can do by navigating the User Interfaces of these applications.

e.g.

A Case that supports orchestration from background BPM can send a message to a system/application and get back a response that consists of new or augmented data.

The message launching must be triggered at a process fragment process step.

Any data essential to the remote processing request must be exported, formatted and then transported (or picked up), such that the local or remote system and application can import the data for processing/data enrichment.

Responses need to be exported from the local or remote system or application, formatted, transported and imported back to the BPMs.

This is not RPA.

Consider, on the other hand, the scenario where a local or remote system or application is NOT capable of accepting\processing messages, except via an official User Interface.

I.e. the application has only one mode of use, that of simulating a logged-in user navigating a menu bar and/or navigating an icon bar within the application.

An RPA app (RPA is both a method and an application system) saves the day by allowing a user to say, "*watch me while I do this, once, then repeat my sequence 'n' times*". (e.g. navigate to a target listbox line item at a local or remote source application, advance the cursor to the "next" line item, copy specific data from a data collection form at the line item, set the focus to a listbox at a second application, advance the cursor to the "next" listbox line item in the second application listbox, and effect a paste).

Note the difference; BPM effects reachout/import to/from application systems **from** a BPM task along a workflow template at a Case, whereas RPA replicates what a user does by navigating the UIs of various application systems.

Both methods bring new/augmented data back to the Case.

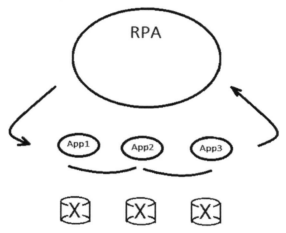

Figure 3-5: Robotic Process Automation at a Case

In this example, a human user copies a data value "d1" from a Case, navigates to App1, where d1 is enriched to a data value "d1, D1".

The user now navigates to App2 where "d1, D1" becomes "d1, D1, D2", then at App3 we have "d1, D1, D2, D3" that goes to the Case.

Because many RPA interventions are one-time interventions and because little or no coding is required to generate an RPA script, scripts can be preserved for future use if you anticipate needing to return to these, or, for a script you are likely to use once and only once, you can cast the script aside after use.

What is important regarding the use of RPA is that it be non-intrusive. The extent of an RPA intervention does not go beyond what a human is able to do at/from a Case.

You won't want or need RPA to go beyond this.

Enter AI

Let's raise the bar by requiring that *some* automated tasks at Cases must be capable of "learning".

Whereas BPM and RPA processing is all about automation of tasks that belong to an organization's "best practices", the introduction of AI allows on-the-fly improvement of these best practices via changes to best practices tasks or by the introduction of tasks not in the organization's best practices inventory.

Tasks that are not fully automated but provide decision-support to humans also qualify as AI.

About "Best Practices"

The term "best practices" deserves some attention.

All organizations have "best practices"; it's what they do.

Best Practices can exist only in the minds of staff, or, they can be on paper, be on-line or be in-line.

In-line best practices are low-hanging fruit for IA because the term "in-line" implies that workflow steps already have plan-side skill category tags plus attached context-appropriate data collection Forms.

Following "compilation" of a process fragment workflow, individual steps automatically post to the attention of the *right* workers at the *right* time at run-time platforms.

These platforms can:

a) support **orchestration** from background BPM,

b) support **efficiency** assists such as RALB (Resource Allocation, Leveling and Balancing

c) support **effectiveness** assists such as FOMM (Figure of Merit Matrices)

What is "compilation"? Software developers who write computer code use compliers to convert their code to .exe files that users can access to launch application systems.

Process mappers build graphic workflows and use compilers that, with one mouse click, carve up their workflows into easily managed "steps" that ACM workflow/workload platforms can post to specific classes of users at their ACM InTrays, at the right times and places. Significant time savings result from dispatching steps to skill categories as opposed to dispatching steps to named individuals (i.e. the first to "take" a task owns the task and is expected to complete it).

Without a process map compiler, the only option you have to manage workflow is to stare at a graphic process map.

CPM (Critical Path Method) users stopped doing this in the 1970s.

AI incorporates "machine learning" by allowing software and robots to perform interventions at Cases that "best practices" process mappers have not anticipated.

Here is an example of processing using AI:

I instruct a robot to go down a hallway, enter the first room where the door is not locked, and wait.

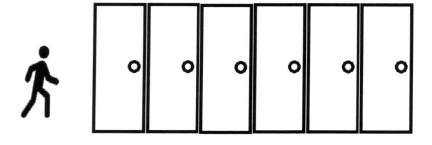

Figure 3-6: Robot, following instructions

If all doors are locked, a non-AI robotic process with an incomplete set of navigation rules will have the robot standing at the end of the hall at the last door.

The same scenario incorporating AI will have the robot back at the dispatch point. i.e. the robot will figure it followed instructions, but given there are no more doors to try, it would be pointless to stay at the end of the hall, so after a brief wait time, the robot decides to return to the dispatch point.

Notice how potentially dangerous AI can be when all outcomes for a scenario have not been anticipated e.g. the point of dispatch/origin is a ship at dock, the robot walks off the ship and the ship immediately leaves the dock. The fix for this might be to have a bodycam on the robot that can sense abrupt changes in height.

It's not easy to differentiate between behavior driven by a set of rules relative to "learned behavior". A generic rule for the robot scenario might be to have the robot be sensitive to lack of movement, except at the home base. This would solve the problem of an infinite wait time where no doors along the hall are unlocked but it could also solve the problem of an obstruction at any point along the hall that would prevent the robot from advancing to the next door along the hall.

Turning to a more practical example of IA, let's revisit our "gatekeeper" process step automation example to see if we can upgrade the automation at this step to Intelligent Automation.

"A 'gatekeeper' process step along a process or process fragment waiting for data to become available, automatically allowing the workflow to move forward as and when data needed at the step becomes available."

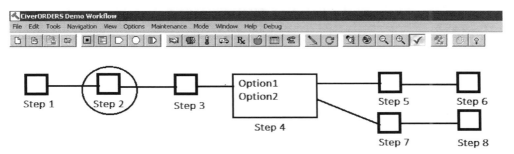

Figure 3-7: Gatekeeper Step along a Workflow

Clearly, the gatekeeper process step (i.e. Step *2*) needs a cycle time attribute to accommodate periodic testing. If Step *2* needs two (2) data values from Step *1*, a rule set at Step 2 along the lines of

If (a=TRUE) and (b=TRUE), then "fire"

will result in the processing moving on to Step 3.

Suppose the above gatekeeper process step (i.e. Step 2) is part of a workflow that has a time goal at the end node of the workflow.

Clearly, we can easily log the number of "tries" at the gatekeeper process step (i.e. looking for data to become available) and have an in-line rule that reads "escalate this process step if the step remains current longer than 4 hours".

The amount of escalation can be adjusted via reference to the time goal of the best practice (less time remaining -> more escalation; more time remaining -> less escalation).

Since the gatekeeper task knows what data it is waiting for, it would not be difficult to scan all upstream current-step Case Forms to discover the source of the needed data and auto-escalate other steps within the Case.

If the needed data comes, in part, from a local or remote application, a similar scan of pending outreach requests for data could identify outreaches where a re-send of the request (with an escalation request) should be effected.

Let's replicate the analysis for the 2nd example we looked at earlier.

"Auto-branching along a process fragment workflow to one or more sub-paths at 'branching decision boxes', based on data values. A rule set is required at each branching decision box option."

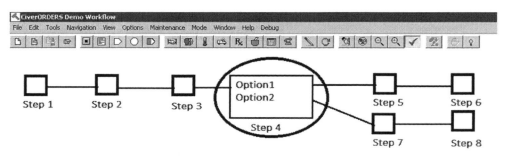

Figure 3-8: Branching Decision Box w/ two Options

Here, without IA, testing for fire/no-fire at decision box options within an auto-mated Decision Box Step 4 will occur according to the sort order of the options within the decision box.

If we add IA, we could have an automated decision box pre-processor task engage an analysis of historical data and apply predictive analytics that would vary the order of testing of the decision box options, favoring, perhaps, a pathway that has a history of yielding good outcomes.

Clearly, if testing of all decision box options takes place in microseconds, there is little point worrying about the ordering of options, unless the first task at the sub-path for an option allocates scarce and competing resources.

Here, testing of options 1-2 re-ordered to 2-1 would allow pathway #2 (i.e. Steps 7->8) to launch, resulting in a delayed launch for pathway #1 (i.e. leaving pathway #1 to wait for resources to be put back into the resource pool).

TEST DRIVING YOUR IA SYSTEM

Say you manage to find:

    a) a process mapping environment,

    b) an ACM workflow/workload management platform (w/ BPM, RALB, FOMM),

    c) links to local and remote systems and applications (preferably via a generic data exchanger),

    d) an RPA application system and

    e) some AI technology,

when following testing of your best practices with a small number of stakeholders; you need to assess efficiency and effectiveness. This is not entirely straightforward because as-is process mapping usually results in improvements to processes with the result that there will be little data available for comparison purposes.

Once you have some data, it is important to assess any changes in efficiency and effectiveness from users who follow best practices relative to users skipping steps, recording data at steps that are not yet current on a best practices workflow, re-visiting steps that are complete, and/or inserting steps not in the workflow.

If you note a decrease in efficiency or effectiveness, or both, you have a problem with your rule sets OR with your users.

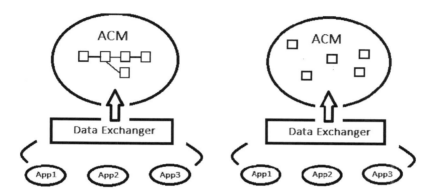

Figure 3-9: Best Practices vs Ad Hoc Insertions at Cases
The processing results should be the same

Rule sets can be upgraded. Problems with users are best avoided by initially categorizing each user as (beginner, intermediate, advanced), where rules are relaxed as the user progresses along the maturity curve.

A good starting position for a new user at an ACM system is no role match with any steps along any best practice pathways. Following training, various skill categories can be encoded to users, resulting in postings of certain tasks to their InTrays.

More training, more access to other tasks.

Once a user reaches a level where they can

   a) stream a Case Record onto a best practice template and

   b) launch process fragment workflows,

pre-processing rules at the 1st step along a process or process fragment can help to avoid problems. (i.e. "are we ready to engage this process?")

Security Considerations

Final QA on a new IA system involves certification of all local and remote systems and applications (i.e. Do these only process de-identified data? If, not, do any of these store transactions sent to them for processing?) If yes to the latter, then your IA system is not secure.

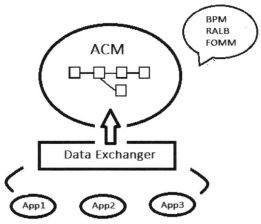

Figure 3-10: A Secure ACM platform only stores data at its Official History

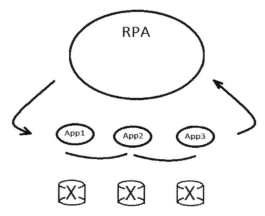

Figure 3-11: A Secure RPA Application Stores NO Data

REPRODUCIBILITY OF RESULTS

Clients often ask whether processing done at local and remote systems and applications can be repeated after the fact. The answer, most of the time, is NO, for the simple reason that executables change as a result of bug fixes, enhancements, etc.

Accordingly, the best expectation is that you have in your Case Histories, a record of data sent and data received.

Looking at these invented IA scenarios, my conclusions are:

- many IA initiatives are likely to increase complexity (something we might reasonably have anticipated).
- most corporations probably have not taxed rule sets sufficiently. This can be explored by calculating the ratio of manual steps versus semi-automated versus automated tasks along "best practices" workflows.

Are we done?

Not yet. The focus in this Chapter has been on Case Management (i.e. doing the *right* things, the *right* way, using the *right* resources, close as possible at the *right* time) but, is your organization exploiting the automation of the right protocols, funding the right opportunities/initiatives and solving the right problems?

NARROWING THE GAP BETWEEN OPERATIONS & STRATEGY

Consider the purpose of an Organization.

There are many definitions; the one I like is *"to build, sustain and augment Competitive Advantage"*.

All organizations start off with a competitive advantage. i.e. that of having sufficient infrastructure and resources to achieve start-up.

Infrastructure/resources include land, capital, access to capital, plant, equipment, tools, staff, suppliers, customers, distributors, partners, etc.

Organizations also need a vision, one or more strategic objectives and a means of evolving initiatives that make "good" use of infrastructure/resources.

Most organizations have more "candidate" initiatives that they can take on at any point in time. For this reason, a means of assessing risks/rewards is needed plus tools that allow ranking of initiatives and shortlisting of initiatives.

RBV (Resource-Based View) is the method of choice for strategic decision-making.

The origins of RBV go back to the late 1950s but the method did not achieve liftoff until the early 2000s, at which time 3D Graphic Free-Form Search Knowledgebases (3D Kbases) became available.

The core message of RBV is you can make better decisions re Resource Allocation when you can see all Infrastructure/Resources at one screen.

A typical RBV sheet can host 5,000 to 50,000 or more outlines/nodes. Alias nodes (as many as desired) allow planners to make provisional allocations of infrastructure/resources to, in this example, strategic initiatives and track residual/real capacity.

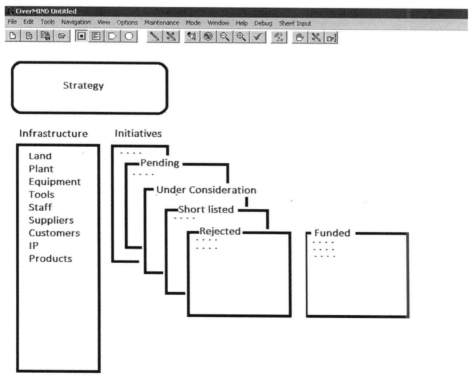

Figure 3-12: *Resource-Based View (RBV) Knowledgebase –*
Strategic Initiatives

Good practice with RBV involves putting shortlisted initiatives "out to bid" (internal or outsourced). Prospective stakeholders prepare Responses which get rejected or funded.

Gap minimization between strategy/operations and operations/strategy is achieved when both groups periodically assess initiatives for their contributions to building, sustaining and augmenting Corporate Competitive Advantage.

Whereas most corporations today use ROI when funding initiatives, some have progressed to SROI (socio-economic return on investment).

RECOMMENDATIONS

Here is a checklist you can use to streamline your transition to IA.

- Get your enterprise architecture right – you need one set of methods/tools for evolving strategy, prioritizing promising initiatives, selecting initiatives and funding selected initiatives. You need a different set of methods/tools for planning, organizing, monitoring and exercising control over initiatives.
- Consider trying to on-board top management with experience in strategy development methods such as RBV (Resource Based View). The core message of RBV is that you can't easily manage assets/resources you cannot see.
    - o RBV platforms allow organizations to view all of their assets/resources at ONE computer screen.
- Don't fund strategic initiatives if operational departments bidding on SOW (Scope of Work) have not included measurable goals/objectives in their ROI/SROI submissions.
- In respect of operational efficiency, bear in mind that the sum of idle times between tasks can easily exceed the sum of task performance times.
    - o ACM workload management platforms reduce idle times between tasks at Cases.
- Avoid meetings where the purpose of the meeting is to decide whether to have a meeting.
- Unless you are a strong aficionado of whiteboards, brown paper or post-its, join the ACM/BPM/FOMM/RALB/RPA/IA generation and work with e-canvases.
- Make sure you make it possible for your users to micro-schedule their tasks (up to a point of supervisory override based on changing corporation and customer priorities). Rigidity in the performance of work stifles innovation and increases job dissatisfaction.
- Give Case Managers decision support on when to ramp up / ramp down resources along Case timelines and give them tools such as FOMM that facilitate periodic assessment of progress toward meeting Case goals/objectives.
- Get your IT to reduce the gap between operations and strategy by consolidating key operational data to strategic planning and KPI tracking platforms. Encourage top management to challenge KPI trends by carrying out free-form searches at platforms.

Using Intelligent Automation to Promote Organizational Agility

Roy Altman, Peopleserv, USA

ABSTRACT

This paper explores why it is advantageous to move to a dynamic team-based approach, and how to overcome the obstacles to become the agile organization.

Key to this approach is the introduction of a new metric; The Agility Quotient (AQ), which is intended to let companies know when they are adhering to agile principles, in order to encourage agile methods.

We address the challenges organizations face and the solutions available to help companies pivot from purely hierarchical structures. But to fully understand the scope of the opportunities of moving to dynamic teams, it is necessary to understand the current challenges.

INTRODUCTION

"In 2018, we are witnessing seismic changes in the workforce, the workplace, and the technologies used in the world of work" cites Bersin by Deloitte. "…we have noted the movement of many organizations toward a 'network of teams' operating model that aims to enable greater collaboration and internal agility."

Companies need to take both an agile approach in management technique, and need new software to support teams and networks of teams as an integral part of their operations. Deloitte's survey of over 11,000 companies and business leaders concluded that many companies are recognizing that current crop of enterprise systems still view the organization as a single hierarchy, which misses a great opportunity to center processes around teams, which will result in increased collaboration, internal integration and engagement, or what Bersin by Deloitte dubs "The Social Organization."[1]

Yet, headwinds remain on adopting the agile approach to organizations due to cultural and political factors as well as lack of understanding of how to become agile.

This paper explores why it is advantageous to move to a dynamic team-based approach, and how to overcome the obstacles to become the agile organization. Key to this approach is the introduction of a new metric: The Agility Quotient (AQ), which is intended to let companies know when they are adhering to agile principles, in order to encourage agile methods.

A BRIEF HISTORY OF HIERARCHIES

The multi-level hierarchical structure has been the dominant way of managing the organization for centuries. However, we are now in the information age, and the hierarchy is no longer the most efficient way to organize work. Although the main hierarchical organization structure is still relevant for some functions, small, nimble teams are better suited to deal with the day-to-day complexities of today's dynamic business environment. Networks of teams provide better support for workers than the single hierarchy. Yet, with all of the advances in management techniques and technology to support business, the hierarchical arrangement of organizations persists, which is holding back progress.

This paper addresses the challenges organizations face and the solutions available to help them pivot from purely hierarchical structures. But to fully understand the scope of the opportunities of moving to dynamic teams, it is necessary to understand the current challenges.

The word "hierarchy" comes from the Greek word *hierarchia* or "rule of a high priest." It is an arrangement of workers whereby one is above or below another. Throughout recorded history, this has been the predominant organizational structure. Hierarchies are all about command and control; one node in the structure supervising others, and in turn being supervised by yet another, until the top node (Chief Executive Officer) is reached.

Hierarchies have the advantage that they are easy to understand. In a hierarchy, the lines of authority are clear; the manager directs work of the subordinates, and confirms that they have performed the work satisfactorily. Communication is two-way, between the manager and subordinate only.

In strict hierarchical structures, there is a redundancy and inefficiency of resource utilization. For instance, if arranged by business, functions like HR or IT are frequently replicated within each business unit. Also, workers functioning in different roles or collaborating across the organization break the strict hierarchical structure. Cross-functional communication and collaboration are not encouraged in hierarchies, because the workers are not responsible to anyone except the direct supervisor. Hierarchies therefore tend to become bureaucratic and siloed.

The hierarchy became a popular way to organize during the industrial revolution, when the assembly line was introduced, presenting a more efficient way of maintaining quality manufacturing as operations scaled. However, we are now entering the third iteration of the information age, which is characterized by nimble decision-making rather than repetitive tasks, and hierarchical management is no longer the best way to manage companies.

THE AGILE METHOD

In February of 2001, seventeen technicians got together at Snowbird Ski resort in Utah to discuss a new way of working. The outcome of that meeting was the now famous Agile Manifesto. The Agile Manifesto favored:

- **Individuals and interactions** over **processes and tools**
- **Working product** over **comprehensive documentation**
- **Customer collaboration** over **contract negotiation**
- **Responding to change** over **following a plan**

The founders observed that planning every aspect of a project is a flawed methodology, because unexpected and unplanned for things happen during projects. Rather, they preferred that technicians work closely with users to get the desired result through iteration, and to be more responsive to unanticipated changes. This dovetailed well with the move of enterprise software to the cloud, which was to become widespread within the following decade. On premise, software is *customized*, so it requires software development to accomplish the desired result, whereas cloud software is *configured*, which lends itself to working closely with the users because the software can be changed quickly.

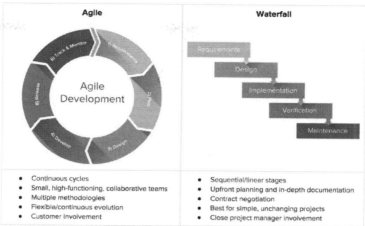

Figure 1: Agile vs. Waterfall software development methodologies

In the intervening years, the agile methodology has been applied to business functions outside of software implementation projects, such as marketing and HR. Most notably, is the move to agile organizations, which represents a fundamental change in the way we manage companies.

THE AGILE ORGANIZATION

Just as traditional software implementation used a structured approach where all activities are anticipated and planned for, organizational operations have used a hierarchical method of organizing jobs, anticipating that all activities will occur as expected. The reality is more unpredictable. People inside and outside of organizations don't react according to plan and business situations change abruptly and frequently. In a perfect world, proactive planning through rigid hierarchical organizational structures should be sufficient to manage complex operations.

In reality, they are woefully inadequate. The underlying assumption is that work is predictable, and success comes from careful planning and executing that plan. In the agile mindset, workers are empowered to make decisions. Work is organized by networks of small teams rather than hierarchies. Instead of managers dictating what is to be done, coaches fill in competencies and advise the teams. The underlying assumption is that workers closest to the problem are best equipped to solve it.

Former boxing heavyweight champion Mike Tyson once said: "Everyone has a plan until they get punched in the mouth." That rings true for many of us. Rather than create hierarchies anticipating orderly business functions, we're better off with structures that are designed to deal with rapidly changing conditions. When organizations are agile, and there is good chemistry among teams, synergies are created in the workplace, whereby results exceed expectations. Much like a finely-tuned sports team or music group, championships are won and great art produced when the participants' interactions mesh well. This analogy also applies to the workplace. It is human nature to try your best to excel when others depend on you. The team concept can have a positive effect on workplace culture when team members support one another.

In an agile organization, the structures are much more fluid. Teams are created to perform certain tasks or projects. These teams network with other teams that provide support or services. Instead of redundant levels of management, there are coaches and strategists that assist teams with experience and competencies that they may be lacking. These teams can reform time-to-time based on the needs of the business and the status of the tasks they are performing. Thus the agile organization can be thought of as an ecosystem of sub-organizational structures, that are better equipped to deal with the unpredictable, dynamic nature of business. The old organizational model no longer serves the needs of business.

Several business/technology trends indicate an imperative to move to an agile organizational structures:

- **Move to the Cloud** – Cloud-based software is configured rather than customized, so there is no need for a team of in-house IT professionals to maintain the system. Since the innovation and support for the products lies with the vendor, the vendor is a closer partner in the success of the company than if development and maintenance was in-house.
- **The Emergence of the Gig Economy** – There is an economic trend toward the "gig economy" whereby a greater percentage of contingent workers play a more important role in the organization. Rather than being a "shadow workforce" that just serves short-term staffing needs, contingents are playing a more active strategic role in organizations, and are able to contribute their expertise to multiple clients at once. Contingent workers who were previously omitted or marginalized on teams are now playing a more vital role.
- **Intelligent Automation** is now acting to enhance human workers and in some cases autonomously handle tasks previously done by humans. Thus the nature of a "job" is being unpacked into a set of tasks, some of which will be accomplished by intelligent automation.

These trends and others necessitate that we reexamine management techniques and organizational structures to more closely align with the way work is accomplished, with a value chain that extends beyond the traditional borders of the company. This includes business partners, contingent workers and automated agents, who are not aligned in bureaucratic hierarchies, but networked structures that optimize assets.

A CALL TO ACTION

The move to team management is in the zeitgeist, as there has been much written and discussed about the subject lately. Here are some recent examples:

- **General Stanley McChrystal**, US Army commander in Iraq, realized that the hierarchical method of decision in the military was too slow when faced with a more dynamic enemy. In his book "Team of Teams," he created a new mode of organization; a "network of teams" with a high degree of empowerment, strong communication, and rapid information flow, to enable more dynamic real-time flexibility within the formal hierarchy. The move was crucial to combatting Al Qaeda in Iraq.[2]
- **Josh Bersin** recently wrote: "What our research discovered, after talking with dozens of companies around the world, is that the high-performing companies of today are not functional hierarchies, they are "networks of teams," and the "network of teams" requires a whole new way of thinking about jobs, roles, leadership, talent mobility, goals, and the tools we use to share information, provide feedback, and measure our success."[3]

- **Peter Drucker**, the highly influential management theorist, observed back in 1988 that organizational changes were coming : "In the information-based organization, the knowledge will be primarily at the bottom, in the minds of the specialists who do different work and direct themselves."[4]

- In "Reinventing Organizations," **Frédéric Laloux** describes the evolution of organizational structures, and recounts several case studies of companies who did away with management altogether, and created wildly successful self-managing organizations.[5]

- **McKinsey and Company** has noted: "The dominant "traditional" organization is a static, siloed, structural hierarchy – goals and decisions flow down the hierarchy...In contrast, an agile organization is a network of teams within a people-centered culture that operates in rapid learning and fast decision cycles which are enabled by technology. Such an agile operating model has the ability to quickly and efficiently reconfigure strategy, structure, processes, people, and technology toward value-creating and value-protecting opportunities."[6]

CHALLENGES TO ORGANIZATIONAL AGILITY

Making this transformation requires that senior executives – the very ones who are benefiting most from the status quo – relinquish their authority to the betterment of the company as a whole. Clearly, there are challenges in achieving this transition. *Agile* is the new buzzword in the industry. However, many business leaders are unaware of agile methods and processes while, at the same time, *professing* a desire to become a more agile organization.

The answer lies in analytics; by measuring certain aspects of our business, we can highlight behaviors that are leading to an agile transformation. Analytics can serve as the "crowbar" to prompt change from the business leaders.

To initiate this transformation, first we need commitment from executives. Without executive sponsorship, no project will be successful. As with any strategic initiative, it is best to start small and build on early successes.

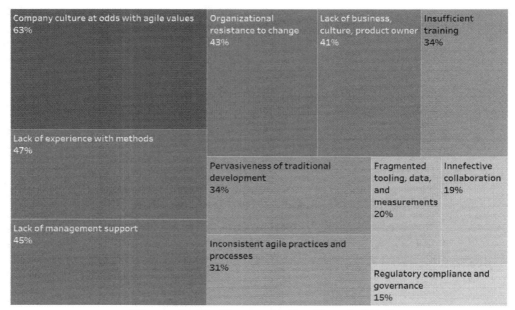

Figure 2: Challenges to Scaling Agility[7]

An Analytics-Based Approach

"No one ever made a decision because of a number. They need a story."[8] Analytics provides us the means to tell that story. And the story that needs to be told is that the waterfall/hierarchical way of organizing work is no longer sufficient for the challenges of modern business. We are not going to become agile unless we adhere to agile principles and practices. We need a way to measure work so that we use analytics to encourage the transition to the agile environment.

WORK REIMAGINED – WHAT DOES THE AGILE ORGANIZATION LOOK LIKE?

Ecosystem of Organizations

An organization comprises many sub-groups. In traditional organizations they are often depicted as either a hierarchical tree structure emanating down from the CEO, or a hierarchy of cost centers, divisions and departments if we're considering the financial organizational structure. Either way, the structures themselves are pretty static, although the people can move around in the organization. Structural changes require a reorganization, which is costly and disruptive. In a traditional organization, there are multiple levels of management. Workers at the leaf nodes of the tree structure are often dubbed "individual contributors." This term should be struck from the business lexicon. Hardly anyone is an "individual contributor." A more accurate term is: "team contributor."

What if we were to reimagine the way work was organized? What if we increased the rewards to people doing the work and decreased it to the ones in the multiple layers of management, whose expertise is navigating bureaucracies and company politics? What if we pushed ownership and responsibility to the ones "in the trenches," those closest to the day-to-day issues? The result will be a company that is better equipped to deal with today's business needs than the 19th century hierarchical model we currently employ.

The organizational structure of tomorrow will have no more than three levels:

- **Workers** – networks of teams of people who do the work. They are empowered to make any and all decisions, and can reach out to other teams or Coaches as needed
- **Coaches** – rather than Managers, we have Coaches that provide competencies lacking in the teams, or advice. Coaches can assist multiple teams.
- **Strategists** – what used to be called "Executives" are those that determine the strategic direction of the company.

Notice in the diagram below the overlapping layers. This is because people at each level can play multiple types of roles. A person who is a coach of one team can be a team member of another. A strategist can also play a coaching role.

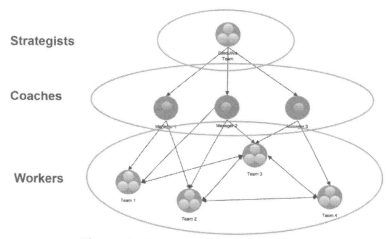

Figure 3: Organization Structure of the Future

COMMONALITIES WITH SPORTS STATISTICS

Sports statistics is an attempt to quantify human behavior on the field (or court or rink) to see how that behavior translates to success in the game. In business, we also try to quantify human behavior with the goal of success in business. The application of analytics in sports, popularized in the book "Money Ball" by Michael Lewis, has reached a level of maturity that exceeds that of many businesses. There are several similarities that can be applied from sports statistics to people analytics.

There *are* some differences, however. Sports tends to be transactional, thus behavior is easy to quantify. A pitcher/hitter confrontation in baseball will either result in an outcome favorable to the hitter or pitcher. Outcomes are less clear when business people meet to discuss and resolve an issue affecting a project. In addition, the universe of possibilities within sports is finite: there are rules for each game, and all the outcomes will be within the scope of those rules. In business, the possibilities are much wider.

The following sections cover aspects of sports statistics that have analogies with people analytics.

Real Plus-Minus

This statistic measures the success of the team, when a particular player is on the field/court/rink. It is relevant because it is a measure of a player's contribution to team success, rather than a measurement of the individual's success. For instance, if a team outscores its opponents by five points while the player in question is involved, that player's Plus-Minus score is +5. Consequently, if the team has a 10-point deficit while the player is active, his/her Plus-Minus score is -10. It attempts to quantify that elusive measure; team chemistry.

In business, we have always focused performance management on the individual worker, yet the agile methodology stresses team over individual accomplishments. We need to judge workers by their contributions to team success.

Wins Above Replacement

Wins Above Replacement is a compelling statistic. It is a single stat which rates the team's additional wins the player as opposed to having the average player. It is a single summative statistic that rates the overall value to the team. The formula behind it is quite complex and somewhat opaque, as one would imagine from at stat which is all-encompassing. The goal of a sports team is to win games, but the goal of an organization may be stock price or net income for a for-profit, or positive outcomes for a health care organization. Comparable statistics may be *Profit* Above Replacement or *Lives* Above Replacement, respectively.

Degree of Difficulty

In Diving (and other sports), participants are rewarded by attempting difficult dives. The overall score is indexed by the degree of difficulty, so that a near-perfect difficult dive would score higher than a perfect easier one. In business it's important to encourage more talented workers to tack tough assignments, knowing that they won't be penalized by outcomes that are harder to attain.

Subjective Scoring

Although many sports are scored by objective criteria (i.e.: point, goals, runs, timings), in some instances sports are scored subjectively by judges. Sports as diverse as figure skating and boxing share this feature. The goal is to standardize the judgements to have the most consistent and fair scoring as possible. To that end, judges have training and experience and standardized criteria which is calibrated across other judges. In addition, there are multiple judges per contest. For instance, in figure skating, they drop the highest and lowest score, and total the scores of the remaining judges from a panel of up to 10. In boxing, three independent judges score a bout.

In business, assessments are often completely subjective, not calibrated among other managers, and the opinion of one person, delivered at infrequent intervals. Although measuring quantifiable criteria is preferable to subjective criteria, when used judgements should be calibrated and based on multiple judges.

Advances in Technology

Around 2005, high speed cameras came into use. In baseball, they were able to measure aspects like exit velocity, swing angle, rotation, axis of rotation, release point, etc. As a result of having access to a great deal more data, teams were better able to predict outcomes, and adjust for them. This is manifested in defensive shifts, along with more evidence-based player evaluation.

Therefore, having access to more data due to advanced technology has had an impact on game outcomes. As we'll see in a later section, advances in Intelligent Automation will result in similar outcomes in the business world.

"Things that Don't Show Up in the Box Score"

This was an expression among baseball announcers to refer to things that help the team in subtle ways but aren't captured as an input into any metric. This shows that despite the plenitude of metrics available in the game, there is still acknowledgement that contributions to team success can evade quantification through statistics.

INTRODUCING THE AGILITY QUOTIENT (AQ)

As stated earlier in this paper, we need an analytic to serve as a "crowbar" to inform management when they are enacting agile practices. This is a new analytic called the *Agility Quotient* (or *AQ*). Much the same way the IQ is a single metric that provides an indication of certain types of intelligence, or the Emotional Quotient, or EQ, is a measure of empathy, the AQ is a singular score of how much the individual or company adheres to agile principals.

Although IQ and EQ are measurements of intelligence and empathy of the *individual*, AQ can be applied at the individual, team or company level. Thus it is a multidimensional measure. As with any metric, the issue becomes how to make the measurement. That's where Intelligent Automation comes in.

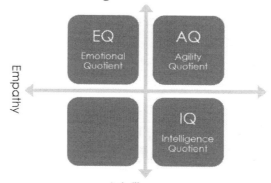

Figure 4: Intelligence/Empathy Grid

Objectives and Key Results (OKR)

OKRs are a way of defining and tracking objectives and their outcomes. Originally developed by Andy Grove of Intel, they are widely used by Google and others, and are spreading rapidly throughout the Silicon Valley community.

An objective is something to be achieved, and is usually qualitative and time-bound. A key result is a quantitative way of determining if the objective has been met. In agile environments, OKRs are often attached to teams as soon as the team is formed. This provides a measurable way of determining if the team has achieved its goals.

As a framework, OKRs are useful for measuring team performance, and providing input into the calculation of AQ. However, they differ from the immediacy of sports statistics because the scope and timeframe are usually bigger than the granularity you have with sports. "Degree of difficulty," or the equivalent can be assigned to challenging objectives, and results are measured by objective criteria where they can be. Where they can't, the score should be based on multiple judgements on calibrated criteria. OKRs should be prorated for the time active, as priorities change throughout the year.

Components of AQ

AQ is essentially a measurement of how people work together in teams. The agile organization is intended to empower teams to make decisions. Team members play roles rather than do jobs, so workers are encouraged to play roles on multiple teams. In general:

- Measurement of how we do in groups is more important than how we do as individuals.
- The lower the level in an organization where a decision is made, the better. Escalations are punished.
- Workers are encouraged to contribute to multiple teams. The more connections a worker has, the better.
- Communication occurs among team members, between team members from another team, or with coaches, rather than up and down a hierarchy.
- Workers are encouraged to experiment and not be afraid to fail because eventually the correct answer will prevail. Multiple iterations of a problem are rewarded.

Therefore, we need to measure team membership, decisions made and outcomes. A working beginning to an AQ calculation could be the following:

$$AQ = \sum (\text{team score} * \text{degree of difficulty} * \text{pro-ration})$$

The team score is captured in an OKR taking into account difficulty and pro-rated for the time span of the task. It is summed, so that all project where the worker plays a role adds to their overall AQ (thus encouraging multiple team assignments). I encourage others to help refine the formula for AQ or modify for relevance for a particular company.

INTELLIGENT AUTOMATION – NON-INVASIVE MEASUREMENT

In sports, most of the time metrics are captured through passive means; we observe play on the field and record the results. As stated in the previous section, all too often measurable behavior at work is too coarse, too infrequent, or we don't have a way to capture a behavior. For instance, if a meeting is convened to make a critical decision on a project, the decision has to be recorded in a place where it's available as a metric. Outcomes from meetings are often less binary than that, which is very difficult to quantify, especially by passive, observable means.

The inverse of the passive practice is the active one, where participants are asked to rate behaviors at various steps along the way. The active approach involves surveys. Although surveys can be useful, it is preferable to measure work passively through the use of an intelligent bot. The active approach is a very popular way to acquiring metrics that defy observability. There are three issues with this approach though:

- It involves an individual's opinion.
- It is invasive in that it requires somebody to do something other than the work they're trying to accomplish. If overused, it can result in a syndrome called "survey fatigue."
- Surveys are lagging indicators.

It is in this area that intelligent automation can advance this thesis tremendously.

Traditional BPM automated repeatable, predictable work by routing transactions among software agents and people. Robotic Process Automation (RPA) went further by applying deep logic to repeatable work to reduce or eliminate human intervention by applying automated rules that previously required human decision-making.

If you know how to solve a problem, you can construct an algorithm to solve it. This is the basis of all procedural programming. For problems we don't know how to solve, we can apply machine learning, which works by using statistical models against large datasets to "teach" the program to find the desired result within a level of confidence. Intelligent Automation picks up where rule-based algorithmic automation leaves off, and is best applied to applications involving pattern recognition, fuzzy logic or complex reasoning.

Internet of Things and Unstructured Data

The Internet of Things (IoT) are the eyes and ears of the web. We learn based on our experiences. Machine Learning algorithms (ML) "learn" based on data. The IoT is a way of providing data to ML. Throughout the digital age, we have adapted to the way computers needed to consume data. The keyboard was the primary interface with which we enter data. As we built systems, we provided integrations so a system can leverage data from other systems. Data that resides in systems is called "Structured Data."

However, we are getting to the point where ML can consume data as it exists on the web, rather than carefully categorized in systems. This is called "Unstructured Data." The ability for bots to consume and use unstructured data represents a quantum leap in the sophistication of how we use data to model our world. IoT is a means of capturing data and making it available to ML. The Economist magazine goes so far to say: "The world's most valuable resource is no longer oil, but data."[9] This is significant because processing perceived information is the way people work. We are getting to the point where computers are adapting to humans rather than the other way around.

Natural Language Processing – Semantic Understanding

Natural Language processing (NLP) has made great strides in recent years, due to ML programming techniques and the vast amounts of data available to train the NLP bot. We are at the point where NLP can recognize speech and provide relevant responses, such as suggesting web sites related to the inquiry. Another use case is a chat bot that can answer simple inquiries in a shared services model. This is useful, if not astounding, technology.

However, we are still in the realm of syntactic understanding (parsing speech), rather than semantic understanding; understanding the *meaning* of speech. As NLP advances to semantic capabilities, it opens up new levels of what's possible with NLP bots. For instance, in business meetings, one person usually takes notes, logs action items, decisions made and parking lot items. This task is usually designated for one of the more junior analysts or managers at the meeting, and with current technology, beyond the capabilities of NLP bots.

However, if these tasks could be performed by a bot, then the bot will have the access to a lot of information about the status of tasks and issues within the project, and can actually score decisions on a project just as we can capture events on the field of play in sports.

How Intelligent Automation Can Advance AQ

The best software fades to the background and is not noticed. Measuring work should not add to work. The active approach to gathering metrics, determining opinions and assessing work represents a good deal of overhead when trying to capture metrics on work evaluation. Using Intelligent Automation with semantic understanding of problems and objectives will provide the ability to measure accomplishments on a granular level as an input to AQ calculation.

AQ calculation using current technology is useful, but is hampered thusly:

- Too infrequent – only captured at the Objective and Key result level, which usually represents several months' work.

- Subjective – much of what's captured are subjective assessments. Calibration and using several judges adds to the overhead.

- Intrusive – capturing OKR results means someone has to log them, rather than spending time on the work tasks.

AQ calculation using Intelligent Automation will bring work measurement on a par with sports statistics and give us the metrics we need to gain insights as to personal and team performance in the workplace.

THE AGILE OPERATING SYSTEM

Enterprise systems also need to adapt to changing needs. Today's applications are structured around the old paradigm of fixed processes, whose workflow adheres to hierarchical structures, where the expectation is that work will be predictable. They need to be rethought to support the agile organization, as the old model no longer holds. For instance, enterprise application systems are geared around completing transactions, whose workflow is pre-determined, rather than to provide the tools to manage uncertainty. I envision an *Agile Operating System* (AOS), providing the automated tools needed to effectively deal with unexpected events. The system would not be centered around the transactions, but more toward decision support and assistance in managing unforeseen situations. The AOS might include the following functions:

- Ability to manage complex and fluidly changing relationships.
- Ability to manage both human and non-human assets.
- Dynamic case management, whereby new cases can be spawned and modified on the fly.
- Embedded advanced analytics, including Organizational Network Analysis (ONA).
- Intelligent Automation, i.e.: chatbots, digital assistants, etc.
- An integration hub, to link together enterprise systems and data sources.
- A flexible workflow engine, to orchestrate across systems, and institutionalize repeatable processes.

Organizational Network Analysis (ONA)

ONA is quickly becoming recognized as a very valuable tool for understanding the inner workings of an organization. One can think of it as "process mining for relationships," because it discovers who are the connectors and influencers based on data in the workplace.

ONA analyzes who connects with whom in an organization, regardless of where they sit on the organizational hierarchy. There are two techniques used to achieve this: passive – based on unstructured data: emails, chat tools, phone metadata, etc., and active – based on surveys. ONA uses analytics techniques to reveal significant relationships in the organization. It can reveal leadership, group dynamics, diversity and inclusion and worker engagement.

Rather than begin assembling teams from the hierarchical org structure, which has little to do with how work gets done, ONA provides a glimpse into the teams that are implicitly forming already and may offer a head-start on creating teams that achieve synergies.

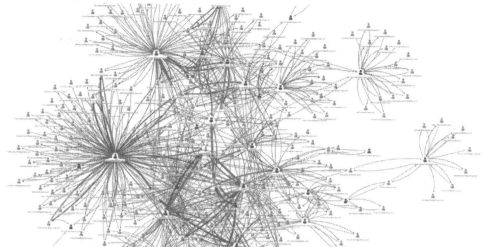

Figure 5: Organizational Network Analysis (ONA) – courtesy of Trustsphere

Dynamic Case Management

Dynamic (or Adaptive) Case Management was popularized in the BPM community since the early 2010s, but hasn't been adopted as widely among other business applications. In a shared service model, the service center uses case management software to track the cases on which they're working.

In the agile organization, *every* worker is essentially a case worker, spawning, working and resolving cases as a matter of course. We have enterprise software that assists in transaction processing, but in the agile organization work isn't arranged in neatly pre-determined transaction processes. Workers need software that will handle all aspects of the unpredictable nature of their day-to-day work.

CONCLUSION

As automation becomes more intelligent, we will be able to more accurately model human behavior and gain insights as to how to optimize the workforce. Intelligent automation, when applied to repetitive tasks, replaces the decisions formerly made by humans. Essentially, it disintermediates the "carbon layer" in the system stack.

When applied to more nuanced decision-making, intelligent automation acts to enhance humans by aiding in organizing and logging human interactions, and also measuring progress so we can test the models of human behavior. I firmly believe that the benefits of measurement of work from Intelligent Automation will prove just as valuable as the enhancement of work.

The AQ is admittedly a crude assessment of a company's agility. I look forward to the time when we are able to measure work in a nuanced way, and agile principles are widely adopted, so we will no longer have the need for AQ. Consequently, I look forward to the time when we can measure traits and talents across the spectrum of traits and talents and no longer have the need for IQ or EQ either. In the meantime, AQ is useful, as a way to nudge behaviors and practices to those which advance the *real* way work is accomplished.

REFERENCES

[1]: The rise of the social enterprise - 2018 Deloitte Global Human Capital Trends, Bersin by Deloitte.

[2]: 'Team of Teams: New Rules of Engagement for a Complex World,' General Stanley McChrystal, et al., Penguin Publishing Group, 2015.

[3]: 'Is It Time to Do Away with the Organizational Chart – Pretty Much,' Josh Bersin, https://www.linkedin.com/pulse/time-do-away-organization-chart-josh-bersin?trk=prof-post

[4]: 'The Coming of the New Organization,' Peter Drucker, HBR, January 1988

[5]: 'Reinventing Organizations,' Frédéric Laloux, Nelson Parker, 2014

[6]: McKinsey and Company, The 5 Trademarks of Agile Organizations, https://www.mckinsey.com/business-functions/organization/our-insights/the-five-trademarks-of-agile-organizations#0

[7]: "HR Goes Agile" – Peter Capelli and Anna Tavis, Harvard Business Review, March-April, 2018

[8]: Daniel Kahneman, The Undoing Project

[9]: The Economist, May 6, 2017

The Role of Data for Intelligent Business Processes

Kay Winkler, NSI Soluciones, Panama

ABSTRACT

New technologies have assured an intuitive, non-programmatic approach for getting the most insights from all your data, intuitively. That, naturally, extends also into the realm of Business Process Management (BPM) and Robots Processing Automation (RPA). The ease-of-use of related platforms, in fact, has grown to such a degree that it has not only become a viable option for C-Level executive to delve into data science but rather a necessity.

Here we will shed light on the different data components that Business Process Management Professionals have at their disposal and how the enterprise can gain a maximum benefit from these. We also look at the typical scenarios when it comes to harnessing the insights stemming from process data and to all the new tendencies as well as technologies in that area, specifically data mining and process mining.

INTRODUCTION

According to Bain & Company, the importance of advanced analytics for managers in the US has increased by a twofold in just over a year. (Bain & Company Inc., 2017) IBM's Chair, CEO and President Ginni Rometty goes as far as urging school systems and universities to fill the current and future skill gap, by adjusting their curricula to delve deeper into data science and machine learning. (Ioannou, 2019)

Data science has become the *de facto* cornerstone for driving digital transformation and, naturally, doesn't stop at the doorsteps of BPM. The complete opposite is true. Currently, it not only happens to be a "nice-to-have" summary of process results into static reports and dashboards but has also become every manager's obligation to have a process ingested and dynamically adapted to complex and everchanging data sets. That, in turn, can be described as the essence of Intelligent Business Processes.

In order to facilitate such an effort, this chapter tries to provide answers to what are the different data components that Business Process Management Professionals hold at their disposal when it comes to intelligent BPM (iBPM) and how the enterprise can gain a maximum benefit from these?

This paper furthermore looks at the typical scenarios when it comes to harnessing the insights stemming from process data and to the new tendencies as well as technologies in that realm, specifically data mining and process mining.

PROCESS DATA 101

When dealing with iBPM and Robotics Process Automation (RPA), business and process analysts typically face at least two important data pillars; transactional BPM-based data and form- and integration-based business data. This chapter will shed light on the innards and usage scenarios of both sets, paving the way toward advanced analytic strategies, using machine learning, decision tree diagrams, sentiment analytics and more. Process users, on one hand, must gain a firm grasp on the run-time behavioral patterns, the in-depth analysis of historical data sets.

On the other hand, they must increasingly combine existing information effectively in order to produce quality forecasts. Reliable predictions will then have to be fed into the process rules logic, adaptively. That's no small feat, especially considering that most users are still struggling with the most basic kinds of process data analytics: the review and interpretation of historical BPM data. It's a necessary undertaking however, if the user wants to climb the next evolutionary step of the process automation and continued improvement ladder, achieving truly intelligent BPM.

Karl Walter Keirstead, for instance, establishes in his chapter, "Managing the Transition to IA" artificial intelligence as a key ingredient for moving to an Intelligent Automation (IA). (Keirstead, 2019) The cornerstone for that and for the central of point of this chapter is the underlying business process data itself.

Figure 1 - Macro evolution of BPM Data; Winkler, Kay; 2019

For many analysts, in order to even include a BPMS into the prestigious *i*BPMS vendor category, they look for advanced forecasting that derives from business process data, has become a standard requirement.

Reports and stored rudimentary raw process data could be described as the last piece of the "basic" elements of a BPM implementation. Now, while certainly advanced reporting, BAM, pattern recognition and predictive analytics are powerful features to accompany a process automation, covering the first elementary step of making sure that all the process as well as the business (form) data is stored in an automated, uniform, accumulative and (very important) scalable fashion – throughout all implemented business processes – is far more crucial (and more often than not something overlooked). This basic step of data collection is key to providing real process insights and such, enabling continued improvements.

The ingredients for viable business reports are, in part, derivatives of the process and form-variable design efforts and in part the understanding of well-defined process metrics.

OF IA DATA PILLARS: PROCESS AND BUSINESS DATA

Having to deal with not only the statistical expressions of the process behavior, but also its effects on the business end of things, certainly adds to the complexity that a BPM analyst faces on a daily level. However, the statistical component of process analysis provides the users with the grand opportunity to gain a better understanding of the causes and effects the process performance exercises on real life business outcomes.

Adding the obvious advantages of continuously optimizing processes, enhanced data sets and the availability of increasingly more intuitive data science applications, the widespread adoption of Data Science Tools among BPM practitioners becomes clear and paves the way towards intelligent automation. Data Mining, for example, has been integrated into process data analytics to such a degree that it has been coined with its own term by industry experts: "Process Mining".

And this for good reason. On a per-process bases, the analyst can achieve quite the effect of scaled economies, given that with a relative few dependent and independent variables, great insights on mission-critical, end-to-end processes can be won (an example of such a variable will be detailed below).

As hinted above, a typical BPMS produces (at least) two distinct sets of data that can be either attributed to information indicative of the elements of the business process as a such or to the data said process handles. This can happen either through its forms and integrations to other processes or through integrations that feed and read data from /to outside applications.

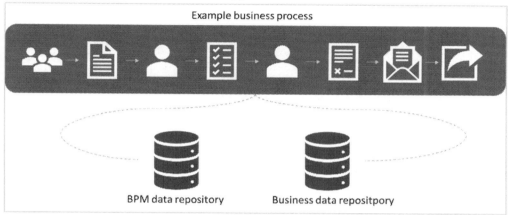

Figure 2 – Business and Process Data in iBPM; Winkler, Kay; 2019

A typical example would be as follows:

For the BPM data repository (not in any specific order)

- ID (Unique process incident or case ID)
- Initial date (Date when the incident/case has been "launched")
- Initiator (User who initiated the incident/case; can be a named or anonymous user that can be later identified through other means)
- Concluded (Tag to identify if and how the incident has been concluded; for example: not concluded/still ongoing, concluded through case abortion etc.)
- Conclusion date (Date stamp if applies)
- Life cycle (Time stamp, if applies of incident/case duration)
- Current process step (In which process step is the incident/case currently located?)
- Assignment date (When has been the incident/case been assigned it its present process step?)
- Assigned Users (To whom has the incident/case been assigned to?)
- Assigned Role (To which role/group does the assigned user belong to?)

In addition to these essentials, of course, there can be many other additional variables that a given BPMS captures. It is important to notice that commonly this information is being "recorded" by most BPM platforms automatically and accumulatively, independent from whatever processes the engine handles.

In that sense, one would have access to all the relevant BPM information, regardless of the user's decision to use the BPM platform for automating a procurement or a vacation request process, for example.

With this information on its own, a lot of knowledge can be harnessed. For instance, time per process and case can be measured (more details below) and process-based KPIs can be formulated.

Analogous to Frank Kowalkowski's chapter "Intelligent Automation and Intelligent Analytics," these data sets are instrumental for the Descriptive and Diagnostic phases of the analytical data science cycle IA normally brings to bear. (Kowalkowski, 2019)

Example: Control a goal for a vacation request not to exceed one working day until decisioning and not more than two working days until an approved request gets logged into the HR systems and a notification is sent to all involved users.

On the other hand, one would have access to the wide array of process-dependent data which clearly depends on the specific business scenario the automation solution has been implemented for. This data can therefore be as diverse as the company's different processes, its forms as well as internal functions (business rules, calculations, integrations and so forth).

In the vacation request process example, typical process specific data artifacts would be:

- Requester name, ID etc. (data likely to be declared in the form)
- Requester department (data likely to be declared in the form)
- Request approvers (likely the result of a business rule in conjunction with an integration to the active directory)
- Requested dates (declared data)
- Remainder of available vacation days (business rule with a calculation and likely an integration to the HR repositories)
- Decisions and reason codes (in case of rejections).

Both sets of information are of very indicative nature on their own but provide exponential insights when combined. Now, interesting correlations can be analyzed in the pursuit of continued operative improvements. Analysts will be able to detect, track and act upon patterns that stem from the influences that a specific user has on response times and case volumes. In our example, it would be of interest determining if vacation requests are being more likely to be reviewed late by a specific user and if these tendencies are altered by seasons, cycles or specific dates.

As a response, dynamic rules can then be implemented into the business process, provisioning alternative or additional resources if a given tendency breaches an established tolerance threshold.

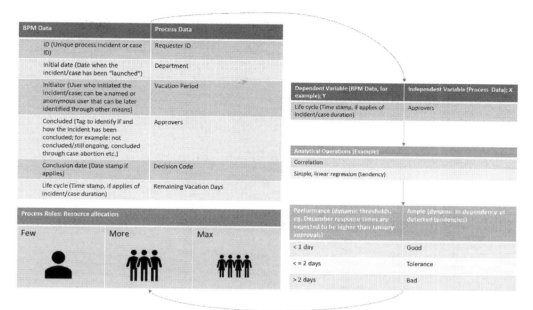

Figure 3 – Business and Process Data analytics example in BPM, Winkler, Kay; 2019

IBPM METRICS, TIME VARIABLE

The Association of Business Process Professional's Business Process Management Book of Knowledge (ABPMP CBOK) lists the process performance measurement as a fundamental element of the BPM practice. Depending on different possible viewpoints within and around the process environment, those measurements may form the foundation to justify a BPM engagement in the first place (project evaluation), identify the ROI of such an engagement; post-project or to pursue continued improvements to existent processes.

Establishing viable metrics can at times entail severe challenges. Trying to establish a robust framework of measurable variables that encompass the most crucial business process patterns without causing an excessive accumulation of sometimes redundant data points, typically requires the design team and the process owners alike to critically boil down the most representative dependent and independent key variables to be measured throughout the company's processes. This definition of measurement variables in turn should then occur ideally early in the process design phase and take into consideration challenges like confidential information (example: hourly costs of employees for human centric processes) that likely won´t be captured on the process level.

One of the most common and intuitive metrics that BPM users, analysts and providers refer to is the *process cost measurement*. In practice, however, especially in human-centric processes, sometimes due to the confidentiality of resource cost information and sometimes because of its unavailability at design time (pointing to whole different set of additional challenges), process costs (ex-ante and ex-post BPM) often can't be exactly and easily represented as monetary values (leading to sub-sequential and colorful ROI guesswork).

An alternate, and eventually more generalized, approach to that dilemma maybe the declaration of "TIME" as the principal and dependent core variable for all economic process measurements, which of course will suffice only for service processes whose material inputs play a secondary role to its results. Different types of TIME can easily and natively be captured by most BPM platforms and later be analyzed and compared within the same company (different processes and versions) and be benchmarked among different corporations. Different economic scenarios, tactics and strategies can then afterwards provide monetary multipliers to the continuously measured TIME variable, delivering a dynamic business context to process owners and analysts, on demand, without being process costs an embedded BPM metric.

The core challenge hereto would be the definition and the coherent measurement of different types of TIME variables. One can differentiate (among other types) between the task lifecycle time in each process and the worked time of different individuals for a task during its lifetime. Drilling down further, one could argue to differentiate between the entire task lifecycle time and only the workday lifecycle time (net lifecycle) of that task and so forth.

Having established TIME as a dependent core variable for process measurements and the possible formulation of behavioral hypotheses, result influential independent variables can now be included into the process metric framework of an Intelligent Automation.

We have found that for most human centric-business processes "net task lifecycle time" as a dependent variable and "quantity of process handoffs," "quantity of monthly process transactions" and "quantity of fully automated core and legacy integrations" – all as independent variables – have shown a significant correlation to each other as a result of BPM engagements. (Winkler, BPM Leader, 2013)

As established, there are several possible definitions of time in a process that can be categorized as:

- Process extension time: The sum of all configured extension times of a process' steps. Typically, during process design time, the process owners define how much time each process step should take. This definition can be different from the task time and worked time.
- Process worked time: The sum of all configured worked times of a process' steps. Typically, during process design time, the process owners define how much working time each process step should consume. This definition can be different from the task time and extension time.
  - o Includes Step Worked Times

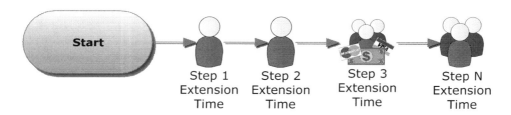

Process extension time = Sum (Step 1..N extension time)

Figure 4 - Process Worked Time; Winkler, Kay; 2019

- Task cycle time: The entire lifecycle of a given task within a process, summing up all cycle times (calendar time or only worked time) of that task within the different process steps until it comes to a cancelation or "natural" conclusion of that task.
  - o The task time takes also into consideration task redundancy cycles due to errors or policy violations (reworking tasks in previous steps).

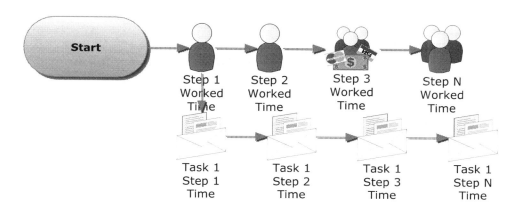

Task cycle time = Sum (Step 1 Task 1..Step N Task 1 time)

Figure 5 - Task Cycle Time; Winkler, Kay; 2019

While "Process Time" is something (as shown in the BPM methodology section) that is defined during design time and is the rigid instruction of the process to-be (time wise enforcement of a worst case scenario that is ensured by a BPMS escalation and notification system), the "Task Cycle Time" would be its dynamic counterpart of the actual process time consumption during runtime. Hence "Process Time" could be classified as a designed goal and the "Task Cycle Time" as a controlled metric. In relation to each other: "Process Extension Time" > "Process Worked Time" > "Task Cycle Time."

For all time types above, the final sum of each expresses a single process run (from "start" to "stop" of the process).

Measuring time is measuring the most important economical variable of human centric processes that then can be freely multiplied with whatever hourly rate and real-life scenario that may apply. In that sense, it also represents, for most processes, the strongest variable to be fed into IA models.

EVOLUTION TOWARDS DEEP LEARNING

Crawling before running is also a good advice when it comes to process performances measuring (PPM). While it is true that PPM itself is becoming increasingly accessible for business and non-technical end users, a couple of basic components must be put in place first, before the desired fruits from machine learning (ML) or artificial intelligence (AI) applied to the process world can be reaped.

As pointed out earlier, there is a great wealth of information to be understood and effectively used for process enhancements, coming from the iBPMS platform alone. Enhancing those data sets with business data that is fed into a unified data mart or dedicated repository, opens the doors for broader correlational analytics through the means, for example, of time series or cross-sectional investigations.

Apart from architectural recommendations like running query-laden studies of process and business data against a database that is separated from the BPM production environment and dedicated to these means, there are other important design decisions the business analysts must take for an IA framework to become efficient.

Many experts in the field recommend establishing strategic measurement goals first, making sure that all required variables are available and complete. A more recent school of thought emerges from the field of Big Data, where the assumption states that basically all existing information is being stored, made available and where, during the data analysis, the pursuit of correlation patterns turns out to be of more importance than a pre-established search and proof of causality.

In both cases however, the integral traceability of transactional data that spans all the different systems that are involved in a business process is of utmost importance. Also, when it comes to system crossing data, it can be initially counter-intuitive but highly recommended to not limit the data-trace and analytics on the iBPMS repositories alone, especially in the case of process mining. There, hash value anchors as well as modern blockchain technologies can be of great use for connecting the dots, not only between different systems but even between different organizations, altogether.

Gaining meaningful and deep insights from business processes can be, understandably, a daunting undertaking and should therefore be organized in stages.

Given a sound system architecture, healthy and integral, transactional and process data repositories, stage 1 would represent the efforts of understanding the trends and possible patterns of the basic process main variables ("time" for instance, as detailed earlier). Applying (lineal, quadratic, simple, multiple...) regression techniques, each process variable should be first analyzed individually and later correlated with other process variables, testing different models for (positive or negative) correlations and predictive qualities.

The process response-time variable, for example, could be reviewed on its own, identifying through a timeseries if specific trends or trend patterns exist. Assuming several years' worth of daily process case registries, indicative observations regarding response time trends, cycles and seasonality can be made. These "vectoral" understandings can be broadened by amplifying process data models with additional "native iBPM" variables.

For instance, the business analyst can put case response times in correlation with process complexities, expressed by the quantity of process steps (handovers), through a cross-sectional analysis. Alternatively, a specific variable can be closer inspected after having determined certain trends, in order to identifying causality. The following example shows how the simple counting of active incident (case) quantities per process step over time, could provide clues to the overall workload or could help explain response time patterns (if observed monthly):

Figure 6 – Net Production; Winkler, Kay; 2019

In this hypothetical case of a lending process, incidents are listed per process step and grouped into statuses "initiated," "carry-over" (from the previous month), "completed" and "aborted" (in real life many additional incident statuses, depending on the BPMS, can apply). The "Net Production" portion of the matrix then details to which originating month the completed production pertains. With such a simple visual arrangement, the answer to the possible question for more resources to face slower response times and bottlenecks can be refined.

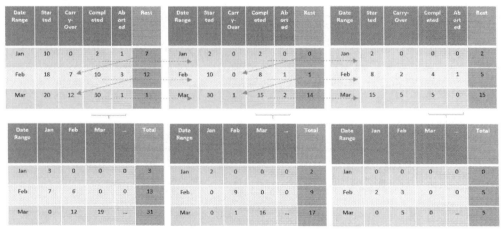

Figure 7 – Net Production amplified; Winkler, Kay; 2019

The continuing stage of data analytics in business processes could be divided into the data visualization phase and basic pattern recognition, as the following or parallel but indispensable step to intelligent automation.

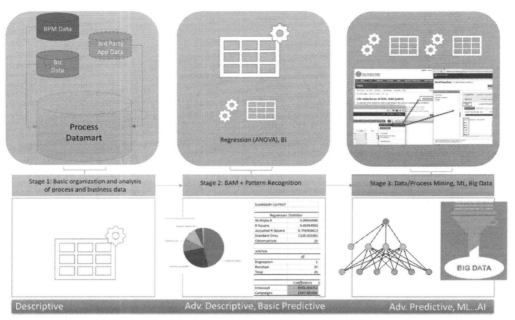

Figure 8 – Stages of Process Analytics; Winkler, Kay; 2019

Typically, the stages of process analytics are not exclusive but rather interdependent and complementary to each other. Also, depending on budgetary constraints and specific business goals, developing a domain expertise within a specific stage may be more suitable for some companies than by default having to achieve "ML level analytics" all the time, as the efforts considerably grow, the further right one evolves within the process analytics spectrum.

THE ADVANCED PROCESS ANALYTICS OF IA

In addition to simple data visualization activities, like the review of the monthly net production resulting from a specific process shown previously, there are numerous other activities the business analyst can undertake from the base BPM and business data repositories:

One such (recommendable) analysis would be, of course, the review of process response times over time to begin with. Here, the evolution of response times could be measured through monthly observations and then put through a time series analysis, validating for trends and statistically indicative forecast models.

A study (Winkler, Benefits of Policy and Rules Driven Processes in LatAm Retail Banking Automation, 2014) from 2014 found that a newly-automated process in the retail banking industry, for instance, typically accounts for approximately 35 percent of savings in worked time, when compared to the non-automated process models. The application of a time series application can then further these statistics over a longer period and start looking at seasonal impacts that may occur.

Time Saving Scales (0 - 400 working hours) ▼	Quantity
Range A -0-9.99	32
Range B -10-49.99	38
Range C -50-99.99	31
Range D -100-199.99	17
Range E -200-399.99	5
Grand Total	**123**

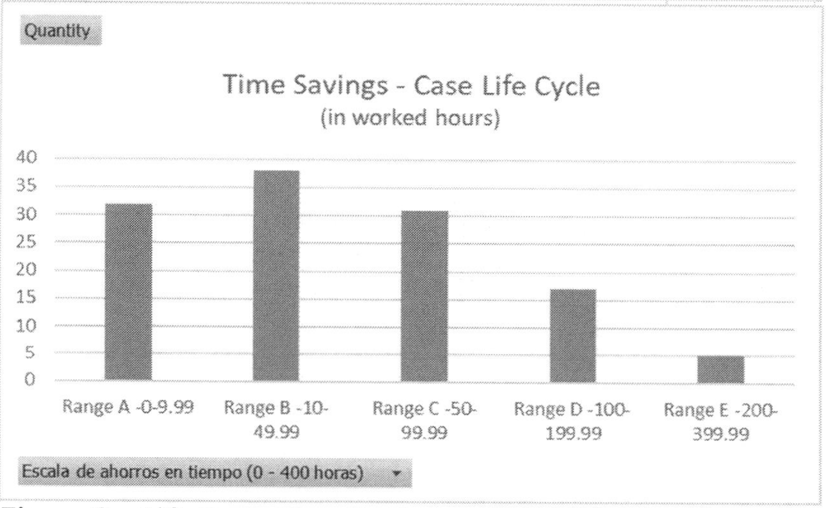

Figure 9 – Life Cycle Time Savings of BPM; Winkler, Kay; 2019

In business process management, good data science practices apply as well. For example, data integrity and completeness are at least as important as a "healthy" amount of quality data points. It just wouldn't be worthwhile trying to establish a tendency of improving response times within a commercial sales process, when only basing the initial regressions on some couple of dozen monthly observations.

That's typically when the companies' BPM and data science maturity comes into play, allowing a certain period of investments to take root before being able to gain the first returns on investment from IA.

Having achieved this level of insights however, furthering investigations will become far more accessible and easier to implement. With a complete and well-structured process repository, modern business intelligence platforms can easily be used as bridges to extend the BPM data sets to the business data and with that offer correlational links and provide visual aids of otherwise complex interdependencies and relationships

Year	Quarter	Month	Count of Incidente
2017	Qtr 3	September	2
2017	Qtr 4	October	23
2017	Qtr 4	November	14
2017	Qtr 4	December	14
2018	Qtr 1	January	23
2018	Qtr 1	February	13
2018	Qtr 1	March	10
2018	Qtr 2	April	10
2018	Qtr 2	May	16
2018	Qtr 2	June	15
2018	Qtr 3	July	2
2018	Qtr 3	August	6
2018	Qtr 3	September	10
2018	Qtr 4	October	12
2018	Qtr 4	November	7
2018	Qtr 4	December	2
Total			**179**

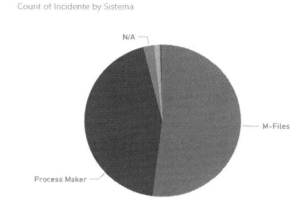

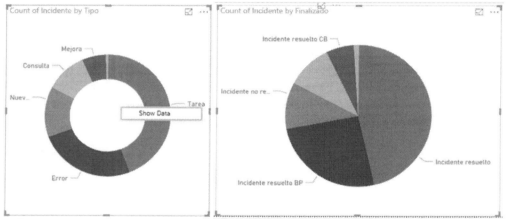

Figure 10 – Support BPM process data presented in a BI Dashboard; Win-kler, Kay; 2019

In the example above, there are different process KPIs that are easily displayed in a unifying dashboard that uses the data output of a process within a BI platform. The resulting console visualizes the concentration of processed cases per request type, user ID, and lifecycle extensions. In that sense, an efficiently-organized representation of indicators relevant to the business strategy is ought to be designed in a way that helps establishing and analyzing the relationships of the most result influencing variables of a business process. What kind of request type, for example, accounts for the highest cycle times and is stemming from which department and which user?

It becomes clear that such a Business Activity Monitor is the natural precursor to a deeper, relational analysis.

Besides the amazing diversity of different technology solutions here, these specific types of data review almost all the time bear just simple regression statistics at their core.

The time-series, establishing time as the independent variable and any other given BPM or business variable as its dependent counterpart, allows for the initial review of process behavior over time and resulting patterns.

Considering several variables at once, permits the business analyst to create more complex data models and the not immediately obvious influencers of process (hence business) outcomes can be contrasted as a result.

In the referenced study, cross-sectional analytics were applied to detect the influences the quantity of handovers and third-party application integrations in process had over time savings and paper consumptions. This study showed that an average of 35 percent of savings on worked time per observed process has been achieved, resulting in about 55 less working hours per case life cycle. More interestingly however, the correlational study of the different reviewed BPM variables also showed that the level of the process as-is documentation as well as the quantity of user managed process policies had the most influence over these savings.

Things become even more thought-provoking when extending time series and cross-sectional analytics to the fields of big data and machine learning for BPM.

Applying the Hodrick-Prescott filter, for example, to-time series such as the GDP over time and process response times in the BI software of your choice, correlations can be researched and categorized in terms of their quality as leading or lagging indicators for business outcomes through process management. A growth in gross domestic production may have a (x number of months) delayed growth impact of process volumes, leading to bottlenecks and these in turn into slow response time trends.

The sheer amount of the increasing number of publicly-available data sets allows for an equally large number of investigations that can be undertaken in the search for formerly unknown relationships of external "stimuli" (or shocks) to the business innards.

As indicated by Cukier and Mayer-Schoenberger in their piece "The Rise of Big Data" in the 2013 issue of Foreign Affairs, analytics in Big Data favors correlation over causality, serving also as the quasi-antidote of the McNamara fallacy when amplified sufficiently. (Mayer-Schoenberger, 2013)

On the opposite spectrum of Big Data, the discipline of data mining has made many important strides, to a point of creating its own niche in BPM in the form of Process Mining. Pioneered by thought leaders in the field, with Wil Van der Aalst at the very forefront, Process Mining has established itself as an important field of investigation among business analysts.

As initial step of the mining process, using unique transactional identifiers, flow sequences can be tracked within a given BPMS environment, as shown in the following scenario within Bonitasoft's BPM platform, leveraging a custom Process Mining module.

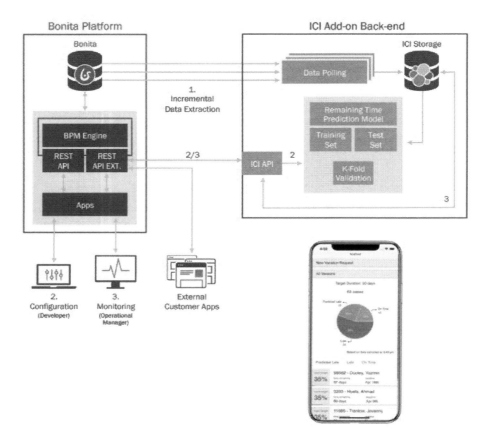

Figure 11 – Intelligent Continuous Improvement - ICI; Bonitasoft; 2018

Automatically tracking the real-life workflow sequence is especially helpful to identify an accurate representation of the process' as-is situation as well to track the delta of how the sequence is thought to progress vs. reality.

Outliers can be caught earlier, its impacts studied, and processes be adjusted more efficiently in alignment to the true operational workings of the company.

When during the data and architectural design phases, the unique transaction IDs have been created in a way that the integrity can be assured even when a case has officially left its BPMS premises and the company's domains, multi-system and, with Blockchain technologies. even multi-company tracking and process mining can be accomplished.

From there, Process Mining introduces entropy calculations as a measure for disorder, enabling the business analyst to visualize workflow patterns in terms of their homogeny into graphical decision trees.

With that in mind, following individual cases down the entire line of company's value chain, the impacts that process deviations within a back-office workflow have on the overall customer churn rate, will become visible and, above all actionable.

In the paper "Decision Mining in ProM" the authors point out that "in order to analyze the choices that were made in past process executions, it is required to find out which alternative branch was taken by a certain process instance. Therefore, the set of possible decisions must be described with respect to the event log. Starting from the identification of a choice construct in the process model a decision can be detected if the execution of an activity in the respective alternative branch of the model has been observed, which requires a mapping from that activity to its "occurrence footprint" in the event log." (Rozinat A., 2006)

If decision or process path mining, Machine Learning offers completely new and additional insights within iBPM.

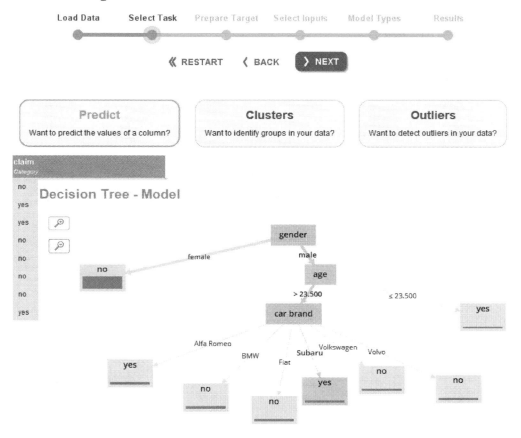

Figure 12 – Decision Tree Analysis with RapidMiner; 2019

The previous graphic shows how modern analytic platforms (in this case RapidMiner) have been become accessible enough for the everyday executive to run even complex queries and operations against existing databases and obtain a meaningful understanding with relatively little effort (in this example the decision tree of different predictors leading to insurance claims).

Intelligent Automation indeed.

A cautionary note: The harnessing of the power of these features, of course, is dependent on the prerequisites of a sound technical architecture, a cultural business mindset favoring data science and the availability as well as the access to the data itself.

REFERENCES

Bain & Company Inc. (2017). *Management Tools: Advanced Analytics*. Retrieved from Bain & Company: https://www.bain.com/insights/management-tools-advanced-analytics

Ioannou, L. (2019, April 02). *IBM CEO Ginni Rometty: AI will change 100 percent of jobs over the next decade*. Retrieved from CNBC: https://www.cnbc.com/2019/04/02/ibm-ceo-ginni-romettys-solution-to-closing-the-skills-gap-in-america.html

Keirstead, K. W. (2019). Managing the Transition to IA. In L. Fischer, *Intelligent Automation.* Future Strategies.

Kowalkowski, F. (2019). Intelligent Automation and Intelligent Analytics. In *Intelligent Automation.* Future Strategies.

Mayer-Schoenberger, K. C. (2013). The Rise of Big Data. *Foreign Affairs*, pp. 28-40.

Rozinat A., v. d. (2006). Decision Mining in ProM. *Computer Science, vol 4102*.

Winkler, K. (2013, February). *BPM Leader*. Retrieved March 22, 2013, from Viable Metrics to Justify a BPM Project: http://www.bpmleader.com/2013/02/11/viable-metrics-to-justify-a-bpm-project/

Winkler, K. (2014). Benefits of Policy and Rules Driven Processes in LatAm Retail Banking Automation. In L. Fischer, *iBPMS: Digital Edition.* Miami: Future Strategies Inc.

FIGURES

Figure 1 - Macro evolution of BPM Data; Winkler, Kay; 2019 52
Figure 2 – Business and Process Data in BPM; Winkler, Kay; 2019   53
Figure 3 – Business and Process Data analytics example in BPM, Winkler, Kay; 2019   55
Figure 4 - Process Worked Time; Winkler, Kay; 201956
Figure 5 - Task Cycle Time; Winkler, Kay; 2019   57
Figure 6 – Net Production; Winkler, Kay; 2019   59
Figure 7 – Net Production amplified; Winkler, Kay; 2019   59
Figure 8 – Stages of Process Analytics; Winkler, Kay; 2019   60
Figure 9 – Life Cycle Time Savings of BPM; Winkler, Kay; 2019   61
Figure 10 – Support BPM process data presented in a BI Dashboard; Winkler, Kay; 2019 62
Figure 11 – Intelligent Continuous Improvement - ICI; Bonitasoft; 2018   64
Figure 12 – Decision Tree Analysis with RapidMiner; 2019   65

Intelligent Automation and Intelligent Analytics

Frank Kowalkowski,
Knowledge Consultants, Inc, USA

ABSTRACT

The level of activity around the topic of intelligent automation (IA) indicates a high level of interest by management in improving the performance of their organizations. Like all waves of ideas and technologies, this one has a history as well as a mix of value and hype. Intelligent automation and intelligent analytics are in the middle of a wave and are a maturing discipline.

INTRODUCTION

There is plenty of material in this book about IA so the focus of this chapter is on the *analytics* and how you position them to take advantage of the smarts in the automation. Automation, especially automation of operational processes, has become ubiquitous in most organizations. Intelligent automation involves applying analytics, and especially 'smart' analytics, to processes, mostly *operational* processes. The goal is more efficient and effective control of the process.

There are, at least, four aspects to intelligent automation in an organization:

1. Adding intelligence to a process, especially operational processes. The key is determining where to add the analytics that will help you decide where to best apply the intelligence efforts.

2. Augmenting decision-making within a process where the focus is on decision support and the ease of use of the analytics that support prediction and options.

3. Monitoring the process for correct operation and managing/adapting to changes in the process to keep process in compliance with organization direction.

4. Applying intelligent automation and intelligent analytics to other perspectives of the organization such as strategic and tactical perspectives and the external landscape.

Managing an organization or governance, especially performance management, depends on proper execution of processes and making good, timely and value-added decisions. Processes are among the key opportunities for intelligent automation and intelligent analytics particularly in operations where most processes are located.

A LITTLE HISTORY

It is useful to have a simple reference point, background or historical baseline that helps us to understand how far we have come in automating things. The history of automation started with automation without any intelligence.

An automation baseline is the expectation, degree and level of automation that is in effect at a point in time. For example, automation in the 1960s focused on numerically controlled tools in manufacturing and simple accounting reporting systems in many organizations.

Later, the manufacturing use of automation depended on concepts, methods and tools such as control theory, cybernetic devices for machines, communication theory and actuators to translate the instructions to a machine action. The same is true of reporting systems and their use of flow charts, computer programs and computers with attendant printing devices.

Thus, we have been automating for many years through a variety of approaches and by industries as well as governments. Here are some examples of automation progress along a timeline from a historical perspective:

- Machines, starting with numerically-controlled tools especially in manufacturing as well as smart robots. Robotic process automation (RPA) is the most common description of intelligent automation today.

- Diagnostics in health care and quality control. Starting with the simple blood test as a data source has evolved to using analytical chips on a card.

- Management reporting using early reporting systems and eventually business intelligence (BI) with dashboards and interactive features allowing the manager to slice and dice data.

- Governance such as compliance monitoring, risk assessment and performance reporting

Analytics are most often used as preparing input for an action (process use) or in making a decision in a process or as a stand-alone effort.

THE CURRENT STATE

The capability to capture, format, save, share and cluster large amounts of data provides the fuel for many analytics that were not viable with the small data sets we had previously. Much digital transport is at the edge of the organization today and deals with the Internet of Things (IoT).

The analytics-supporting processes became increasingly sophisticated until the emergence of Artificial Intelligence (AI) that includes machine learning and neural nets added to traditional statistics that support processes and decisions. We also added the use of software robots. Robots validate that a process is working correctly. Their ability to make intelligent decisions makes them valuable. They manage process change and adaptation.

Intelligent analytics help you anticipate situations and put you in an action-taking proactive mode rather than reactive mode. As such, they leverage the discovery and diagnosis usually found in operational analytics as input to predictive and prescriptive analytics. Predictive and prescriptive analytics are intelligent analytics. They suggest where things are going and what you might do with that knowledge.

A recent Gartner study put the use of predictive analytics at 30 percent in organizations and prescriptive analytics at only three percent. Basic predictive analytics have been in use for some time. The techniques include classical regression analysis with trend lines, correlation analysis, correlation matrices and affinity analysis.

The latter two were used extensively in marketing. They answer questions like 'people who bought this product also bought that product.' The goal is to increase cross sales.

Ultimately, intelligent automation depends on lifting process intelligence, making the process smarter. Operationalizing AI is one way to do that. Knowing where to apply the AI is a key factor in successfully automating processes with AI. It's all about processes, decisions and their support with analytics. Organization governance, especially performance management, depends on proper execution of processes and making good, timely and value-added decisions.

Analytics started with process monitoring in the early 20th century with the advent of workflow measurement, especially in manufacturing, to control costs and predict production. Processes evolved using new automation methods such as those used in manufacturing. As other technologies became available, the analytics sophistication increased. For example, control theory developed to manage and govern physical systems, much like the thermostat in a house governs the temperature, using a feedback approach. Computers made accounting processes and jobs automated and so on.

Consider that a process consists of steps/actions and decisions that route the flow, plus the enablers supporting those decisions or carry out the steps and actions in the flow. Both are candidates for automation and intelligent analytics. The use of analytics in a decision is different from the use in the steps of a process. Process steps mostly have discovery and diagnostic analytics while decision have mostly predictive and prescriptive analytics that *depend* on discovery. Here are some points to note about decisions:

- Effective decisions need a core diagnostic input that helps answer 'Why' something is happening as opposed to just 'What' is happening. We can easily get the 'What' from reporting systems and BI but *understanding* the reasons behind this information leads to better improvements and opportunities.

- Effective and value-added analytics provide a hint of direction with risk/reward for each option.

- These decisions need a measure of automation and semi-automation (meaning manual help) especially where factors are not clear, or risk reward is marginal or indeterminate.

THE DATA SCIENCE APPROACH

As smarter processes evolved using automation, the more we needed improved, better and smarter analytics. We needed robust methods because the usage became more critical and the volume of data grew huge. Data portion evolved to support analytic algorithms and eventually the ideas of data science emerged as an umbrella approach to analytics.

The data science approach is typically used to create viable analytics that support some organizational need. The approach consists of five major stages of analytics that vary a bit depending on who is defining them. This is the most common set of analytic categories today:

1. **Discovery/Descriptive** – Looking at *what* is going on related to some interest of the organization such as problems, opportunities, competitive interests and other triggers of interest. Clustering is an example.

2. **Diagnostics** – These try to identify *why* something is going on and the analytics differ from the discovery analytics but overlap. Ranking or semantic sentiment analysis are examples.

3. **Prediction** – Estimates the path if the situation continues. The common example is simple regression used to predict a trend line such as for sales or expenses.

4. **Prescription** – Decides between courses of action and suggests one or more possible solutions.

5. **Tracking/Monitoring** – Watches for variances of performance parameters or other situations such as economic trends. Uses alerts management and a data science analysis cycle for new and existing performance indicators. This is typically done with business intelligence systems and dashboards.

The diagram below gives a bit more detail on what goes on in this cycle. The method is typical of developing machine learning, neural net, statistical and other analytic models. Keep in mind that analysis always starts with some need of the organization. It could be an opportunity, a problem, an area of interest, a competitive response or any myriad reason.

Analytic Methodology Overview

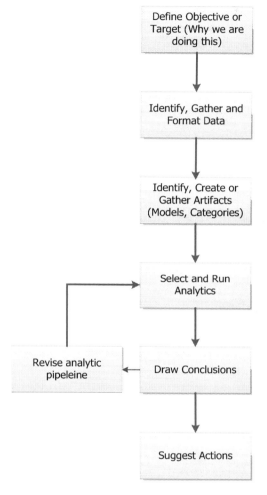

The start of any analysis begins with the goal, questions, area of interest or target

Then the types of data are identified both quantitative and semantic. There can be many sources of data, spreadsheets, documents, keyed in data etc.

The data is grouped into clusters based on discovery and diagnostic algorithms. Both quantitative and semantic analytics are used.

Depending on what is the target, an analytic or multiple analytics are run on the data. Results of analytic operations may be saved depending on the type of analytic. An analytic pipeline may be used.

Reviewing the results the analyst then draws some conclusion about the analysis. This is where the insight comes into play, the 'AHA' moment when some pattern or value is identified. As an alternative, another analytic sequence may be defined and run

Persuasive presentation graphics are selected that urge the analyst. manager or whoever chartered the analysis that they should take or avoid an action.

WHERE AND WHAT TYPE OF ANALYTICS ARE MOST USEFUL?

It is easy to *talk* about concepts and theory, but it is much better when you can *see* some examples of what it means. The rest of this chapter is devoted to reality.

The goals of intelligent analytics are driving growth, effectively dealing with competition and market position, translating direction to action and optimizing efficiency. This set of goals, and there are more depending on the organization, implies that there are different analytics and different uses of the same analytics for the different perspectives that spawn these goals.

For example, while *strategically* the organization is focused on growth, *operationally* they may be focused on efficiency or optimization. This means you need to know what kind of analytics to apply to each situation and where to apply them. They may be applied to decisions or processes or to an enabler such as a database or application.

These analytics vary according to the management perspective. There are four perspectives used today by most managements. The use may be very formal and extensive with well-developed tools and methods as used in large organizations or it could be more basic and ad hoc when used in small and medium organizations. Depending upon need and scope of the analytics, analysis can range from sophisticated analytic tools to using Excel.

It helps to understand that there are differences in the focus and use of analytics and the types of processes and decisions they support. There are some 65 different management models that support these perspectives. Here is a brief comment about the four levels using decisions, process and an example to illustrate the opportunity. How the analytics are determined and how they cascade in a useful manner is key to their successful use.

Few analytics have great value in isolation. They are much more valuable in combination and when applied to the business context from the external landscape through to operational execution.

THE REALITY OF APPLYING ANALYTICS

Organizations have key pain points that they deal with depending on organization size, markets, products and services, history and several other factors. They must work with the processes, decisions and insight for *each* pain point and *collections* of pain points. Each perspective has the following four points that show how analytics are identified and applied to that perspective:

- The *questions* – These show up usually as management is trying to understand what should be done for a specific perspective.

- The *processes* - There is a set of processes that define how an organization deals with a perspective. There may be only one or two processes or there could be many, depending on size and formality of the organization. The goal is in applying intelligent analytics to processes with an assessment of the impact of change on those processes and development of operational excellence. Operational processes are the largest set.

- The *decisions* – The decisions are usually made based on insight, experience and analytics. The goal of intelligent analytics is to decrease the uncertainty with better analytics. Decisions are usually defined by their conclusion or outcome.

- An *example* of the type of analytic used for that perspective. There are at least 20 easy-to-use and understand classes of quantitative and semantic analytics like ranking, semantic comparisons and others. Within each analytic class there are options on how they are applied and what their result tells you.

AN INTRODUCTION TO A FEW ANALYTICS

There are varying options that identify how the analytics are used and to what kind of data they are applied in order to support the analysis. In this chapter only a few of the analytics are shown along with some variations or combinations. Ranking, for example, is used both in landscape analysis of external impacts as well as market analysis when evaluating the strategy perspective for setting market direction for the organization. Most analytics are applicable and useful when applied to any of the four perspectives.

Landscape analytics

Landscape analytics address the external environment of the organization and focus on opportunities and threats. These approaches are focused on macro-economics and segments of economies. The PESTLE (Political, Economic, Social, Technology, Legislation and Environment) approach is a good example as are econometrics that use equations to estimate things like GDP, income growth and so on. Analytics of impact analysis are used here, especially predictive and prescriptive analytics. The results of this type of analysis are input to the strategic perspective.

Questions

- What events or trends are increasing/decreasing?
- Are they emerging or maturing in the external environment?
- Which ones are the most important to us?
- What types of landscape risks exist and how are they ranked?
- What is the market profile for markets of interest to us?
- What technology trends may impact us?
- And so on…

Processes

Landscape analytics feed the strategic planning process. Key steps of the planning process require certain types of analytics to identify what factors are of interest outside the organization. These factors impact the strategic direction of the organization pursues. A lot of this analysis is about discovery and diagnosis of those factors that impact the strategic actions of the organization either increasing or decreasing the emphasis on strategic direction. Typical processes are those that gather some form of intelligence such as:

- Environmental scanning (e.g. PESTLE data gathering)
- Semantic analysis of news feeds (frequency of word or term use, company mentions etc.)
- Competitive intelligence gathering
- Target intelligence (industry oriented) gathering
- Conferences, trade shows and other feedbacks

Decisions:

From the questions, you can see the decisions that an organization faces. This is defined by the outcomes from the analytics. Here are some typical examples of decisions and results that are made in scanning the landscape.

- The number one market opportunity is in X region
- The number one risk to success is 'social trends' (a PESTLE component)
- What technology X is the most likely innovative one in the next five years
- What technology is most impacted by economic change?
- Legislation on data protection is the number one barrier to new markets
- Economic trends show a decrease in disposable incomes impacting our products

Analytic Example

Consider the question above of economic impact on technology. This is a pretty typical question for an organization to ask if they are especially dependent on various technologies or if they are interested in getting into a technology market. This is a classic impact analysis example of trying to identify what parts of the organization might be impacted by changes external to the organization and to what degree those changes might impact the organization.

The analytic provides a basic assessment of impact of change. In this case, we are concerned with economic impact on our markets and then subsequent impact on technologies as seen through those markets.

The result points to those technologies that need monitoring for future impact on the organization. It is a prediction of likely *degree* of impact and not a *probability* of impact. Additionally, subjective probabilities can be provided that would filter the ranking and focus the monitoring effort on economic indicators, markets or specific technologies.

The idea is to predict which technologies are likely to be impacted by economic factors in specific markets. We start by linking two matrices. The first one relates economic impact (19 factors) to markets (10 of them). A second matrix relates the 10 markets to the major technologies. For this analytic, we need to see the input matrices and the resultant matrix.

Model A is the Economic Factor to Market relationship input matrix

Model A	Model B	Inference Data	Inference Counts				
Model Name: External Impact on Markets, Total Cells: 190, Relationships: 96, Density: 50.53%.							
Row Item	erica South	Asia Pacific	China	European Union East	European Union West	Middle East	Total
Aggregate Demand		●	●	●	●	●	7
Aggregate Supply		●	●		●		5
Business Formations	●		●	●		●	5
Consumption							1
Disposable Income		●		●		●	6
Economic Growth			●	●		●	5
Employment	●		●		●	●	6
Exports	●	●	●		●		6
Firm Revenue		●	●		●	●	5
Government Spending			●	●		●	4
Gross Domestic Product		●	●		●	●	5
Household Formations		●		●	●	●	5
Imports		●	●		●	●	7
Inflation	●			●			5
Investments	●		●	●		●	5
Total	7	11	14	11	10	11	

The 19 factors are related to their markets and the relationship is denoted by the dots. Values (like 1 to 5) for degree of impact can be assigned instead of the dots to filter the results for high hit factors.

Model B is the Markets to Technologies relationship input matrix

Model A	Model B	Inference Data	Inference Counts		
Model Name: Market Impact of Technology 01, Total Cells: 250, Relationships: 79, Density: 31.60%					
Row Item	Security Technology	Toxic Material Technology	Warehousing Systems	Web Support Technologies	Total
Africa Northern			●	●	7
Africa Southern				●	4
America Central					2
America North	●		●	●	13
America South					4
Asia Pacific	●			●	10
China	●		●	●	13
European Union East	●				5
European Union West	●			●	9
Middle East	●		●	●	12

Next, we look at the matrix relating markets and technologies. Similar to the dots in Model A, these dots denote a perceived and verified relationship between markets and technologies. It means a specific technology is important to that market. The relative degree is determined with quantitative estimates not shown here.

The inference counts are the result of analyzing Model A and Model B together

Model A	Model B	Inference Data	Inference Counts		
Row Item	Agile Software for Mobile Devices	Chemical Solvent Technology	Communications Systems	Electr	Total ↓
Aggregate Demand	4		1		69
Imports	4				68
Firm Revenue	3				57
Gross Domestic Product	3				57
Exports	2		1		53
Tariff Wars	2		2		51
Aggregate Supply	2				49
Disposable Income	3		2		49
Household Formations	2		1		49
Economic Growth	3		1		47
Employment	3		2		47
Investments	3		2		41
Price Level	2		1		41
Consumption					4
Business Formations	2		2		38
Total	44	0	23		

Finally, an algorithm is used to determine the inferred impact and the results are shown in the results matrix presented above.

Only the first few columns can be seen in these screen shots. What we see in this shot is that Aggregate Demand and Imports have a large impact on the Technologies. So, these two economic factors should be closely monitored.

As noted earlier, quantitative values that indicate importance, subjective impact, risk, volatility etc. can be assigned to each of the factors in the input matrices and used for filtering the results.

The conclusion is that the most impacted technologies based on economic factors and markets are the following:

1. Networking (66)
2. Security (66)
3. Information Technology (65)
4. Internet of Things (65)
5. Sales support technologies (58)
6. Material Move systems (55)
7. Handheld Devices (53)
8. Robotic Process Automation (47)

The result means that the technologies the company should be closely monitoring are Networking, Security, Information Technology and Internet of Things as these have the greatest possible predicted impact on their direction and operations.

Strategic analytics

Many strategic approaches and methodologies have emerged over the last 50+ years. These are described in the many management models available, such as 5 Forces, Blue Ocean/Red Ocean, Value Chain management and so on. There are some 65 different management models that span all perspectives.

Questions

- What external events or trends impact the strategic direction of the organization?
- Which has the greatest impact?
- What is the risk of going forward or not responding to a threat or opportunity?
- What is the competitive situation in each market?
- Is it worth going into an emerging market or should we take a defensive posture?
- And so on...

Processes

The core of strategy management is the strategic planning process. There may be support processes around it and usually the analysis of the organizational landscape is included. Most processes involve the word *assessment*. This is a keyword about finding out why things are happening, estimating the trend or future point and then proposing actions to meet the conditions. The processes are defined and designed to answer sets of questions about what direction the organization should pursue.

The following processes are typical of most organizations.

- Situation analysis (where are we? how did we do?)
- Identify and define direction, objectives and strategies
- Analyze resources internal and external
- Identify strengths and weaknesses (e.g. SWOT analysis)
- Review mission and objectives for practicality and likelihood of success
- Formulate strategies (direction statements)
- Develop implementation action plans

Decisions

From the questions, you can see the decisions that the organization faces.

- Here are the markets we will pursue
- This is the degree of market activity we will support
- These trends will be ignored

- These trends will be monitored
- These trends require a response
- These competitors require blocking
- We will enter these markets
- And so on

Analytic Example

This example is one of composite ranking, that is a ranking with multiple factors. The ranking algorithm is set up first with a configuration screen that lets you decide how you want the algorithm to interpret the rank order. Sometimes, the largest number is what you want as number one and sometimes, it is the smallest number. Notice that all the factors are checked here and that the ranking will include all of them. Such rankings are done with different combinations of factors to highlight a direction. Some factors may not be important to the current ranking effort.

Here, the lowest rank value determines the best market.

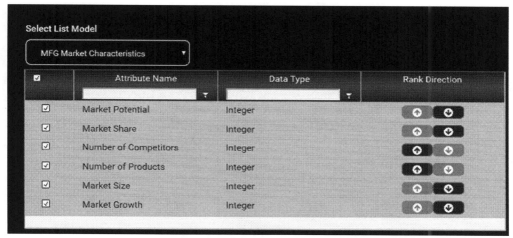

Once the algorithm knows the factors to include and the order you want to use for the ranking, it can calculate the best market to pursue.

In the result shown below, the best market is Asia Pacific market as it has the lowest rank value. The least likely markets to enter are the European Union West and the Central America market (a tie)

Result1	Result2	
		Attribute Ran
Position	Item Name	Rank
1	Asia Pacific	3.50
2	America North	3.67
3	Africa Southern	4.33
4	China	4.50
4	America South	4.50
5	Africa Northern	5.00
6	Middle East	5.17
6	European Union East	5.17
7	America Central	5.33
7	European Union West	5.33

These analytics are easy to use by a manager without needing any expert help regarding analytics. The manager or analyst focuses on the business use of the analytic not the technical capability.

Tactical Analytics

Tactical analytics support the linkage between strategy and business structure. What the organization must change needs to be identified. Impact analysis and identifying the relationships is a typical analytic used here.

Questions:

Typical questions deal with the structure of the organization and the charter for key departments or operating units. Some typical tactical questions are:

- What does it take, and should we consolidate processes?
- Should we eliminate processes?
- What does it take and is it feasible to consolidate operating units?
- Are any processes nonperforming?
- Are there any opportunities for AI augmentation?

Processes

The processes for the tactical level deal with the monitoring and restructure of the organization, often across organizational units. For example, consolidating operating units or processes to get a standard process such as for hiring or supply chain etc. Some of the processes are:

- Reporting (summarizing operations)
- Tactical planning (change management, initiatives for strategies etc.)
- Performance analysis
- Process management (consolidate, simplify, eliminate etc.)
- Organizational development
- Knowledge management
- Product development and engineering
- Information technology management

Decisions

Decisions are focused on organization structure and performance overall. As such, they deal with making changes, solving organization-wide issues and developing plans to implement.

- We can combine these two processes
- We can merge these operating units
- Take this risk for this yield
- Apply AI to improve this process or decision

Analytic Example

Looking for significant and hidden relationships is a task all organizations need to do. Linking the structure of the organization parts together is one of the best ways to do that. Algorithms do the work and diagrams like the ones shown below uncover the result. The point is to see what economic factors relate to the core processes of the organization.

The first cycle of analysis usually provides a diagram like the one below. This is clearly difficult to work through as it has a lot of detail. What you really want to know is based on the most important economic factor or some other parameter, which core processes, seen on the right are affected.

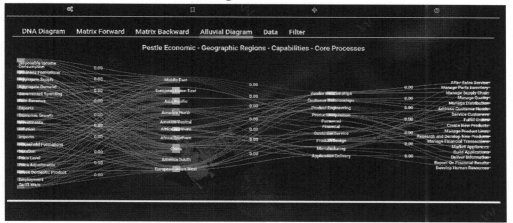

To determine that we use filters that will sort the economic factors base on parameters such as importance or risk or subjective impact and so on. The result is usually a simpler picture like the one below.

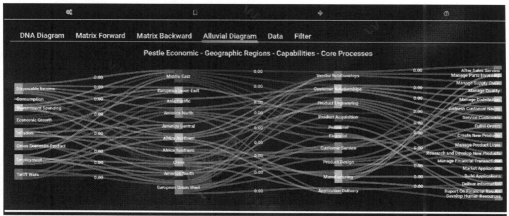

Operational Analytics

Questions

Questions about operational processes deal with quality and performance.

- Are the outputs correct?
- What are the error rates?
- What is the average cycle time?
- What are the throughput measures?
- Are documents positioned on time?
- Are the parts the correct quality?
- And so on

Processes

The processes are the typical operational processes that do the transformation of input to output. They follow simple value chain and process flow structures. Processes are often modeled, reviewed, implemented and monitored. These processes include the basic function of any organization whether product, service, government, charitable, religious etc. oriented. These usually include the following or some variation. These processes are currently the focus of most automation efforts.

- Supply chain
- Customer service
- Production or service operation
- Employee management (HR)
- Finance
- Accounting
- And so on

Decisions

Decisions are typically embedded in the process flow or are handled as a supervisory or expert decision resolution. Today, the focus is on augmenting human decision-making and, in many cases, replacing with smart analytics, usually with AI.

Some decisions are about the operations themselves like evaluating process performance. Some are normal organization criteria for proceeding through a flow to a conclusion such as evaluating a loan application, assuring parts are present for assembly, all documents are present and correct for a permit and so on. These are the everyday decisions made in the normal operation of an organization.

Analytic Example

Suppose that management likes to use cycle time and transport time with cost as a basis for ranking. This is a reasonable approach as one of the better improvement targets is transport time, the time it takes to move from Process A to Process B or Step 1 to Step 2. The chart below shows one way to view the data using a logistic recession with bubble to indicate the size of one of the variables.

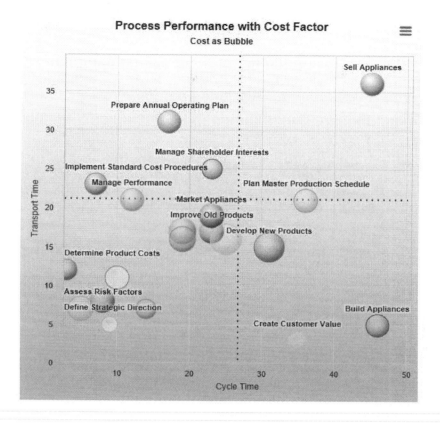

Process Performance with Cost Factor
Cost as Bubble

Interpretation

Based on plotting only cycle time and transport time performance with cost shown in the bubbles, the following interpretation of the four quadrants makes sense:

1. **Upper left quadrant** – The usual starting point for many process improvement projects lies in shrinking the time between actions. For example, improve the transport time and reduce the overall cycle time in doing so. These improvements are very visible and are good for establishing credibility. In this situation, start with 'Prepare Operating Plan'.

2. **Upper right quadrant** – A good opportunity for fixing two things at once. This quadrant is where management likes to focus efforts for that very reason, fix two things with one project. 'Sell Appliances' is the target starting point in this situation. While addressing two things at once has good yield, it could also pose some added risk and complexity

3. **Lower left quadrant** – This probably is the last place to go to fix anything as the performance looks OK. However, there are always exceptions, such the squeaky wheel syndrome of someone complaining. Here, the process is fixed to address the customer complaint instead of performance reasons.

4. **Lower right** – Fixing cycle time is the most difficult as it involves a combination of enablers such as skills, technology, policies, procedures, etc. The full suite of enablers does not affect other factors as much as transport time, queue time etc. They may have one or two of the enablers (like cycle time) but rarely all of them.

Suggesting improvements

Here is the order you might use for process improvement based on this simple 4-box analysis:

1. Sell Appliances
2. Prepare Annual Operating Plan
3. Manage Shareholder Interests
4. Implement Standard Costs

ANOTHER EXAMPLE OF INTELLIGENT ANALYTICS

Smart' or 'intelligent analytics' gives you something of insight about an item of interest, problem or opportunity. For example, the highest risk option or the highest yield option on a specific action. Better yet, what pairing of yield versus risk will show a range of options where you can choose the risk and yield level? Here is an example that ranks AI projects based on a composite of all the AI project factors versus the estimated number of neural goals (a high-risk factor):

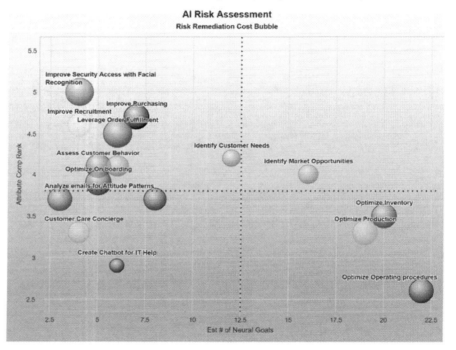

What does all this mean? How do you interpret the diagram? Here is a simple example:

1. **Lower Left**: Not very important, but likely success, low risk (some small projects)

2. **Upper Left**: Important, high success, low risk (full of small projects, good yield, low risk)

3. **Upper Right**: Important but likely failure, high risk (larger projects and more complex but still good yield)

4. **Lower Right**: Unimportant and likely failure, high risk (very complex with low yield)

These are advisement analytics that suggest actions that may be taken. Analytics from software algorithms do not recommend but merely present a ranking or result that a person needs to interpret. A recommendation made by software, and implemented by an organization with bad results, may have legal liability connotations for the software vendor. A human must interpret the result and make the actual recommendation.

HOW DO YOU GET TO INTELLIGENT ANALYTICS?

Tools

The intelligent /AI type of analytics space is very fragmented right now. The tools range from sophisticated algorithm suites for development of applications to canned tools like chatbots and facial recognition to coding environments using AI development platforms. The real need is for tools that are simple yet powerful; visually pleasing but informative; data independent but with access to multiple sets of data. The industry needs tools that management and staff can get up to speed quickly and productively like they did with BPM tools, spreadsheets and simple dashboard products. The screen shots in this chapter are from such a tool.

These must contain business-oriented analytics with simple, easy-to-use interfaces. There is value to using the technical data science tools or creating algorithms using Python, Panda, MAPR and other development tools. However, it should be clear you need a development staff for this or a really good development partner. The real value is from tools that have widespread application with managers and staff providing a large range of value at the point of use. Here are some useful hints for sources of intelligent analytics applications.

Processes:

How do you know where to position process analytics? Start by looking for key verbs in language that define the task. For example, in the flow diagram below the step 'Assess Indicators with Strategy' implies the use of some analytic or analytic sequence (an analytic pipeline). Looking at the flow you can also see the discovery part in the step 'Extracting row data' implying a database access to data related to the indicator. The step 'Preparing the Indicators' is another preparation analytic.

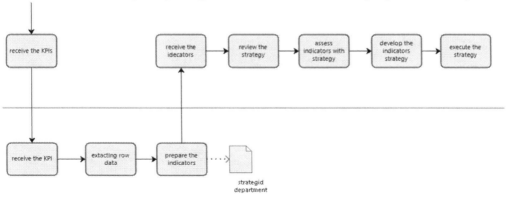

Process flows are a rich source of identifying points of analytic use.

A FEW CONSIDERATIONS ON APPLYING INTELLIGENT ANALYTICS

As you begin to understand intelligent analytics and determine where they can play a role in your organizational improvement efforts, you should keep the following suggestions in mind:

While there are cautions in applying intelligent analytics, the value far out-weighs the effort and cost to apply them. The key is having a compliant staff and expertise that helps you understand where to apply the analytics, what result you need and how valuable they are to the organization.

1. Educate managers and staff as to the use and value of the analytics and lessen any threat to jobs

2. Start simple. Pick an easy issue to deal with or an upgrade of an existing issue. There is a lot of value to mundane things like tracing hidden budget moves to improve budget management and avoid end-of-year sur-prises.

3. Avoid a grandiose starter project like automating an entire operation or replacing a staff with AI, etc. Most of these fail because they are not properly socialized into the organization. This is also part of *start simple* where there is little threat and people have time to adjust. They become great supporters and identifiers of the application of analytics if they are part of the change.

4. Always do some simple pilot efforts to see what your issues will be. They may be the same as other organization or they could be quite different.

5. Get good reliable expert help. It is difficult to create an instant expert staff or expensive to hire several experienced and well-trained data science ex-perts. Plus, there are not many of them yet and they are hard to find.

6. Finally, make sure you understand the data needed, its ease of access, protection issues, formats and availability. This applies to both internal and external sources of data.

Operational Excellence with Digital Process Automation

Dr. Setrag Khoshafian, Gerry McCool, Carolyn Rostetter
Pegasystems Inc., USA

ABSTRACT

This chapter delves into the pragmatic aspects of operations improvements through the various Digital Process Automation capabilities including dynamic case management, robotic automation and artificial intelligence. It will also illustrate how digital enablers such as digital channels, cloud, and connected devices can be leveraged in DPA-enabled operational excellence best practices.

It delves even deeper into a DPA-enabled continuous improvement approach that aligns digital capabilities to lean methodology best practices: an approach that is much-needed and long overdue. It also covers the full excellence cycle from innovative ideation to dynamic execution with intelligent processes coupled with performance monitoring and best practice governance. The authors also discuss various personas in Digital Enterprises that will benefit from this pragmatic *operational excellence* approach; powered through DPA.

INTRODUCTION

In this Digital Transformation (DX) era, the importance of operational excellence and lean principles are becoming even more – not less – critical. Global, social, technology, and marketplace changes are happening faster than ever. Today, every business is a digital business. While some organizations are chasing the latest technology fad, digital leaders are finding success powering lean and operational excellence with Digital Process Automation[1] (DPA).

This paper will delve into the pragmatic aspects of operations improvements through the various DPA capabilities including dynamic case management, robotic automation and artificial intelligence. It will also illustrate how digital enablers such as digital channels, cloud, and connected devices can be leveraged in DPA-enabled operational excellence best practices.

For organizations that face enormous challenges in transforming for tomorrow while realizing business benefits now; delayed gratification is not an option. The objectives of practical operational excellence with lean, focusing on value-added work, are even more compelling in the digital era. The paper will delve deeper into DPA-enabled continuous improvement approach that aligns digital capabilities to lean methodology best practices: an approach that is much needed and long overdue.

The paper covers the full excellence cycle from innovative ideation to dynamic execution with intelligent processes coupled with performance monitoring and best practice governance. It will also discuss various personas in Digital Enterprises that will benefit from this pragmatic *operational excellence* approach; powered through DPA.

---

[1] https://www.pega.com/products/pega-platform/digital-process-automation

DIGITAL PROCESS AUTOMATION

In the past few years, the entire realm of *Business Process Management* has been disrupted. Digital Technologies such as Social, Mobile, Cloud, Internet of Things, Artificial Intelligence and Robotic Process Automation have each had their share of influence on BPM. The new digital-era business process platforms now incorporate Low Code/No Code capabilities to support Citizen Developers. Further-

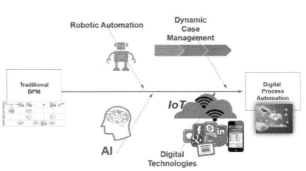

Figure 1: Evolution of DPA

more, the process flow-chart and swim-lane paradigm is now superseded with Dynamic Case Management (DCM) (Khoshafian, 2014) capabilities.

Each of these disruptions are contributors – think of them as major "features" of modern-day DPA. DPA is a prime candidate for Digital Transformation: the catalyst to shift the enterprise from legacies to a digitally transformed organization.

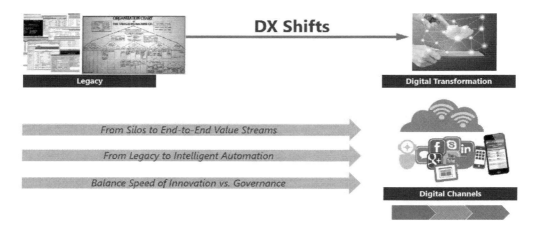

Figure 2: Cultural Transformations

It is sobering to realize that, despite the enormous advances in digital technologies, legacy organizations and legacy applications have survived.

Organizational Shift

The impact on Organizational Culture is one of the most fascinating realities of the digital era. Digital technologies are simply enablers of cultural trends that are transforming all demographics at an accelerated rate. Culture is always more important and impactful than pure digital technologies (Khoshafian, 2018), as impressive as the latter are. The potential cultural impacts on individuals as well as organizations are tremendous. To succeed and innovate with digitization, transformation best practices should challenge long established cultural norms.

It is interesting to note that one of the most archaic organizational structures that has survived decades if not centuries is the ubiquitous vertical "Org Chart." It simply does not inspire agility or change – with layers of management exerting control, functioning through power-driven bureaucratic practices and suffocating innovation, if not the very life, of the organization! The digital era fosters challenging the hierarchical and centralized control-driven organizations with alternative more democratic robust models that empower the participants.

Most organizations are still organized vertically, and each business unit focuses on their measurable objectives. Value streams go horizontally across business units attempting to optimize customer experiences. The Cultural change needs to capture, digitize, and automate the value stream for optimized visibility and control. The value stream digitization and automation are the important pillars. Organizationally, the culture needs to encourage empowered ownership of the value stream across silos.

Digital Process Automation achieves the digitization and automation of value streams through Dynamic Case Management (DCM). It is important to point out that the meta-model of DCM is at a higher and more powerful level than business process flowchart or swim-lane meta-models. So, the evolution of BPM elevated the meta-model of "processes" from flowcharts to digitization of value streams (aka value chains) that have milestones. These milestones in the meta-model hierarchy can involve individual automation steps, robotic automation or process fragments that are swim-lanes or flowcharts. The key point is that the DCM is a higher-level construct that captures and digitizes value streams.

Implications for Operational Excellence

The problem of silos is pervasive. It causes considerable amount of waste and adversely impacts the customer or stakeholder experience. A customer touch point will typically need many business units, teams, or participants towards resolution.

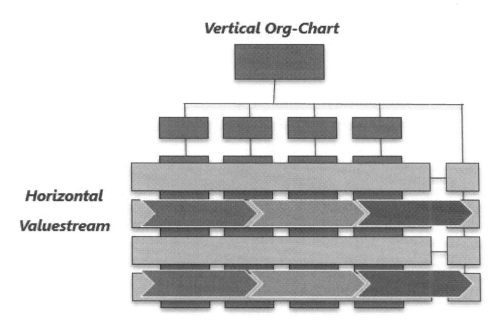

Vertical Org-Chart

Horizontal Valuestream

Figure 3: Horizontal Valuestreams

Typically, these are silo-ed and the communication is done through manual handoffs. It is interesting to note that digital technologies and even digital transformation practices have had little impact on vertically organized siloed organizations. The organization hierarchy has persisted. Value streams go horizontally often with an empowered owner for its operational excellence. If the value streams are not optimized through DPA there will be considerable waste and inefficiencies.

Intelligent Automation

DPA automates work. However, there is a spectrum of workers and a spectrum of work categories for automation.

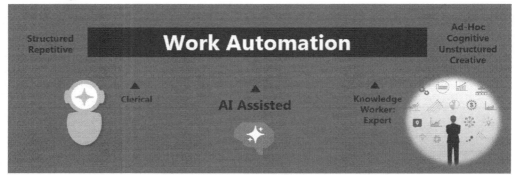

Figure 4: Spectrum of Work Automation

Repetitive Work Automated through Robots and Robotic Automation:

Increasingly, robots are replacing routine, predictable and repetitive *manual* work. This is sometimes characterized as the "long tail" of tasks that are allocated to relatively low-paying repetitive jobs that are managed by the business vs. IT. These can now be automated with robots. These include actual *physical* robots that can, for instance, manage a warehouse moving boxes around or clean the floor in large plants and, of course, you have extensive robotics in Manufacturing.

Smart Manufacturing (aka *Industrie 4.0),* especially due to the Industrial Internet of Things (IIoT), has given rise to the *Adaptive Digital Factory* (Rostetter et al., 2016). That is the industrial Operational Technology (OT) side. On the Information Technology (IT) side we are seeing increasingly Robotic Process Automation (RPA)[2] solutions leveraged successfully in customer relationship as well as back-office operations. It is truly a pragmatic approach for automating work—especially in organizations that have many legacy systems.

AI Assisted Work:

For more mission-critical and higher business value (and typically higher transaction volume) tasks, you now have AI-assisted workers that are guided by increasingly intelligent software that leverages business rules, analytics, and machine learning. It is like having an intelligent Siri or Alexa helping the worker complete their tasks.

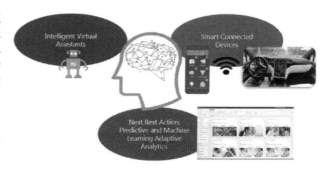

Figure 5: AI Assisted Work

---

[2] https://www.pega.com/rpa

Workers are assisted by bots and Intelligent Virtual Assistants with increasingly sophisticated Natural Language Processing capabilities combined with *knowledge* that is contextual for the task or interaction at hand. The intelligent system now provides the contextual actions to the AI assisted workers: prioritizing various decisions. In many industries, the connected devices themselves are also assisting the worker, even pro-activity: for instance, a smart vehicle warning or making recommendations to the driver (Khoshafian and Rostetter, 2015). AI assisted solutions are becoming increasingly intelligent: especially in the context of end-to-end value streams empowered with underlying rich intelligent capabilities such as rules, predictive analytics, machine learning, adaptive analytics, and Big Data recommendations. The overall end-to-end value stream of different types of work requires orchestration with humans, robots, virtual assistants, and robotic automation when applicable.

Involving Cognitive or Knowledge Workers:

Knowledge workers are the experts. They are the cognitive workers (Khoshafian, 2011). Some have accumulated considerable knowledge and expertise in particular domains. Many organizations are facing a crisis as these workers start to retire and their sometimes-irreplaceable knowledge is lost. A complete digitization strategy needs to also capture, digitize, and automate this knowledge. It is another category of intelligence—this time emanating from *human* intelligence or know-how. Work is not always predetermined or structured. There are some-

Figure 6: Knowledge or Cognitive Work

times—more often than we give credit to—unanticipated exceptions: ad-hoc, dynamic, or unplanned tasks. The cognitive workers need to be involved to solve the difficult challenges. In some cases, their expertise is invaluable. No "Artificial" intelligence will be able to replace this category of workers. They innovate and often come up with the policies and procedures in the organization. They can react on the spot, knowing what to do in an exception situation.

Knowledge workers can be engaged to resolve cases or processes. They can also analyze the reports and the performance of operationalized processes. The knowledge and know-how of this important category of workers need to be harvested and digitized. Ideally, they need to work closely with data scientists: to complement human knowledge with data and machine discovered models. Most importantly their knowledge needs to be harvested and digitized in the context of end-to-end value streams.

Implications for Operational Excellence

Supporting the entire spectrum of automation is a core value proposition for Operational Excellence with Digital Process Automation. Equally important is the flexibility in moving from one automation capability to the other. Sometimes enterprises have used different solutions for the various categories or ignored others. This could create even more inefficiencies. Not everything, for instance, is a Robotic Process Automation problem. If only a siloed RPA tool is used, you could end up with many fragments of robotic automation with no end-to-end automation or orchestration. A bad approach is still bad if it is simply automated. A Digital Process Automation approach for operational excellence combines support not only for the automation spectrum and the worker spectrum, but also for the flexibility in moving from one automation paradigm to the other with ease.

Innovation and Governance

Innovation is critical for survival. Approaches such as Design Thinking[3] for innovation design methods and processes are strategic. Design Thinking helps organizations innovate through empathizing with their target customers, ideate and quickly prototype with innovative solutions. This is often followed by testing and deployment. The whole process is dynamic with multiple continuous iterations and tollgate reviews between the phases. The DX organization needs to encourage and promote design thinking initiatives. It implies focus on innovation with budget, time, and resource allocations. Design Thinking engages multiple disciplines and creates a prioritized backlog of innovation solutions - balancing ease of development, optimized customer experiences, market opportunities and business value. Technology alone does not cause innovation or disruption.

When it comes to prototyping and productizing innovative solutions, DPA supports accelerated speeds of innovation. A new generation of tech-savvy workers are entering the workforce. At the same time, a new generation of application development environments are getting much easier to use – also known as low-code or even no-code development[4] - allowing *anyone* to build small and robust enterprise applications. Citizen developers can also contribute in the development of more complex automated value stream applications - collaborating with their peers and IT. In fact, traditional IT is not able to keep up with the demand of increasingly innovative enterprise applications. With these unstoppable trends, Citizen Developers are filling the gap for innovation in the enterprise in close collaboration with IT.

However, the empowerment of Citizen Developers has to be governed. There needs to be a balance between Digital Innovation Speed – as captured in the Citizen Developer, Citizen Data Scientist and Design Thinking approaches - and Digital Competency Best practices (Khoshafian and Roeck, 2016). This is achieved through a

Competency Center (aka Center of Excellence (CoE)). Connected and Decentralized worlds are mega digital transformation trends.

As organizations try to leverage digitization *specially to automate work,* they are often faced with a healthy tension between two compelling approaches:

- *Digital Innovation Speed:* accelerated and expressed digital application development for automation
- *Digital Competency Best practices:* enablement, methodologies, governance, and re-use to optimize delivery of work automation solutions

---

[3] https://en.wikipedia.org/wiki/Design_thinking

[4] https://www.pega.com/technology/low-code

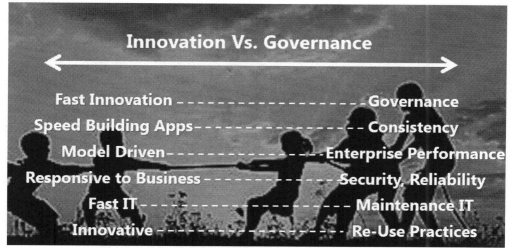

Figure 7: Innovation Vs. Governance Tug of War

The CoE is the clearing house of this balance: innovate fast but also govern with best practices. Four major areas that are covered by the CoE:

- *Enablement:* The onboarding and training of team members for DX

- *Continuous Review of DX Projects:* Project selection, design review and expert services

- *Governance:* The governance for adoption of automation best practices, methodologies (agile and lean), and guardrails to guide team constituents

- *Re-Use:* The creation and management of reusable assets: process fragments, case types, business rules, analytical models, UI/UX design, integration assets, etc.

Implications for Operational Excellence

Innovation is a catalyst for new products and services. But it can also be a catalyst for innovation in operational excellence. Furthermore, having a common language among IT–Business–Operations avoids waste in communication and unmet expectations. CoEs are often either ignored or they starve for authority or budgets. This has serious ramifications for operational excellence. The Competency Center for Digital Transformation makes sure Operational Excellence objectives in building innovative solutions are also met. DX organizations need to think big, think digital but to start small with pragmatic quick wins. They also need to fail fast and succeed faster. All this needs enablement, governance, and agile methodologies – precisely the charter of the CoE. The CoE is not a concept. It needs to be budgeted. Resources need to be trained and empowered to realize the formidable task of alleviating Digital Transformation Debt.

OPERATIONAL EXCELLENCE: CONTINUOUS IMPROVEMENT

We have been – and continue to be – on the Operational Excellence path before; especially through well-established Lean Six Sigma methodologies. There are those who would consider "Lean" and "Six Sigma" as passé. Understandable. These are decades old methodologies.

However, the core value proposition of:

- Lean – reduce waste and improve process efficiency – and

- Six Sigma – reducing variance and improving process quality –

are *more* compelling in the digital era! No other methodology or approach for reducing waste and improving quality has replaced Lean Six Sigma (LSS). This is in sharp contrast to, for instance, development methodologies such as Agile completely replacing or obliterating Waterfall (see Chapter 10 of (Khoshafian, 2014)).

The emergence of Low-Code/No-Code together with key enablers such as Dynamic Case Management digitizing value streams, robotic automation, and AI decisioning within DPA are providing an even *more* compelling incentive to finally realize the promise of Lean and Six Sigma (see Chapter 8 of (Khoshafian, 2014)).

The main difference is that best practices, techniques and the transformational potential of Lean and Six Sigma are now made part of the DNA of continuous improvement methodologies within DPA practices. There are many enterprises that are realizing Lean and Six Sigma optimizations, without rigorous and sometimes over-engineered LSS practices.

> ***Instead of separate LSS practices and certifications and then DPA practices and certifications, the two disciplines are coalescing.***

The DPA approach has profoundly changed LSS. The optimal approach is to leverage the best disciplines and measures of the well-established LSS practices and embed them within DPA methodologies and competency practices. The "Black Belt" thus transforms to DPA practice, while leveraging the best of LSS.

The transformation to embedding LSS disciplines within robust and fast paced DPA implementations that often start with a Design Thinking approach is no small feat.

CONTINUOUS IMPROVEMENT

The continuous improvement for Operational Excellence with DPA is achieved as follows:

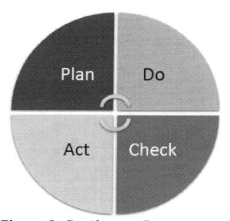

Figure 8: Continuous Improvement

- ***Process efficiency in planning and deploying innovations:*** manufacturers use business-friendly value stream zero-code modeling tools to capture their business requirements directly into the system; automating the system implementation and maintenance phases of the project lifecycle. We call this *Plan*.
- ***Process efficiency in automated execution:*** DPA dynamic cases, AI, robotic automation, and digital capacities orchestrate and automate the work in all categories: avoiding errors, reducing waste, and eliminating manual hand-offs and rework. We call this *Do*.

- **_Process efficiency in process monitoring and improvement:_** Out of the box business activity monitoring dashboards, reports, and automated alerts dynamically monitor if work is processed on time, contractual SLAs are being met, and if processes are running optimally. We call this _Check._

- **_Adjust process efficiency through re-use and specialization_**: Standardize processes across products, LOBs, and regions, while allowing for specialization where needed. Manage the complexity of "1,000 processes" which are really 100s of processes with 10 variations. We call this _Act._

WHO BENEFITS AND HOW?

Leaders Need To:	Digital Process Automation provides:	Who Benefits:
Simplify, streamline and automate key business processes to increase efficiency, minimize errors, adhere to regulations, and deliver better customer and employee experiences Remove waste and effort in handling exceptions, collaborating across siloes, and dynamically managing ad-hoc changes to the case Reduce repetitive tasks and non-value-added work Enable straight-through processing	**End-to-end automation and robotics.** End-to-end automation with case management to orchestrate work across organizational, systems and data siloes - bringing together the people, processes, data and technology to deliver key business outcomes quickly	COO, CFO, CIO Value stream owners Business and IT together Program managers Business analysts Manufacturing SMEs Operators Customers Internal / external auditors
Continuously improve and optimize the business to deliver better results: increased productivity, quality, customer satisfaction, compliance, and cost effectiveness Reduce waste that results from complex forms and manual data retrieval Skill based routing, guided prompts to the service operator, and better user interface and customer experience Decisioning with Next Best Action to reduce effort to figure out what up-sell / cross-sell recommendations or actions for service Reduce waste in trying to figure out the best policy, procedure or information for a given context	**Real-time omni-channel AI.** Intelligent automation—such as for email—that automatically turns unstructured documents into end-to-end work Workforce Intelligence to discover new opportunities for improvement, and powerful business rules to enable the contextual and situational execution of work	COO, CFO Value stream owners Operations / Plant Managers Shared Services Managers Operators Aftermarket Services

Provide faster time-to-value and return on operational excellence efforts in 90 days or less Reduce waste and effort by adopting an agile approach - from requirements gathering all the way through to continuous development, testing, integration, automatic documentation and faster deployments Remove waste in introducing minor or major changes – while leveraging existing investments Avoid unnecessary errors and obtain just-in-time information at any step Empower business users to make changes in a controlled environment on a no-code enterprise scale platform	**Journey-centric Rapid Delivery.** A journey-at-a-time approach that starts with a single case type (i.e. Order Fulfillment)—or even with a small desktop automation like "Start my day"—and lays the foundation for future expansion.	Lean, Six Sigma, and Digital Transformation leaders Value stream owners Kaizen teams Operators Customers Suppliers
Standardize and optimize processes across products, business units, and regions, while allowing for specialization where needed Introduce substantive efficiencies through re-use of no-code assets (case types, processes, decisions, UI) Built-in audit trails and real time visibility into process performance via dashboards and reporting Simplify specialization and avoid waste synchronizing multiple repositories	**Re-Use and Specialization** An architecture that captures business dimensions in reusable layers, enabling logic re-use while allowing for specialization where required.	COO, CIO Value stream owners Business and IT Change managers Operators Auditors
Satisfy security and data residency requirements, while ensuring they can easily connect to legacy systems and on-premise data Remove waste and effort of multiple siloed applications Reduce waste in redundant legacy applications – reduce errors and improve speed	**Cloud Choice.** "As-A-Service" capabilities built for the enterprise, with the flexibility to run in the cloud or within an on-premises architecture, as required.	CIO, CTO, CISO, CFO IT and business stakeholders Program managers Change managers

CONCLUSIONS

Enterprises face enormous challenges in transforming for tomorrow while realizing business benefits *now*; delayed gratification is not an option. The objectives of Lean, focusing on value-added work, are even more compelling in the digital era. Yet most experts estimate 90 percent of lean initiatives fail. Many improvement efforts stall and some fail to meet their full potential when faced with silos and the weight of legacy systems and organizational structures. Operations are plagued with waste and changes to legacy systems are slow and costly; losing valuable momentum needed to seize the real improvements that your teams worked hard to secure. How can you avoid becoming another statistic? How can you innovate and be more responsive?

Companies and their processes are increasingly reliant on digital technologies. Today's operational excellence demands agility to bring full-spectrum solutions which combine the physical and digital in an agile way that allows digital processes to change and evolve as quickly as your people and your business, and as quickly as your customers and market, demands.

While it sounds simple, this requires a unified platform with business-friendly tools to quickly capture business requirements; change processes, rules, and other elements; test processes; and go live, online in days and weeks; not months and years. This also requires an execution engine to orchestrate, automate, and monitor work in real time, allowing your team to see the flow of value as well as problems, and fix or prevent those problems before they disrupt flow.

Enterprises need cutting-edge tools to quickly offer more efficient ways to get work done with less waste, better cost efficiency, and with consistently predictable results. Additionally, enterprises need the ability to create and operate entirely new customer offerings.

To deliver these benefits, they need to have complete control of their processes; but also of any manufacturing process: from innovation, to implementation, to execution. With Digital Process Automation, enterprises can digitize and automate their value streams: orchestrating all phases of end-to-end internally or externally managed manufacturing workflows. Eliminating silos across functional areas provides unprecedented process innovation and efficiency for the manufacturer and their suppliers, partners, and customers. These advancements don't replace your lean methodologies; they accelerate them.

REFERENCES

Khoshafian, S. (2011). "Knowledge Assisted Workers." ZDNet innovation article. https://www.zdnet.com/article/knowledge-assisted-workers/

Khoshafian, S. (2014). *Intelligent BPM: The Next Wave for Customer-Centric Business Applications.* Pega eBook publication. https://www.pega.com/insights/resources/intelligent-bpm-ibpm-next-wave-automation

Khoshafian, S. and Rostetter, C. (2015). "Digital Prescriptive Maintenance." In *Internet of Things, Process of Everything, BPM Everywhere* edited by Layna Fischer. Lighthouse Point, Florida: Future Strategies, Inc., Book Division. http://futstrat.com/books/BPMeverywhere.php

Khoshafian, S. and Roeck, P. (2016). "Digital Transformation Competency Centers." In *Best Practices for Knowledge Workers,* edited by Layna Fischer. Lighthouse Point, Florida: Future Strategies, Inc., Book Division http://bpm-books.com/products/best-practices-to-support-knowledge-work-ers-print

Khoshafian, S. (2018). "How Culture Always Trumps Technology," TEDx talk: https://youtu.be/Z1M2DUparIk

Rostetter et al., (2016). *Adaptive Digital Factory*. Co-authors Carolyn Rostetter, Setrag Khoshafian, Kenty Adams. Pega eBook publication. https://www.pega.com/insights/resources/adaptive-digital-factory

The Man and the Machine and the Future of Work

Alberto Manuel, Microsoft, Singapore

ABSTRACT

Cognitive functions that fundamentally depend on creativity; for example, scenario conception, reasoning and problem solving, are tasks for which humans are, and most likely, will always be better. Machines might mimic these functions, but are not likely to duplicate them, and they will need to lean on human beings for that creative spark. Artificial Intelligence paradigms such as agent systems, evolutionary programming, reinforcement learning, automated theorem-proving, and probabilistic reasoning are looming in different industry sectors. This creates a challenge as we move toward creating a new kind of digital mind that is enhancing the ability of humans to execute their work.

This ground-breaking chapter provides new horizons for what the future of work can look like by combining and blending the man and machine interface with a new set of emerging technologies.

INTRODUCTION

The achievement of singularity is perceived or motivated by advocators that show fear of death or want to reach a stage of immortality. It is therefore irrational, combined with the looming ubiquitous computing in which it was made to appear everywhere and anywhere[1], with possible endless combinations of workloads, omnipresent, making computing an embedded, invisible part of today's life. The stage of distinctiveness or singularity is perpetually arriving 14 to 25 years from now and the future is being delayed[2]. Supporters of singularity tend to forget about the computing limitations on some of the use cases that are just about to become a reality.

Let us take brain simulation as an example. To simulate 10 seconds of real brain-time would require about one year of computer simulation [3] with the current most powerful existing supercomputer.

Only creatures with nervous system and brain would have feelings, which obviously are not present in machines. In the past decade, there was an intense debate on whether machines can or will feel. Emotions are considered as non-detachable part of intelligence. Emotions can be catalogued as rage, fear, panic, love, happiness and which can be driven to take actions. Humans classify emotions and assign them some other emotional values [5]. Advocators of distinction or singularity tend to invoke that cognitive systems designed in advanced forms of machines, like living systems without a nervous system are also able to define a domain of interactions in which it can act with relevance to self-maintenance [6] and as such, are also able to execute the process of cognition.

While the condition is truly related to organisms with and without a nervous system, consciousness is a function of emotional interaction in the societal environment in which humans live or are surrounded. What can be condemned in one society can be accepted in another. The meaning of the emotional values is the basis for conscious experience. Therefore, understanding the cartography of human interaction with the environment is critical in understanding the nature of consciousness [5] that is non-existent in machines.

Humanity questions its own existence and limitations vis-à-vis with the perpetuated advent of new technologies that are transforming our understanding of our societal context. On the other hand, it is almost as easy to start by saying that technology is becoming shaped by universal culture: "How do we enact our changing understandings of ourselves through new technologies" [7].

Our universal individuality cannot be separated by the sacred, profane and spirituality [8]. The flow of other people, nature, environment and ancestor influence that provided us the life principle guidelines we adopt or tend to ignore, that is a consequence of what surround us and make us unique individuals. Because machines do not and most likely will not possess consciousness, they do not describe self in a recursive manner and do not become self-observing systems - out of their defined scope of intervention - that generates the domain of self-consciousness as a domain of self-observation, they are incapable of having free will and intentionality, something that is an essential criteria for moral agency [6].

The fusion or combination of man-machine can be considered in the form of a cyborg – that has certain physiological and intellectual processes aided or controlled by mechanical, electronic, or computational devices [9]. In current thinking, the challenges related with man-machine interface or human augmentation are often concealed, because it is more appealing to discuss whether machines are going to take over human existence.

The Viable System Model (VSM) is probably one of the most elaborated man-machine representations [10] and the importance of the role played by information in control systems and decision making. The VSM was then a vision of the organization in the image of the human species. Functions of management and control were envisioned along the lines of the human brain and nervous system. The brain and nervous system were simulated by a combination of information technologies and human interaction.

STEPPING INTO THE FUTURE OF WORK

Due to accelerated technological improvement and ubiquity, machines in the work environment are more capable of executing repetitive tasks, support a spectrum of manual tasks, including tasks requiring non-cognitive skills. This has led to a demand for a new kind of workforce to complement machines and specialize in new kinds of roles, as well as, talent marketplace aspires a new value proposition, where they can self-realize beyond being treated as a cost-competitive advantage, infusing technology broadly, alongside creativity and increasing their own productivity.

New technologies create new jobs and career changes are widened by their adoption and talent scarcity. Companies expect to hire new employees already possessing skills relevant to new technologies; they seek to automate repetitive work completely and retrain existing employees. The probability of hiring new staff with relevant skills for permanent positions increases the likelihood of strategic redundancies of staff lagging in new skills adoption.

However, nearly a quarter of companies worldwide are undecided or unlikely to pursue the retraining of existing employees, and two-thirds expect workers to adapt and pick up skills in the course of their changing jobs [11], [12]. Other hiring strategies can include resorting to third-party contractors or freelancers. However, these external resources will also need to be proficient in new technologies and new ways of executing work, that is easiest for knowledge-oriented tasks, compared to work environments that include industry sectors like healthcare, manufacturing, transportation, energy and resources.

Throughout history, looming technology development has been propelled by news about human redundancy. Even though new technologies like artificial intelligence will eliminate some jobs [13], they will create new ones and more importantly, they will support new ways on how we carry out our professional activities. Humans have never demonstrated that they struggle with innovation and technological development. Putting political views aside, they have been liberated from the labor burden in terms of how efficiency has contributed to higher net income. Simultaneously, they have the opportunity to take advantage of technology progress and to achieve something which they dream about but see to perceive that will be realized only for the younger generations [14].

Having worked with many customers in different industry sectors, I observed that the way people work has becoming frustrating and unproductive, despite the fusion of cloud services, social, and bring your own software/device. There are definitively productivity improvements, mostly in terms of mobility. Individuals can work anywhere at their own pace and have access to information they commonly use every day. However, mirroring self-expression, self-development (be digital-ready), generating representations of our interactions (the individual social graph [15]) and being able to interact with several social graphs simultaneously and to repeat this process recursively in a single working platform are yet to be accomplished.

Individuals aspire toward a future wherein, in order to participate in a meeting, they don't need to search for meeting content in "teams' workspace", don't need to connect to a projector, don't need to write meeting notes, spark and track action items. People expect that they can use technology to help them make better decisions and concentrate on the decision-making process, instead of manually curating different information sources and imperfect models. In practice, it is about augmenting human intelligence. This is not a futurist idea. This a desirable outcome that humans anticipate and want technology to realize it.

THE FUTURE OF WORK SCENARIOS

To address the desire of what the future of work should become, it is necessary to rethink how technology should pursue a human-led design strategy:

- *Help people achieve what is important to them.* This is something that, during all the years, companies have worked in operational improvement, which did not fully deliver. For example, can't we let people organize and define their own User Interface in a way that they can focus on what is most important to them?

- *Building relationships.* There is an intense debate on methods to discover how to get to know individuals and understand their real needs and wants based on trust, instead of creating personas framed on stereotypes into which we must be forced to fit.

- *Design technology that seamlessly integrates into the human world.* Design for the capabilities and limitations of the human body. Adjust to the human needs dictated by the physical conditions of an environment or device. For example, designing an application to be operated in an explosive and noisy environment is different for designing the same solution to be operated at the office.

A spectrum follows of possible scenarios to explore in terms the future of work..

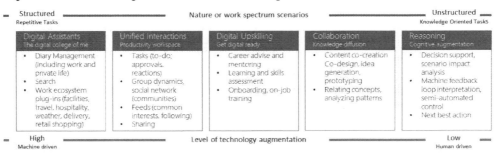

Figure 1 : Collection of Future of Work Scenarios

In summary, the guiding principle of each of the scenarios is focusing less on job descriptions and how jobs will look like in the future, and more on the nature of the work produced.

DIGITAL ASSISTANTS

Managing daily work life can be time-consuming and a major source of distraction and unproductivity. For example, simply agreeing on a meeting slot can involve a considerable effort that could be automated. Aligning private life preferences and professional life duties are another challenge. Incorporating and mirroring private life habits on work life are also a desire. Instead of manually requiring effort to combine commoditized services, e.g.: transportation, into diary management, the expectation is that technology can make a decision on behalf of the human in order to set us free from time consuming tasks and focus on what is relevant, in terms of work activities.

A digital assistant is a solution anchored on the agent systems concepts and it must be responsive to events that occur in its environment, wherein these events affect either the agent's goals or the rules which underpin the procedures that the agent is executing in order to achieve its goals [16].

The agent observes behaviors based situational awareness that will evolve by itself, as a human or the agent proficient level improves about work preferences, build and maintain work rules; search information about the work environment context and filter it according to relevance for task orientation; predict and remind about important actions to accomplish – goal-oriented rules - based on the nature of the work performed; will automate actions like reorder tasks list based on goals and risk factors; manage the agenda in a way that executes the balancing act of collaboration and focus work, adequacy between commitments, workloads and travelling schedules and ultimately, is able to interact with other agents to jointly manage common goals and share information. In this sense, a human will coexist with its digital assistant slowly evolving to a digital twin – morphing private and work life.

Cooperation between a digital assistant and a human requires the implementation of these four kinds of relations to create a trust relationship: augmentative (for mutual incompleteness), integrative (of different views), debative (in sharing critics and criticism) [17] and private (data protection).

UNIFIED INTERACTIONS

Unified interactions enable employees to take actions on tasks, gain access to the data feeds they follow, and collaborate with other individuals, without leaving a single customized interface and hardware according his needs and wants, without changing from one application to another. The use of adapted social network services facilitates team communication, incorporate location-based services for context-aware information (e.g. process machines feeds and signals, service/product quality parameters.

The services incorporate input from team members), real-time information sharing based on role execution and preferences or allow facilitating subject matter expert interaction, communities, third parties (e.g.: suppliers, governmental agencies), and dynamic intelligence. An adaptive collaborative environment enables connectivity with other individuals based on their expertise or access to supporting information for problem-solving.

Human augmentation is enabled by enhancing the human with hardware which has the capability to interchange messages, share information and reactions, as well as, smart things (physically-connected assets) for improving operations in both process and asset level. Technology will adapt and organize the appropriate human "cockpit view" in a single interface discriminating among what is now relevant to act on and what is not, for assisting the human in bringing situation awareness.

DIGITAL UPSKILLING

The continuous rapid development and penetration of digital technologies implies that the workforce must be digital-ready to demonstrate formal authority to execute based on readiness levels [18]. The near-term comprises a pattern of repetitive task automation[1], while in the mid-term, technology will head toward knowledge-oriented activities.

The future of work is related to employee upskilling and retainment - flexibility in terms of employee experience will contribute to retention of talent for the next generation of workers using hyper-personalization engines based on human social graph[2], role definition, performance execution requisites and performance review feedback that will include reputation measured by other individuals.

Workforce upskilling is about bringing more content to the natural work environment. Digital twins will be common, simulations for tweaking and work environments will be duplicated, allowing immersion for training purposes including other physical assets and people that are necessary to work with like virtual managers, equipment and environments. Learning on the job in the twin, virtual space, will be the primary leaning environment, that also include occasional interactions in nomadic spaces for human-only interface. Being able to execute your role to do certain tasks in the work environment – will be linked to training readiness accomplishment.

COLLABORATION

Autonomy and synergies between human and machines co-exist in collaboration, and their proficient levels improve through learning and practice.

In a live enterprise network, technologies will integrate communication between human and machine, socialization; to improve and distribute resource allocation (humans and / or machines) based on ability and authority to execute [18] tasks that contain an intention (request, promise, question, assertion) and a proposition (something that is or could be the case in the social world).

---

[1] Robotic Process Automation is a solution that is being extensively used

[2] It uniquely defines the human: identity, role, relationships, working patterns [15]

This allows the human and/or the machine to optimize operations and transfer execution to become fully-automated, like for example self-healing mechanisms; hybrid with human reasoning or be done manually if no automated solution is met. As a digital extension of individuals' senses, contextual knowledge support serves as an interface of humans to the physical world. Enhancing human capacity to perform can either actively execute requests that machines will answer or, passively, where machines will provide information or decision-making support based on contextual awareness (location, execution conditions and goals).

REASONING

Machine-assisted reasoning - characterized as necessarily independent of formal language [19] - will improve human capabilities to adaptively interact with machines realizing the cyborg concept by means of interoperative man-machine gateways that assumes in increasing interactions between them, accepting their conflicts and letting them cooperate with each other to change a current conflict status into a new coordinated one [17], designed to align the human cognitive needs by means of adopting unified interactions.

Technologies such as agent systems, reinforcement learning, automated theorem-proving and recommendation engines are used to support knowledge-oriented activities. Incorporate specialized Artificial Intelligence technologies processing functions tuned specifically to answer questions, create models, improve operations and support decision making, towards an autonomous, adaptive, learning system, in which the cooperation between man and machines in cognitive functions enables the emergence of other form of evolved intelligence[3].

The key components of assisted reasoning are:

- *Data integration agents*, consisting of automatic disparate data source integration into a common data repository environment, with data cataloguing, ontological construction, multidimensional discovery integration, domain model creation and self-learning and unified data search interface;
- *Analytics agents,* executing cognitive analysis of data, and creating data relationships [20] like for example: association, in which patterns, are related with patterns that they have previously been associated with in some way (social graph); differential attention allocation, in which patterns that have been valuable for goal analysis achievement are given more attention, and prioritized to humans in giving rise to new patterns and supporting to create new models; pattern creation, in which patterns that have been valuable for goal analysis achievement are mutated to yield new patterns and are combined with each other to yield new patterns; hierarchical network, to enable to several large-scale emergent domain knowledge pattern networks and retaining memory of which patterns have previously been associated with each other in any way. This will allow humans to reason under uncertainty and incomplete knowledge;

---

[3] Trying to avoid using conflicts terminology; for example, "General Intelligence"

- *Visualization agents,* data visualization scenarios construction supported by querying via natural language processing, speech recognition and human emotional response to evaluate results satisfaction evaluation.

CONCLUSION

The future of work will bring new forms of interaction between humans and machines, and how humans overall will benefit from human-machine symbiosis. The nature of work might be simplified and at the same time enhanced, that will increasingly augment the human performing his work. However, this won't happen by itself. A clear identification of the difficulties and necessities occurring when trying to make the fusion between man-machine and how that will shape the nature of work, can therefore speed up future development in this area. A human-led approach can only be realized if different groups of interest come together to develop a shared framework for such symbiosis to be realized.

Organizations have a responsibility to prepare the workforce for a future as such and anticipate what professional skills they'll need. Training will play an important part of preparing humans to interact with the next generation of technologies and change in work practices because they will be profoundly different from what we already know today.

REFERENCES

[1] Guide to Computing Fundamentals in Cyber-Physical Systems Concepts, Design Methods, and Applications – Dietmar Möller – ISBN – 3319251767

[2] How We're Predicting AI or Failing To – In Beyond AI: Artificial Dreams - Stuart Armstrong, Kaj Sotala –edited by Jan Romportl, PavelIrcing, Eva Zackova, Michal Polak, and Radek Schuster, 52–75. Pilsen: University of West Bohemia

[3] The Digital Mind: How Science is Redefining Humanity – Arlindo Oliveira – ISBN – 9780262535236

[4] In the Strange Order of Things: Life, Feeling, and the Making of Cultures – António Damásio – ISBN – 0345807146

[5] The Brain and the Inner World: An Introduction to the Neuroscience of the Subjective Experience – Mark Solms – ISBN – 1590510178

[6] Autopoiesis and Cognition: The Realization of the Living – H.R. Maturana (Author), F.J. Varela - ISBN - 9027710163

[7] Indiscretions: of body, gender, technology - Ira Livingston – in Processed Lives - Gender and Technology in Everyday Life, edited by Jennifer Terry and Melodie Calvert – ISBN – 9780415149327

[8] Design Anthropology, Indigenous Knowledge, and the Decolonization of Design – Elizabeth Tunstall, Fabrica, 2011

[9] Cyber-Humans – Our Future with Machines – Woodrow Barfield – ISBN – 3319250485

[10] How Many Grapes Went into the Wine: Stafford Beer on the Art and Science of Holistic Management – Roger Harnden and Allenna Leonard – ISBN – 0471942960

[11] Towards a Reskilling Revolution - World Economic Forum 2018

[12] Future of Jobs - World Economic Forum 2018

[13] The Future of Jobs, 2027: Working Side by Side with Robots – Forrester Research 2017

[14] The Human Condition - Hannah Arendt – ISBN – 0226025985

[15] A Social Platform definition - https://ultrabpm.wordpress.com/2012/01/09/a-social-platform-definition/ - Alberto Manuel 2013

[16] Agent-Oriented Software Engineering: The State of the Art - Michael Wooldridge and Paolo Ciancarini in Agent-Oriented Software Engineering 2001

[17] Modeling and Analysis of Human Interactions with and within Complex Systems - Tetsuo Sawaragi - IEEE International Conference on Systems, Man, and Cybernetics 1999

[18] Social Network Analysis – part two - https://ultrabpm.wordpress.com/2012/03/25/social-network-analysis-part-two/ - Alberto Manuel 2013

[19] Autopoiesis and Cognition: The Realization of the Living - H.R. Maturana (Author) and F.J. Varela - ISBN - 9027710163

[20] The Novamente Artificial Intelligence Engine - Ben Goertzel and Cassio Pennachin – in Artificial General Intelligence – ISBN – 9783540237334

Section 2
Award-Winning Case Studies

Alquería, Colombia
Process Intelligence / Intelligent Business Operations
Nominated by AuraPortal, Spain

1. EXECUTIVE SUMMARY / ABSTRACT

For 59 years, Alquería, Colombia has specialized in the processing and commercialization of long-life dairy products and is now positioned in the Top Three companies in the Colombian Dairy industry. Alquería has always sought constant evolution for business processes in its value chain, especially in critical processes such as supply and the optimization of fresh milk collection.

To stay ahead of the market, Alquería made the decision to digitally transform the company, using a Digital Business Platform to achieve real-time control of their daily processing of 1.2 million liters of fresh milk, integrating many processes including purchasing, collection, farm visits and supply to production for the entire company, which is consists of 11 collection centers, three plants and over 1800 farms.

The new system involves many roles, including Operators of receipt and discharge, Quality Analysts; Information Analysts; Suppliers; Heads of collection and information, and Transport control, etc. Before the implementation, Excel sheets and manual documents were used to record how much milk was wasted or rejected due to non-conformities; and information was often processed with a 15-day delay. Additionally, a great deal of time was required to take control of payment and discount variables for farmers and transporters.

With the tool, the company, farmers and transporters involved have real-time information analysis which results into faster decisions in the event of an anomaly. The strategic value of the information obtained by the platform is the differential point for the entire supply chain.

The competitive advantage gained is the ability to control relevant information for price calculations, including the certifications of each farm, analyzing volumes and centralized information of all the processing to analyze efficiency, pinpoint issues and calculate the probability of obtaining greater margins.

2. OVERVIEW

The implemented platform is mission critical, as it operates 24 hours a day, every day of the year and impacts 100 percent of the industrial process. It controls the entry of more than one million litres of milk per day at a national level. All operators in each collection center use very efficient capture screens which give the company total control of the process.

All the basic parameterization of the dairy farms, stock, routes and vehicles is the basic information required by the platform. Then the waybills are drawn, and another department is responsible for scheduling quality samples, followed by sending of information on scheduled task to a cellular platform to perform the collection work.

Once the collectors start their work in the cellular platform, the data is taken and controls the milk per supplier and consolidates it for each compartment of each vehicle to allow an operator to start the download process, which consists initially of taking temperatures and quality samples. Once this work is done, it goes to the quality area for analysis with minimum and maximum compliance parameters. In case of a non-conformity, the system rejects the milk and uses the tools traceability to show the quality operator where the milk was collected and the compartment in which it was stored, to analyze a counter sample and determine which farm or vehicle caused the non-conformity and automatically charge for the defected milk.

Once the milk has passed the quality control, the analyst gives the order to unload each compartment of each vehicle, at which point the unloading operators receive a task containing all the necessary information for them to empty the vehicle. This indicates the compartments to unload to ensure the complete traceability of the process and take an online inventory. From a button on a form, the integrated mechanical pumps are turned on to unload and automatically weigh the milk. The information that is given by the scales is compared with the data collected in the farms and real-time information of losses is reported. The data controlled by the platform is integrated into our ERP to carry out the manufacturing process and payments to dairy farmers and transporters.

Depending on the region, each stock and plant has set parameters for milk loss that cannot be exceeded which vary depending on the temperature of the milk when collected. If the shrinkage of the unloaded vehicle exceeds the set parameters, the system registers the liters unloaded and automatically charges the relevant supplier in the same way, that milk which does not meet the requirements is also charged to the dairy farm or vehicle contractor that the system determines as responsible.

The system allows traceability from the farm to the final silo of the milk that is being collected, as well as the milk losses and charges to each person in a detailed manner; it also controls all the characteristics, pays transportation rates for each vehicle and records the quality at arrival. At present, the freight rates of more than 120 vehicles are controlled daily with the data managed by the platform and sent to the ERP for their respective payment.

3. BUSINESS CONTEXT

Before implementing the application, many people had to keep control of how much milk was discharged due to wastage or non-conformities using Excel sheets. This information often had a 15-day delay. Additionally, a great deal of time was required to take control of payment variables for freights and discounts to farmers and transporters.

4. THE KEY INNOVATIONS

By having the process online, Alquería can control and monitor real-time accurate information on inventories, shrinkage; traceability, quality and control points of the supply and transport processes. Furthermore, it is very versatile in terms of controlling the transport scheme of the milk from farms to stockpiles to ensure efficiency in transportation costs.

4.1 Business

With the tool, the company, dairy farmers and transporters have the timeliest information analysis which empowers faster decision making in the event of any anomaly and the strategic value of the information obtained by the platform is the differential point for the entire supply chain. The next stage of the implementation is an extranet for the farmers to have their information online for us to access and support them with quality and efficiency issues.

4.2 Organization & Social

The people involved in the processes, ranging from operators to area managers, know the impact of their work on each part of the workflow. Furthermore, control points were designed for the tool to detect important variations. In such cases, it sends the process to review, and we are making the most of the detailed information that the platform collects from the subprocesses.

During the Project, we drew the diagram of normal operation and emphasized the points that were critical and had an important economic or time impact on the operation. There were two premises, primarily for it to be simple and practical for the users and secondly, for the implemented controls to be automatic and of great value.

We evaluated the integrations with the other applications that had to interact and the most relevant were the mobile application, the ERP and the mechanical measuring systems.

Several roles intervene but the most representative are:

1) Operators of receipt and discharge
2) Quality Analysts
3) Information Analysts
4) Supply role
5) Heads of collection and information
6) Transport control

4.3 Case Handling (if any)

Visually we can monitor how each process is flowing according to the different activities and how each used case or exception behaves, thus making it easy to pinpoint issues or points for improvement. When we need to make instant changes, we use the simulation tool to evaluate the impact and determine the best modification. We have linked information from one process to others, such as visits to farms where there is a continuous improvement scheme proposed to each of them. Likewise, our processes undergo continuous optimization to ensure we take full advantage of the controls we put in place.

We now have agility and flexibility to undertake all kinds of changes immediately with complete control and security. Moreover, we use the tool's integrated capabilities that empower the management of all types of cases, and these capabilities include:

- Monitoring, control and analysis of the execution of each process and the analysis of each case and the combined results of several cases.
- Agile Creation of Management Applications to control the different types of cases and elements involved in these cases.
- Integrated Tasks and Dynamic Forms that have the capacity to make items appear when required.
- Business Rules Management.
- Agile Management of Documents and Content to provide a source of organized information, where all users can share information, thereby increasing knowledge and achieving greater efficiency.
- The complete vision of all business activities (in addition to having the option to enter data, make changes or terminate a process at any time).

5. HURDLES OVERCOME

Before the implementation, many of the subprocesses involved a lot of manual work, therefore we requested a human management professional to hold a change management workshop. The goal was for the workers to understand their new roles and what was required of them, and to explain the importance of each person's work in the process flows. This helped boost acceptance to change and so far, the result is total approval by the end user.

5.1 Business

We have achieved a competitive advantage because having the entire process automated and online allows faster decision making in terms of inventory management, price proposal and cost reduction.

5.2 Organization Adoption

As the Project progresses, the scope of control possibilities and improvements increases, and the organization adoption expands. At present, after the ERP, the BPM implementation is the largest and most critical process in the company, so the impact on the company is immense.

6. BENEFITS

6.1 Cost Savings / Time Reductions

100 percent reduction of time and money used in consolidating information to pay transporters and farmers, since each load used to take several hours of work and with the application, it is now automatic. The new system of inventory control has also resulted in savings because we have shipment planning and waste control that is much more detailed than before.

6.2 Increased Revenues

In the current phase, with the information provided by the application, we can evaluate the possibility of analyzing variables included for milk payment and obtain a higher margin in the product price.

6.3 Quality Improvements

The supply process has been optimized. By doing everything online, the real inventory is known at all times. The freight value and milk quality are meticulously controlled, with complete traceability. The information that was captured is of high value to the company and control points placed throughout the process show all possible inconsistencies that could affect the quality of the product.

7. BEST PRACTICES, LEARNING POINTS AND PITFALLS

7.1 Best Practices and Learning Points

- ✓ *Something we learned from this implementation is that the process must be dimensioned so that it not only meets the Manager's requirements but also that it can be easily adapted by the operators.*
- ✓ *Start with the subprocess that generates the most value to the company and takes the least time to implement to obtain quick wins.*
- ✓ *In processes as critical as the one we implemented, we must guarantee that the integrations are always available. Our process auto-detects if the connection is optimal and waits a while to validate again and thus, we guarantee that if the ERP is disconnected, the system has full control of when to integrate the information.*

✓ *In industries such as Alquería that require massive processes, it is necessary to identify what can be done sequentially and what must be done simultaneously to achieve the result that users expect in terms of the application's performance.*

7.2 Pitfalls

✗ *Avoid automating processes without real control points.*

✗ *Failure to consider all the possibilities that a process may have before reaching the final result.*

8. COMPETITIVE ADVANTAGES

The BPM processes we have implemented controls the largest input required by the company, so the competitive advantage we have is the possibility of controlling relevant information for the calculation of prices. This includes controlling the certifications of each farm, analyzing the volume to determine when it should be sent to make powdered milk and centralizing of all the information gathered from preparations to see efficiency issues and the ability to obtain greater margins.

9. TECHNOLOGY

Absolutely all the development, processes and controls were done in the AuraPortal iBPMS tool. We integrate the information provided by the platform with the ERP; and this integration is continuous and bi-directional. Additionally, we have integrated the AuraPortal instant workflow app with information boards and a cellular platform developed in Android that allows us to collect information we never had previously.

10. THE TECHNOLOGY AND SERVICE PROVIDERS

We have received training from INDEPRO, a Partner of AuraPortal (http://indepro.com.co). After completing a short training course and a lot of reading and practice, we decided to carry out the development ourselves. One person was responsible for the development and if a technical question arose, we consulted the INDEPRO consultant. The results were very positive.

California Resources Corporation, United States

Nominated by ProcessMaker, USA

1. EXECUTIVE SUMMARY / ABSTRACT

About CRC

California Resources Corporation (CRC)[1] is a publicly traded oil and gas exploration and production company and the largest oil and natural gas producer in California on a gross-operated basis. CRC operates a world-class resource base exclusively within the state of California, applying complementary and integrated infrastructure to gather, process and market production. Using advanced technology, CRC's workforce of approximately 5,000 employees and contractors focuses on safely and responsibly supplying affordable energy for California by Californians.

Project Scope – Optimizing Parts Management

CRC was interested in improving the process of linking field assets to their inventory of spare parts and optimizing parts management. To accomplish this goal, a cross-functional team was established to study the problem and recommend a solution. The study produced a complex workflow that diagrammed a parts procurement workflow that traversed multiple CRC departments and external parties as well.

Several sub-problems within the parts procurement workflow were identified to create a multi-phased approach to the project.

1. Create a comprehensive end-to-end workflow to fully understand the parts procurement and management process between CRC departments and between CRC and various vendors too.

2. Link field assets (such as oil producing wells) to the CRC inventory of spare parts in a 60,000 square foot warehouse. Obsolete parts no longer mapped to active wells in a timely fashion and sync data sources.

3. Transform time-consuming word-only description searches to precise metadata searches via part numbers, supplying vendor names, SKUs, contract numbers, etc. allowing users to search for parts using a variety of attributes; reducing the time needed to locate parts in CRC warehouse.

4. Consolidate parts data from disparate sources.

5. Resolve lack of searchable metadata fields that make finding parts difficult as they are indexed under slightly different names in various disparate systems.

6. Create an automated solution for inventory management and use its data to improve contracting and lower expensive off-catalog purchases.

---

[1] http://www.crc.com/

7. Ensure the metadata of newly ordered parts were captured and mapped to active wells to achieve the goal of all parts in the CRC warehouse being tied to active field assets.

2. OVERVIEW

Executive Support

To tackle the project of this extreme complexity and size, the first step was building executive support. Field-based executives, leaders in IT, procurement and relationships with vendors were all brought to the table. What could have been a political hot potato was nipped in the bud as soon as executives provided guidance to check "the blame game" and get the process fixed right.

Mapping the Process

Once executive support was marshalled, the initial core team got to work diagramming the vastly complex procurement workflows associated with securing parts for field-based assets. It took several months to diagram the entire process. Discussions within one functional area lead to hand-offs to other departments and additional pieces that needed to be incorporated into the larger workflows. Similarly, parts vendors with whom CRC contracted needed to be included in the broader workflow. In total, more than eight departments and multiple vendors participated in the creation of a comprehensive parts procurement workflow.

Search Before You Buy!

The single most important step in the procurement process was searching inventory already on hand. CRC inventory stored in a dozen disparate systems, including external vendor systems. Many searches across so many systems were time-consuming. They were also frustrating because parts were cataloged based on descriptions rather than part numbers, vendors' names or other methods of identification making it difficult to locate parts in existing inventory. The first big step in the project was the integration of these systems of record into one Google-like searchable database. Once this phase of the project was complete, CRC was able to implement the "Search Before You Buy!" protocol.

By searching the comprehensive inventory database, parts on hand could be quickly located and dispatched for oil well repair. To ensure the inventory control was constantly being improved, the data entry workflow was amended. Now, when a part being searched is determined to be a one-off item, a new database entry is created, and the part mapped to an active field-based asset before procurement activities with external vendors can commence. Another essential element of the controlling part inventory was to create stock numbers and to associate them to field assets. Frequently-used parts were identified. Those parts used less frequently (that could be sourced locally) were transferred to vendor contracts with strict SLA times for delivery.

Introducing Automation

Everybody on the CRC team agreed that understanding and automating the "Search Before You Buy!" process was key to the project's success. CRC used tabs to display responses from various systems of records in a central location. Once that was done, the automation of the entire process began. CRC selected a new BPM vendor after a robust due diligence process. The vendor's professional services worked closely with IT colleagues at CRC to build an automated process for parts procurement that automated the searching of inventory and provided reports that allowed unprecedented visibility to CRC parts inventory. This new clarity allowed for the identification and procure of more parts from existing inventory – faster.

Advantageous contracts with vendors for locally sourced parts were negotiated based on data gleaned from new BPM reports and dashboards. CRC was also able to streamline warehouse operations for additional savings.

Results

Once the automated procurement workflow was deployed, CRC experienced an immediate and profound reduction in phone calls and emails chasing down parts. Reports that contained data not previously available showed which parts were used frequently and where they could be procured. Conversely, parts that didn't turn over frequently (or at all in some cases) were also identified. This new information helped CRC identify inventory that was not being used or were not mapped to field-based assets and queued for clean-up.

3. BUSINESS CONTEXT

CRC is the largest oil and gas exploration and production company in California on a gross-operated basis. With a workforce of 5,000 employees and contractors and a 60,000 square foot warehouse to store parts for their many field-based assets, and a dozen disparate systems to search for inventory, the procurement process was complex, frustrating and in need of automation.

4. THE KEY INNOVATIONS

The "Search Before You Buy!" procurement protocol immediately reduced calls and emails between departments, among the requestors and the warehouse and with external vendors too since parts were being found faster and more accurately within existing inventory. Searching for part descriptions was centralized to one data source and the search process itself was upgraded to include part numbers, vendors and other attributes that made finding the right part significantly easier. Collectively this parts procurement automation project greatly reduced the number of off-catalog purchases. Each off-catalog purchase was likely to incur an up-charge of 20 percent or more scaled across the volume of requests.

Additionally, metrics were reported on many new pieces of data. This information allowed for insight into frequently used parts and it also helped determine the demand for various parts that would be sourced locally. It's preferable for the vendor to incur the cost of inventory and have the service level agreement to deliver to CRC for local parts.

Finally, this automation project allowed CRC to begin understanding what was in their 60,000 square foot parts warehouse. Parts that were not able to be tied to active field-based assets were obsoleted. Some were recycled, sold for scrap or otherwise disposed of. The newly-freed warehouse space eliminated the need to procure additional storage space too.

Because variation in the parts ordering process was reduced and transparency to inventory created, CRC was able to translate these learnings into better contract terms with suppliers to reduce non-catalog purchases.

4.1 Business

Using the metrics generated through the new BPM solution, CRC gained new visibility into their operations such as the identification of frequently used parts. Conversely, demand for parts that don't frequently turn over or that never are used were also noted. Because variation in the parts ordering process was reduced and transparency to inventory created, CRC was able to translate these learnings into better contract terms with suppliers to avoid non-catalog purchases. This information allowed CRC to develop smarter contracts with local suppliers, often transferring the cost of warehousing inventory to local vendors. CRC was also able to negotiate local vendor delivery of less frequently used parts according to agreed-upon service levels, further optimizing the CRC warehouse. The capital investment tied up in inventory was reduced as the procurement process became more efficient.

4.2 Process, Platform and Automation

- Any use of digital technologies as they are leveraged in Bakersfield planning and operations, including mobile, social collaboration, cloud, analytics, IoT, and especially digitized theater value streams through iBPM and Dynamic / Adaptive Case Management

- Nearly a dozen legacy procurement systems were actively used by CRC at the time this project was initiated. Through the application of ProcessMaker BPMN workflow solution, an automated process that combined a Google-like search of disparate inventory sources was created. Because of this new capability, CRC was able to introduce a "Search Before You Buy!" protocol that has made procurement more effective, contracting more advantageous and wells are now repaired more quickly – all of which have a positive impact on oil production.

4.3 Organization & Social

Because of up-front executive support at CRC and commitment to "no finger pointing," internal departments and vendors alike were willing to constructively participate in this massive workflow project. Also, the key to the project's success was the fact that the two project leaders were well-tenured within the company. One was from the IT department and the other had significant field experience. Collectively, their expertise equipped them with the right knowledge, skills and abilities to assemble a superior team, marshal executive support and get the work done.

The previous friction of searching many disparate systems for parts on hand by procurement specialists was frustrating and time-consuming. When the "Search Before You Buy!" process went live, it was rapidly adopted by procurement specialists due to its ease of use and automation. This made the procurement process more efficient and wells were able to be repaired faster, boosting production.

Contracting appreciates the new system, because it gives them visibility to inventory. They now know what was being used, where it was sitting, etc. Using this new-found information, they are able to renegotiate contracts so local vendors inventory and deliver parts that are used less frequently. This reduces CRC capital tied up in inventory.

5. HURDLES OVERCOME

5.1 Management

Because a bit of due diligence was done by the two project leaders and presented to executives backed with data, the decision to tackle this project was an easy one. The executive team showed impressive leadership and support when they instituted the "no finger pointing" rule to the project. They were able to see the benefits such a project could offer to CRC and set aside their pride to get it done.

5.2 Business

Getting control over the inventory in a 60,000 square foot inventory space that was augmented with a network of vendor suppliers, each with different descriptions, item numbers, etc. was an enormous challenge. Automating the parts inventory systems and consolidating them into one search was the key to success for this project. Without the capability to "Search Before You Buy!" the project would not have enjoyed the success it did.

5.3 Organization Adoption

Because the procurement team was able to quickly and easily "Search Before You Buy!", the adoption of the new automation went incredibly smoothly. Because automation delivered such rapid value to end users, there was no need for a comprehensive rollout strategy, at the elbow helpers during go live, etc.

6. BENEFITS

6.1 Cost Savings / Time Reductions

Reduced time-to-market, cycle time, etc.

- Reduced warehouse costs that have already exceeded $1 million dollars in obsolete inventory that could not be mapped to active wells
- Increased productivity of procurement staff. No more calling and emails searching for items by description only. Part numbers, vendor names and other fields are now searchable in an automated fashion.
- Increased use of pre-negotiated contracts helped lower cost of inventory.
- Metrics, reports and dashboards created visibility into inventory and its use. This allowed for the establishment of par levels of inventory and smarter inventory control decision making.
- Increased use of local vendors for less frequently-used parts storage and deliver reduced capital needed to maintain par levels of inventory.
- Every off-catalog purchase that was eliminated, reduced costs by at least 20 percent.
- Less frustration, email and calls – priceless.

6.2 Increased Revenues

While it's clear that getting oil-producing wells repaired more quickly and productive again producing leads to a healthier bottom line, the exact contribution to this metric is not available.

6.3 Quality Improvements

7. BEST PRACTICES, LEARNING POINTS AND PITFALLS

7.1 Best Practices and Learning Points

- ✓ *Working together with business stakeholders to gather feedback and support up front allowed this project to be highly successful. Communication is an important component for a project of this magnitude to ensure success.*
- ✓ *Implementing the "Search Before You Buy!" capability for procurement fundamentally changed the procurement experience – reducing friction for employees and vendors alike and improving the find rate of parts on hand for field assets in need.*
- ✓ *Each off-catalog purchase that was eliminated saved CRC at least 20 percent*
- ✓ *Intellectual capital lost due to retirements or separations for other reasons does impact the organization. Visibility to larger processes to become fragmented and less efficient across the organization.*
- ✓ *Process maps are amazing tools to memorialize processes, people by role, resources and more. No matter who needs to know or why they need to know*

about the process at some time in the future – the entire process is well doc-umented.

7.2 Pitfalls

×   *Ensuring parts were consistently mapped to field assets improved partner-ships with vendors when legitimate off-catalog requests cropped up. This al-lowed for more strategic partnering with the vendor to provide CRC enhanced inventory management services at the margin and the service level.*

×   *Because CRC only had their parts inventory cataloged by description (a field with lots of variabilities) it was very difficult for procurement as well as CRC vendors to rapidly search inventory and locate needed parts. As a result, off-catalog requests were too high, and the cost of parts procurements was at least 20 percent too high for this type of request.*

8. COMPETITIVE ADVANTAGES

By bringing together inventory data from disparate sources, standardizing and im-proving indexing criteria and making it available for downstream decision making, CRC is transforming their business and becoming a much better steward of finan-cial resources.

This project has fundamentally changed procurement, inventory management, contracting and vendor relations strategies in the oil and gas industry in California.

By having access to the right data in an easy-to-find, structured process, variability (and cost) are driven out of the procurement, contracting, vendor management and inventory management processes.

By obsoleting and recycling or otherwise liquidating old inventory, warehouse stor-age is more efficiently used, eliminating the planned expansion into new warehouse space.

9. TECHNOLOGY

CRC selected ProcessMaker as their Business Process Management solution. Pro-cessMaker Enterprise Edition was deployed on-site at CRC so they had total control over the system.

The vast procurement process was diagrammed first by CRC and its vendors. The Process Map was built in ProcessMaker and fine-tuned by both professional ser-vices and CRC staff. ProcessMaker professional services worked closely with the CRC team for about four months to develop an automated and searchable procure-ment solution.

The go-live of this solution allowed CRC to launch the "Search Before You Buy!" protocol and to enjoy the many fruits of this labor.

10. THE TECHNOLOGY AND SERVICE PROVIDERS

CRC staffers were augmented by two highly-skilled professional services consult-ants from ProcessMaker. Together, they spent four months developing the procure-ment BPM solution that is live at CRC today.

ProcessMaker is a workflow management software solution that automates docu-ment-intensive, approval-based processes to improve the way information flows be-tween people and systems. ProcessMaker can assist organizations of any size with designing, automating and deploying business processes or workflows. Process-Maker's built-in flexibility makes it easy to integrate with external applications and leverage your investment in legacy solutions while at the same time, streamlining operations.

City of Fort Worth, Texas USA
Nominated by BP Logix, Inc. USA

1. EXECUTIVE SUMMARY / ABSTRACT

The City of Fort Worth is ranked 15th largest in the U.S. and is home to 800,000+ residents. Fort Worth's goal—to be the most livable and best-managed city in the country—prompted CTO Kevin Gunn to envision and implement a BPM initiative. Gunn leads the City's efforts to digitally transform its business processes, beginning with garnering the support necessary to embark on a project that touches Fort Worth's citizens, businesses, and employees. Launched one year ago, the initiative's first phase includes a City-wide implementation impacting nearly 7,000 users.

Fort Worth's digital Forms Portal—a cornerstone of the project—was conceived as a vehicle to gain rapid acceptance and demonstrate ROI. The City leverages the technology in unique ways: through the creative implementation of placeholder forms, the City was able to go live with over 400 City forms *on day one*. This innovative approach allowed all forms to be categorized, promoted (where appropriate), and made searchable while producing valuable utilization data. This actionable information provides City management with statistics that help focus efforts on areas promising highest ROI through additional automation.

Fort Worth is currently rolling out the second phase: the Citizens Portal, thereby extending the benefits of the City's phase one achievements to its residents, and to those who do business with the City. Based on the positive results so far, Gunn expects this next phase will contribute to Fort Worth's goal of favorably positioning the City as it vies to keep and attract residents and businesses.

2. OVERVIEW

With a vision to become the most livable and best-managed city in the country, the City of Fort Worth relies on BPM technology to digitally transform itself into a more user-friendly and accessible city for all stakeholders.

Phase 1, beginning October 2017, successfully established an internal Forms Portal now hosting over 500 forms, and averaging over 3,700 forms accessed per month. The forms portal is a keystone component in the automation of the City's business processes as it is the source of initiation, tracking, and interaction with City services. The implementation has allowed the City to design, develop, and deploy new applications, and improve existing applications that have greatly enhanced how it handles its day-to-day operations. As a result, Phase 1 is meeting its goal of gaining rapid acceptance and measurable return-on-investment.

Fort Worth's CTO, Kevin Gunn, selected *Process Director*, an off-the-shelf BPM solution, as the core technology for this and subsequent phases. Gunn and his team leverage the platform in unique ways, and development time and cost are kept to a minimum by using core product capabilities to perform a majority of the required functions. Through the creative use and implementation of placeholder forms, the City went live with its internal portal featuring over 400 City forms.

The City's innovative approach provides for all forms to be categorized, promoted (where appropriate), and searchable—and produces valuable utilization data in the process. The ease of finding and submitting any form needed by City employees drove quick acceptance of the new portal, resulting in an estimated savings of

$1,040 per month alone from time saved by locating forms. The usage statistics collected by the portal provide valuable input into prioritizing competing opportunities for automation.

Internal Forms Portal – Home Screen

The greatest benefits, however, arise from the reengineering of the City's business processes, which also presented some of the larger challenges. The tuition reimbursement process was one of the first to be reengineered; affecting employees who work throughout the 680 facilities distributed across the City's 350 square miles. The current process involved five separate forms and spreadsheets plus rules, regulations and instructions located on three different websites. The process starts with the user filling out documentation and obtaining signatures to get pre-approved to take courses and remained active throughout the entire semester completing with payroll reimbursement and filing of the forms. By leveraging the BPM solution, we were able to automate much of the data entry, both through pulling employee information from our ERP system and by copying and transforming data within the form as it progressed through the process. Leveraging the dynamic nature of the forms and external data sources allowed us to eliminate several steps in the process associated with validations and filling in data that an employee would not have readily available. Previous planning spreadsheets were eliminated by including the calculations in the form along with validations and prompts that helped clarify limitations to the reimbursements. It was challenging to reach consensus on reducing the number of previous touch points and standardizing the processing across 24 departments.

Previously, a file folder was maintained within HR throughout the semester and when grades were submitted, they were manually matched up to the original request, compared against the approved courses and the reimbursements were manually tabulated. Leveraging the power of a BPM solution allowed the forms to remain active throughout the semester in case the original submitter had a course change. Two weeks before grades are due, the system sends a reminder to submit grades along with a submission link . Once grades are submitted, they are reviewed, and payroll disbursements are compiled.

The final step of the process posed a technical challenge, requiring filing the completed form and supporting documentation into the City's document management system. The City already had a document management system in place prior to implementing the BPM solution but there was no interface that would allow the BPM solution to pass the documents and associated metadata needed for automated filing. This technical challenge was overcome by leveraging the power of the Process Director software development kit to build a custom task that would create the required interface. Once developed, the custom task was easily reused for all subsequent forms, as the SDK allowed for the development of a generalized parameter driven interface that draws upon the power of the BPM solution and is consistent with the custom tasks that ship with the software. The complete automation of the tuition reimbursement process eliminated several man-hours of work for each form that was processed and greatly sped up processing time.

As an example, during the introduction of the forms at a department head meeting, a fire chief offered his praise for the form, stating that in the past he literally had a fire truck pulled out of service so that they could take a firefighter to City hall to manually walk the form through the process and get it approved.

Even with a significantly reengineered process, the tuition reimbursement form contains 13 touch points and leverages more than seven of the core BPM functionalities. As it was our first complex form being rolled out, the IT team kept in routine contact with the administrator of the tuition reimbursement process and kept tight control of any deviations that were needed in the defined process. After the first complete semester cycle, the lessons learned allowed for additional rights to be assigned to the process administrator, which turned out mainly to be in the ability to assign alternative approvers. We also took the lessons learned and applied them to the creation of a template that is used as the starting point for future process reengineering efforts.

The following shows the complexity of the tuition reimbursement timeline:

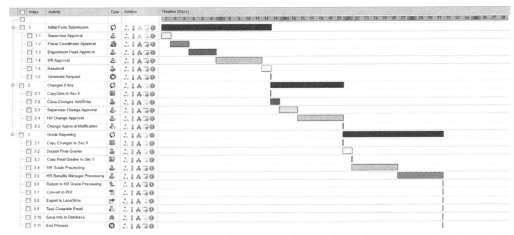

The City has continued to leverage the BPM solution in unique ways that have led to the development of seven additional custom tasks that further extend the functionality of the product. During process reengineering meetings with customers, we were able to change the narrative of the customer from asking "what can the solution do" by informing them that in almost all cases, we have found ways to configure or extend the product to address most everything. We have changed the customer narrative to "what is needed to best support the business needs."

This shift in mindset led to ideas such as one that was brought up for issuing security badge access where the customer wanted to be able to select a building and the floor at which point, they would be presented an image of the floor with callouts for the badge access points. Next step required the customer to be able to click on the callouts in the image to select the doors where badge access was to be granted. Checking with the vendor, it was determined that there was not a known solution to the challenge. We then utilized common HTML image-mapping techniques and combined them with JavaScript APIs offered through the BPM solution to create the desired functionality. Our ability to make the BPM solution produce the results required to effectively support the City's business requirements has led to a continued increase in demands to reengineer processes. Recently, a new HR form was introduced at a meeting with human resource coordinators from all 24 city departments to rounds of applause by those who would be using the form and benefitting from it.

The initial effort was focused on making all City processes easier to initiate, to leverage existing data in other repositories, systems and locations while extending it to where and how the customer needs to participate. The effort evaluated current business practices and reengineered them to streamline the processes while integrating with other systems to optimize customer needs and engagement.

Fort Worth is currently rolling out the second phase of its Citizens Portal and is extending the City's previous years' achievements to its residents and those who do business with Fort Worth. The City's goal is that by re-working all city processes so we are more efficient, and providing a Citizen's portal for improved access and communication, this will result in a positive response from the community, and improved reputation as a city that "CAN."

City of Fort Worth leadership was aware of the challenges inherent in transforming how a large city operates and the risks associated with such an encompassing business transformation project that would involve years of planning, implementing and fine-tuning to meet its needs and those of its employees and citizens – and ultimately changing the way it handles its day-to-day operations. Most important to City management was the concept of becoming a model city in how it is operated and is managed and to become the most livable city in the country. But it had to start on its internal operations first, on a massive city-wide Intranet project that involves 7000+ employees. Fort Worth is on a mission to transform and morph into a progressive city; the best in the U.S. To achieve this goal, its management is taking steps to replicate its initial successes and transformation seen with its Forms Portal and create a Citizen-facing platform that will aid in the creation and delivery of services to retain and attract residents and businesses to the area. Making Fort Worth an example of an innovative, forward-thinking city was key to the success of the City's initiatives.

3. BUSINESS CONTEXT

The City of Fort Worth was previously operating in obsolescence and disorganization, and the few automated processes the City offered were undeniably antiquated. Progress was slow, getting business accomplished was painful and there was absolutely no visibility into any established processes. The City realized that in order to be known as the best-managed city in the U.S., it would have to undergo a major renovation of systems and processes and become accountable as improvements began to take effect. The City had a grand vision but required a partner with which to make drastic changes that would position the City differently going forward.

To succeed in meeting its vision, the City needed to replace outdated processes and systems that were no longer effective, efficient and step up the way the city operates, both internally and externally, by leveraging BPM technology. Fort Worth desired a cohesive and robust system to help digitize, streamline and attribute accountability along the way, with added visibility into those processes with necessary metrics to continue making positive changes as the City transformed itself. By implementing the first phase of its digital initiative, the Forms Portal, Fort Worth was able to creatively implement what would ultimately work for the City's Intranet.

4. THE KEY INNOVATIONS

The Forms Portal replaced various forms that were distributed across the Intranet, and other forms which were hard to find in other systems, were consolidated into one portal. More importantly, the bigger picture was a tremendous effort by the City to rebuild the processes behind each one of the newly accessible forms. With over 500 forms now, each process behind the forms is being reengineered and streamlined, or eliminated altogether, making the City much more efficient and saving both time and dollars.

Impact:

- Legal compliance – previous manual processes were limited to sporadic random audits and lacked the controls to ensure we were in legal compliance. Through BPM, we can ensure that actions are happening when required, information is validated and is routed for action when required.
- Centralizing information and data (SQL & Laserfiche) - Prior to implementing Process Director, forms were often filled out and filed locally. The data collected was not readily available and did not exist in a format that could be leveraged.
- Auditing – forms remain electronic and, once complete, are stored centrally in the City's document management system with appropriate records retention applied. This eliminated driving to each of the 44 fire stations to conduct manual audits, for example.

- Reduced lead-times - with a City that provides services 24x7x365 from over 680 facilities spread across 350 square miles, people involved in executing a business process may span several shifts and be in disparate locations. Keeping the process fully electronic, making it available from the Intranet as well as the Internet and having it be device-agnostic has greatly reduced processing times. Forms that would have taken days or weeks to completely flow through the business process are now being completed within hours.

- Reduction of forms through automation - many existing paper forms can be combined into a single form by utilizing the dynamic properties of the BPM solution.

- Elimination of unneeded business processes - in some cases, we have been able to eliminate complete business processes when the reengineering effort has discovered competing processes that accomplish the same function. We ensure the reengineered process addresses the business needs that both original processes set out to accomplish.

- Elimination of participant interaction - many of the processes involved steps that used to require someone to validate the information entered or for a down-process participant to fill in information not known to the process originator. Through leveraging information in other systems, we can pull that data into the process much earlier on and not require further validation.

- Automation of key performance indicators (KPI). - During process reengineering, we determine if KPI stats are collected for the process and if so, what benchmarks are being reported. We have automated the collection and compilation of that data, making the numbers reported more precise and system recorded.

- Records Retention - forms and supporting documents are now filed into records management faster due to their being electronic throughout their entire lifecycle and accurately by eliminating transcriptions of data as they are filed. Some of the forms had never been filed into the document management system previously due to the limitations and challenges presented by their disparate use. Now, they are centrally housed electronically, eliminating scores of file cabinets across the City and allowing accurate records retention policies to be applied.

For the **Citizen Portal**, which is rolling out now, the impact we expect to see is outlined below:

Currently, the majority of all citizen-facing forms are PDFs that need to be printed out, filled out and then submitted by scanning them and emailing them, faxing them or mailing them in. For those forms that are already electronic, often as part of a specialized third-party application with a citizen-facing component, the forms are often hard to locate. The Citizen Forms portal provides a centralized point where a citizen or business partner can locate a form, no matter where it resides. The forms portal is also designed to be mobile-responsive and browser-agnostic, so it is designed to conform to our citizen and business partner needs.

Beyond that, the City is working on rolling out a creative solution by taking on-premise third-party vendor applications and cloud-hosted solutions and using Okta Identity Cloud to provide authentication. We are also working on leveraging

Okta for our BPM solution. This will allow for the dynamic creation of citizen and business partner accounts that can span all the systems where they may interact with the City. This unique approach allows BPM processes that require citizen or business partner authenticated access to utilize a standardize authentication that can be shared by other systems. Due to our unique method of leveraging metadata to control a forms presence on the citizen portal, we are able to show all citizen forms to anonymous users and invoke authentication only when a form that is selected requires it.

Citizens and business partners expect interactions to be fully electronic, accessible from any Internet-connected device, easy to use and resulting in a rapid response. The forms portal is a major contributing factor to the City of Fort Worth being able to meet those expectations. By cross-referencing forms available through our citizen customer relationship management platform, to bill payment forms, to our BPM hosted forms, there will be a single source to find the form needed. Our initial launch will include approximately 200 citizen-facing forms.

4.1 Business

The immediate benefit to the users was to provide them with a single location to easily find any form that they needed regardless of where that form resided, which was accomplished by easily integrating with other systems and repositories so forms could be located regardless of location. The portal was designed to provide multiple intuitive methods to locate a form including a text search, a view by business unit, a categorized view and promoted forms. The forms portal also integrates into the user touchpoints of the BPM technology that is leveraged, providing a consolidated interface to interact with automated forms at any point in their processing. All stakeholders are benefitting from this portal that has become a source for improving how processes are set up, the usefulness of all forms, and spearhead the City's automation efforts with metrics.

The Citizens Portal delivers even greater benefits to customers and key stakeholders. The Citizen Portal starts out by providing citizens and business partners with a single location to find all publicly available forms. By providing a form-specific search, categorizations and trending forms reduces the time needed to locate City forms. By providing an easier method to locate forms, it reduces frustrations and calls to City departments seeking to locate the forms. By extending our BPM solution to citizens and business partners, we are able to replace our current static paper forms with dynamic forms that remain electronic and trackable throughout their lifecycle. The forms are platform-agnostic and leverage the capabilities of the platforms they are being run on. For instance, when contesting a parking citation, you will be able to do so from a mobile device and use that device's camera to attach photos of supporting documentation.

With the integration among our BPM platform and our single sign-on platform along with reengineering our existing static forms, the portal allows citizens and business partners the ability to create an account that they will be able to utilize across City applications and City forms. By having a single sign-on account, forms will be able to store and retain data across interactions. For example, apartment complex owners who currently annually fill out a lengthy multi-family rental registration form will be able to have the system load their previous information and provide updates. Forms will also be able to draw data from other City applications to pre-populate data within the forms, such as pulling data into a form from our customer relationship management system.

We also plan to leverage our BPM platform in creative ways when extending it to our citizens and business partners. For instance, "Alexa, I need another City recycling bin" may process through and cause a form to be launched to initiate a request for a recycling bin.

4.2 Process, Platform and Automation

Due to the fast development times that we have been able to achieve with our BPM solution, the City has leveraged it in some very creative ways to tackle some critical needs. In one case, the City was deploying new mobile data computers (MDC) in the police cars and fire trucks but they started receiving reports of the computers blue screening. These computers are critical in protecting life and property, so assessing and addressing the situation was a high priority issue. In a day and a half, we were able to utilize the BPM platform to develop a solution that would allow assessment of the blue screen situation near real-time with data being updated every 15 minutes from the MDCs. The solution allowed them to instantly identify the MDCs having the most instances of blue screening, application of bios patches and blue screen events post patching. Within seconds, they were able to run analysis that had been taking them between four to eight hours a day to compile. This freed them up to actually address the issues, instead of spending a majority of their time trying to develop operational insight. Not only did the solution provide them with a clear picture of the issue, but it also identified several previously unknown issues that they were able to further address.

The following is a screenshot of the solution:

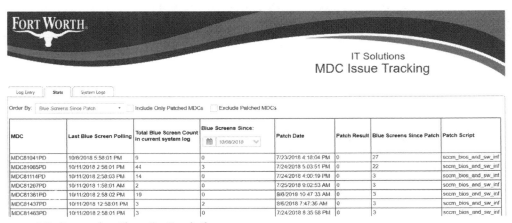

4.3 Organization & Social

Ease of use has been achieved with the Intranet portal, where employees are now able to quickly find what they are looking for, accelerating time-to-value and saving with productivity and payroll hours. From the Citizens portal, it has been creatively developed to allow an employee to sign in and have access to all internal forms as well. The ultimate goals were to make this as intuitive and user-friendly as possible. Results have been amazing, with the City receiving accolades on the uniformity, structure and user-friendly portal, which pulls material together regardless of where certain forms are housed.

5. HURDLES OVERCOME

5.1 Management

The forms portal and BPM implementation were presented at a department heads meeting and several citywide managers meetings along with an explanation of how the City will be reengineering business processes in order to maximize the benefits of implementing a BPM solution. The biggest challenge with management was the result of the department having previously selected a much less capable BPM solution that caused frustration and a delay of the planned deployment timeline.

5.2 Business

The City's departments often operate like 24 semi-independent entities, which can make obtaining consensus on standardizing citywide processes a challenge. Through careful inclusion of stakeholders with competing requirements we were able to bring them together to reach a common approach to most processes. There were situations, such as meet and confer contracts, where we had a legal requirement to handle situations with certain groups differently. We would document the exceptions, the methods required to identify them, and, by using dynamic responsiveness of the forms and conditional workflows we were able to combine them into a single process with variations in content, validations and processing.

5.3 Organization Adoption

Adoption started with the presentations at the department head and managers meetings where the forms portal, Process Director and tuition reimbursement form were all introduced. The tuition reimbursement form is complex and leverages a lot of BPM benefits to greatly transform the process, so we took care to ensure our first form was impactful citywide and demonstrated benefits on multiple levels. The result was that the form was a success and that drove interest from the departments to request to have their processes re-engineered and encouragement to re-engineer other citywide pain point processes. As more forms have been deployed and more people start using them interest has increased demand for further adoption.

We also encouraged adoption by extending development opportunities to the departments. We developed templates to give them a jumpstart while enforcing standards. We offer training classes and we have a resource site where we put all kinds of content needed to learn how to utilize the tool and leverage what we have already accomplished. By having development, test and production environments we are able to give access to the development environment to users with little risk. We do have a "getting started" document that employees must read before they start to ensure they maintain the integrity of the environment.

The following is a screen shot of our SharePoint site where we host the development content.

Overview Videos Getting Started Media Custom Tasks Resource Links Templates FAQs and Tips   Search this site ▾ 𝒫

Process Director

Process Director Overview

Process Director by BP Logix was selected as the business process modeling platform to transform our paper based forms into electronic business processes. Through re-engineering efforts Process Director can leverage data from other City systems to improve the efficiencies and accuracy of forms processing.

Videos
Various training videos including an overview video and the original set of five training sessions that started us on our path to Process Director development.

Getting Started with Process Director
How to get started developing in Process Director and important things you need to know to ensure the integrity of our development environment and your forms.

Media
Media that is loaded onto the Process Director servers that help ensure consistency and ease of migration between environments.

CFW Custom Tasks
Custom Tasks that were developed here at the City along with instructions on how to utilize them to enhance your forms.

Resources
Links to our Process Director environments and various development resources

Templates
Get a jumpstart on your forms development by using a template. We have created templates modelled on some of the most common use case scenarios that allow you to go from concept to functional form and processing rapidly.

FAQs, Tips and Tricks
Things we have learned along the way and have documented here to make your development experience easier.

6. BENEFITS

6.1 Cost Savings / Time Reductions

The implementation not only improves the day-to-day operations of the City, but also saves money, accelerates time-to-market, thus speeding employee and citizens' digital journeys when dealing with City processes. The forms portal is saving an estimated $1,040 per month in employee hours looking for forms. Additionally, the forms portal also allows users to track the progress of automated forms through the system. This functionality has contributed to even greater savings as we automate and track status on forms. Combined, the City is saving over $2K per month on increased productivity of employees.

The City implemented 26 forms within the first year by eliminating paper-based forms and manual routing and approvals. Some of them have a smaller 'per form" impact, but they may have a much higher usage rate often saving an equivalent amount annually. The tuition reimbursement form is a bit more impactful than some of the other forms, where the average form has a $5,000 per year cost improvement impact. This means that in the first year the forms we automated have resulted in a financial impact of $130,000 per year, a number that will increase as we further reengineer our forms. One of the most important impacts is to free up personnel to perform more value-added tasks and to keep our public safety employees protecting the lives and property of our citizens and businesses.

The phase 1 implementation results:

- Saving $2K per month attributed to improved workforce productivity
- Elimination of two other forms of solutions, saving $87,000 annually
- From the initial 26 forms, we are saving $130,000 per year
- Increased time to value by 25 percent
- Forms usage rate increased to 800+ forms per month (a 30 percent increase)
- Improvements in compliance and security
- Ability to rapidly transform processes due to low coding required
- Ability to now track processes until completion within the platform
- Free up personnel to perform more value-added tasks

For the Tuition Reimbursement Form project alone:

- HR hours reduction in processing time, each semester, from 40 hours to eight hours (saving 96 man-hours per year)
- For submitter, saving 225 hours per year in time spent filling out, submitting, and tracking
- Overall, saving 321 employee hours a year
- Financial impact, $8,025 savings per year

Phase 2 Citizen Portal "Projected" results:

- Increase user communication/participation by 25 percent
- The overall reduction in costs by 30 percent with improved processes in place
- Increase user communication/participation by 25 percent
- Provide fully electronic processes that provide visibility and accountability for our citizens and business partners
- The transformation from print and fill forms to dynamically responsive forms that are platform-agnostic.
- Decrease calls by 75 percent for instances of being citizens and business partners not being able to locate forms.

The City expects those savings will ultimately follow a similar model to the internal forms, as they will provide a lot of the same opportunity points to reduce transcriptions, manual validations, manual filing, etc.

6.2 Increased Revenues

Our target is not to grow revenues at this point. From a revenue perspective, we are looking to achieve cost savings that can be reinvested into more value-added activities and initiatives.

6.3 Quality Improvements

- Reduction of data loss due to form loss.
- Elimination of transcription errors in forms processing.
- Reduced entry errors because information is imported from other systems of record to pre-populate forms.
- Improved accuracy of collected data through validators and restricted input.
- Data consistency through pre-defined choices.
- More accurate filing on documents in our document management system due to improved data accuracy.
- Collected information is more complete.

7. BEST PRACTICES, LEARNING POINTS AND PITFALLS

7.1 Best Practices and Learning Points

- ✓ Collaboration with BPM provider to support requirements Forms Portal placed on its server
- ✓ Creation of control panel built to track form access and provide utilization statistics for automation ROI
- ✓ Analytics used to prioritize forms for automation and determine which ones to retire or re-construct, and which processes to make more efficient
- ✓ Automation ROI from form utilization insights
- ✓ Data transformation best achieved via intuitive, graphical configuration of the entire application, from the user interface to process behavior, data transformation, reporting, etc.

7.2 Pitfalls

- ✗ *Involving too many people before, the core team has learned the product and were capable of supporting less experienced and non-technical users.*
- ✗ *Project assessments needed to be more thorough before starting development work. We started developing some forms that appeared to be simple only to learn that they may feed into a much larger business process that needed to be reengineered.*
- ✗ *Dedication of long-term resources to the project to maintain the environment and act as subject matter experts well beyond the initial rollout.*
- ✗ *Obtaining customer assessments for forms used enterprise-wide. We had the primary stakeholders involved but found that within the organization forms may follow different business processes depending upon the department they are initiated within.*

8. COMPETITIVE ADVANTAGES

To become the most livable and best-managed city in the U.S., it was important for all city management to be on board with the digital transformation that was being planned for a year prior to the initial implementation (first phase). With a firm commitment to leading a progressive City and providing new ways of collaborating with and communication within the City, competitive strategies increased productivity, improved visibility into processes, and enhanced perception as a progressive City. As a result of investing in its future with BPM, the City is creating new market opportunities and expanding the existing business by developing digital innovations that are enabling Fort Worth to be a model city of the 21st century; with the development of processes, people and culture underway .

9. TECHNOLOGY

The forms portal was designed as an extension of Process Director by BP Logix. The portal is built as a Microsoft ASP.NET MVC project with limited coding, mainly associated with the search input field. The real power of the portal is derived from inline frames referencing knowledge views in Process Director.

The innovation is best described as the way in which Process Director is leveraged. Custom placeholder forms were created in Process Director that launches existing forms from wherever they reside. The placeholder forms are tagged with Metadata that allow them to be sorted into categories by department and to be promoted. The forms are now organized and searchable, even though the forms themselves are scattered across various websites.

Proliferation: Our approach was to enable our business customers to be able to do various levels of forms development in order to facilitate a faster acceptance and conversion to BMP driven processes. To support this effort, the IT department created an entire developers resource site that is cloud hosted. Included in this effort is a developer's site, establishing standards, creating templates, do demo's at departmental meetings and conducting training classes.

The City has found many ways to creatively use/leverage the BPM technology where it appears that it has not been utilized in that manner before.

Our ERP solution did not have a way to convert and pass off images to our Document Management System. We utilized our BPM solution as an intermediary between the two systems, converting and preparing the images to be imported and filed from ERP to the Document Management System.

Example: The Fire Apparatus Maintenance Daily/Weekly form is dynamically rendered from inspection items stored in a database. The BPM solution did a good job of setting up the form from the data, collecting the inspection information and rendering the completed form. However, we needed to write the response to each inspection item to the database and flag those items with issues and the BPM solution did not have an iterative way of performing this task. We developed a custom task using the SDK that allows each inspection finding to be written to a database. This allows us to drive the business process and is used by the form to pre-populate subsequent uses of the form to display known issues for the equipment.

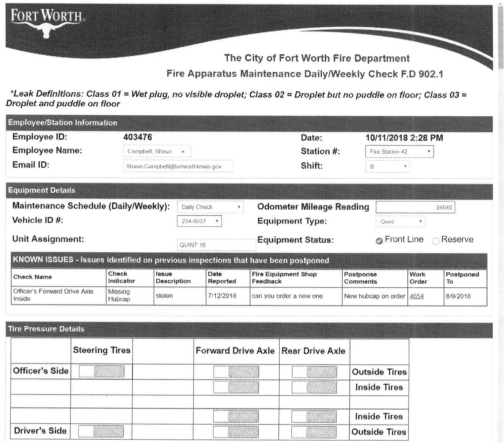

The tire pressure details are dynamically reconfigured when you select equipment with other tire configurations:

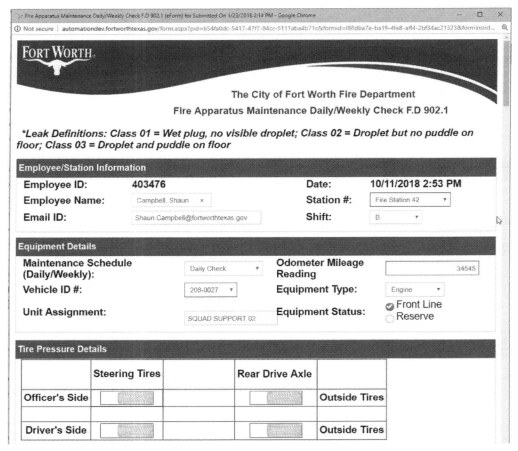

10. THE TECHNOLOGY AND SERVICE PROVIDERS

BPLogix Process Director is the BPM technology that enables the City to develop, deploy, and enhance critical digital applications and achieve new benchmarks in market agility, customer engagement, and regulatory compliance. As a result of using Process Director, Fort Worth is transforming its business, improving city-wide processes and increasing purposeful collaboration with employees, residents and businesses. www.bplogix.com

Discovery Benefits Inc., USA

Hyland, USA

1. EXECUTIVE SUMMARY / ABSTRACT

Benefits across the organization – and beyond

Since 1987, Discovery Benefits Inc. (DBI), one of the fastest-growing employee-benefits administrators in the industry, has simplified its process so its employers, participants and consultants can focus on the things that matter most. They do this by offering cutting-edge technology, instant access to information and expertise, and superior customer service. One component of that cutting-edge technology is its effective use of case management capabilities.

Most of DBI's 800+ employees interact with its case management solution on a daily basis. Its clients do as well through an online portal that allows customers to launch their own cases by submitting service requests.

A truly enterprise-wide solution

Prior to its deployment of an enterprise-wide case management solution, DBI faced a classic challenge: lack of insight into customer and employee information. To wrestle control over the issue, DBI created a purpose-built CRM solution using the data management capabilities of its content services platform. On that same platform, DBI configured a variety of case management solutions, leveraging the information within its CRM for a number of case-driven applications across the organization. Some of those applications include invoicing, client implementation and renewals, awareness situations, client health dashboards, surveys, contracts, integrations with Salesforce and UltiPro, and many more.

Building for success

Much of its case management success is driven by the way DBI built its case management solution: with a future-proof, planned growth philosophy. The DBI team can quickly build case-driven applications for its internal clients that provide valuable time savings and allow employees to strengthen customer relationships and client experiences. With its own initial launch of the case management solution, DBI realized ROI within eight months.

2. OVERVIEW

Prior to its deployment of an enterprise-wide case management solution, DBI, a third-party administrator of consumer-based health plans and COBRA, faced a classic challenge: lack of insight into customer and employee information. They struggled to determine where data was, who had access to it, and how it was gathered, analyzed and acted upon. This lack of visibility strained relationships with clients by extending the time it took to resolve issues, like approving claims, or to discover problems, like workflow process issues.

Case management in control

To wrestle control over the issue, DBI created a purpose-built CRM solution using the data management capabilities of its content services platform. On that same platform, DBI configured a variety of case management solutions, leveraging the information within its CRM for a variety of case-driven applications across the organization. The CRM acts as DBI's central nervous system. All 800 employees use the system intracking data and information such as customer services issues (externally and within its internal organizational structure), on all of DBI's clients and its employees.

By utilizing the same content services platform to build both its CRM solution and related case applications, DBI has the extraordinary ability to service various departments within the organization, as well as to communicate and work with clients externally. Each of these applications, many covered in the content below, call to the CRM as necessary to access information needed to complete tasks. Some of those applications include invoicing, client implementation and renewals; awareness situations; client health dashboards; surveys; contracts; integrations with Salesforce and Ultipro, and many more.

One of those applications is the company's customer-lauded online portal, LEAP. LEAP, accessible from the company's website, offers DBI clients a cross-section of companies from multiple industries and unprecedented access to information. From the portal, customers can set up contacts, do self-reportingl submit service tickets and more. If a client loses an employee who actively accesses the portal, the company can immediately rescind that employee's access by using the portal to do so. On the other hand, if a client hires a new employee who needs access to the portal, the company can provide that access from the portal by filling out an electronic form and opening a case. This ensures the employee gains the correct access to the account. Information like this submitted by the client is automatically updated in the CRM.

Contract signatures and client notes

Here's another way DBI uses its case management capabilities to both manage work and protect the company. DBI struggled with securing and filing client contract signatures and managing that process. In the past, DBI's onboarding team would create a contract and provide it to the client to sign. Once the client signed the contract, DBI expected the client to return it to the company. In most cases, that process flowed smoothly. Nevertheless, DBI found it difficult to track whether or not a client returned its contract. Moreover, if they did, it was just as hard to track whether they signed it properly. This was a challenge DBI needed to solve quickly.

DBI restructured the whole process, creating a legal tab in its CRM system that tied every one of the fees, a per employee fee for any of the services it offers, to one of nine different agreements needed in a contract. For clients who arrived with FSA/HSA/Cobra, three different contracts, the solution would create a report to track those signatures.

Similarly, after a sale based on fees, the CRM creates a contract, using a document packaging solution, and then sends it out via DBI's newly implemented cloud-based signature solution. Once signed and returned, all necessary fields are updated in the CRM. Now, not only does DBI know if a contract was signed. Its employees can go back and review both a client's current and past contracts.

DBI also uses case management capabilities to manage client notes and call tracking. When DBI sets up an account and notices something unique about a client, DBI's Client Health Action Plan application tracks it as a customization. Similarly, if something significant occurs with a client or client group, such as a customer service issue, that interaction is included in client notes and the application tracks the issue. Now, when a participant calls in, the case management solution makes all that information immediately available to the call center, enabling better client service.

These are just a few examples of how case management capabilities not only make a difference at DBI but also puts the company in a league of its own within its industry. For example, after implementing its case management solution, DBI customer service representatives were able to use an Outlook integration to kick off a client case without leaving their familiar email client. Cases are automatically routed to the appropriate parties for follow-up and further action. This time savings alone helped DBI realize ROI within eight months of implementation.

In short, there isn't a third-party administrator in the country that can do what DBI has done, with the efficiencies it has realized.

3. BUSINESS CONTEXT

Since 1987, Discovery Benefits (DBI) has simplified employee benefits administration so its employers, participants and consultants can focus on the things that matter most to them. It does this by offering cutting-edge technology, instant access to information and superior customer service. It is one of the fastest-growing third-party benefits administrators in the insurance industry.

Its stated mission is to transform the complexity of employee benefits administration with innovative solutions and extraordinary customer service. There was a time, however, when that mission was tough to complete.

Until 2008, DBI was still completing many processes, including its claims process, via paper. One of DBI's senior engineers in IT refers to stacks and stacks of paper at that time. Much of that information came in via fax provider. As faxes printed out, DBI employees would collect the faxes, batching 25 documents together at a time. After inputting data from the faxes, employees would return for another group of 25, move to their desks and get back to work. It was a manual, time-consuming process.

Exacerbating the situation was a lack of insight into information: Where was the data, who had the data, how was the data gathered? This lack of visibility was creating issues with clients and damaging customer relations by extending the time it took to resolve issues or discover problems before they became issues.

DBI resolved its paper problem by leveraging the content management capabilities of its content services provider. However, even that step would not fully resolve its visibility challenges.

DBI was running Oracle Siebel, an external system, and one in which DBI didn't own its data. The company found the solution a bit generic, "like anything else." They were building solutions in Siebel but found it difficult to customize those solutions to best meet their needs. To gain some insight into the health of its client relationships, DBI relied on SAP Crystal Reports, running about 30 or more reports a day. Those reports were fed into its content management solution to feed datasets and lookup tables from a number of different systems and vendors.

Employees were doing their best to maintain those datasets, either manually or through electronic forms. That process weighed on employee time commitments. For example, when an employee switched teams or departments, updating datasets wherever that information lived could take an entire morning to accomplish. If DBI added a new position or title, it could take updating more than 15 different forms, adding the new title to numerous drop-down menus.

"We were pulling reports out of our previous CRM every day just to get that information into the autofill table so we could do lookups and workflow," says Dean Johnson, OnBase Manager.

DBI's case management solution would eventually solve that issue. Now, an employee title changes or team move is pulled from DBI's core system, which then auto-updates information across the board, so employees no longer have to manually do all the work.

Workflow helps but doesn't solve every challenge

While DBI had a robust workflow solution, without case management it was still struggling to identify how to best route information from the moment of intake. For example, email communication from one of DBI's 11,000 customers would arrive. The customer service representative receiving the information would create an electronic form in its content management system and then manually choose where to route that information. The process looked something like this:

- CSR receives an email
- Records claims issue
- Fills out an electronic form
- Selects a claims team from a drop down
- Submits electronic form
- Hopes it was the right team

This process presented several challenges. If you were a newer employee at DBI, you may have no idea to whom in the 800-person company you should route the form. Similarly, if a client submitted information through DBI's external portal, they received no verification that it was properly submitted and made it into the system. Clients would regularly call to check on the status of their entry.

DBI would turn to case management to help solve these challenges. In turn, one success leads to another. Before long, DBI has established a number of case management applications that not only streamlined work and brought transparency to the process but also made DBI a leader in its industry.

4. THE KEY INNOVATIONS

As described above, the impact of case management on DBI is felt throughout the organization. Below are just a few of the applications in which DBI leans on case management capabilities to make a difference.

4.1 Business

LEAP & DBI'S Client Health Action Plan

DBI relies on case management capabilities to make its customer-lauded online portal, LEAP, a success. LEAP, accessible from the company's website, offers DBI clients unprecedented access to their information.

Customers can take charge of their own policy renewal through LEAP, control which employees have access to their account and more. They can set up contacts, do self-reporting and submit service tickets. If a client loses an employee for whatever reason, they can immediately rescind the employee's access to the portal. On the other hand, if a client hires a new employee, they can access the portal, fill out an electronic form, and open a case to ensure the employee gains the correct access to the account. Information submitted by the client is automatically updated in the CRM and in DBI's case management solution.

Data from LEAP helps inform DBI's Client Health Action Plan application, an application DBI built from its CRM, which measures the health of each client and consultant. In this instance, "health" reflects DBI's relationship with the client:

green for steady, yellow for concern and red for emergency. When working within DBI's CRM, employees have an immediate view of each client's health report.

If an indicator measures as yellow or red, employees access the Client Health Action Plan application. Through the app, DBI teams create an action plan to help resolve customer issues. For example, if a team experienced a bad renewal with a client, the team can design a plan focused on addressing the issue the next time around. Once the steps are followed and the issue is resolved (with all information tracked in the system), the case is closed and the client's health status is moved from red or yellow back to green.

Case management capabilities help DBI track all the information that fuels the Client Health application. Beyond the health of the customer, DBI also tracks other customer data, including the number of times the client has called on a participant level, how many cases they have created, how many claims they have submitted and even revenue. That information is stored in a data warehouse and the company builds detailed reports on that data that help guide organizational decisions.

Case Management and Claims

Case management also plays a small but significant part of DBI's claims process. DBI processes nearly 15,000 claims a day for its clients, everything from daycare expenses to medical claims. A quick lookup in its case management solution can provide the information an analyst needs – if a policy is claims-based, for example – to best process the claim.

Human Resources

Another case management application in use at DBI focuses on HR processes. DBI relies on Ultipro as its HR solution of record. The HR case management app pulls information from Ulitpro daily to remain up-to-date with every employee's most relevant information.

Electronic forms are used to populate the app, and information from the forms help populate and build a case, as well as assign tasks. For example, a manager can fill out an employee transfer request via an electronic form. Once submitted, the solution calls to the database to see if a desk change is also required. If so, the solution will automatically create a ticket for the IT team to do the move.

The HR app pulls 25 or more different fields from Ultipro on a daily basis. The first thing the case management solution does is check to see if each employee record exists in the app already. If not, the solution will automatically create a new record. If it does exist, the app updates that record with any pertinent information. If an employee changes department, is assigned a new supervisor; is promoted and so forth, that information is also updated.

Everyone in the company uses the app and utilizes it for multiple reasons. Teams build filters so they can review, run reports and build cases tied to team members. For example, the Client Services Department, a team of more than 170 people and eight sub-teams, uses it to route cases to the right sub-team – finance, company profiles, employee issues– and assign work to team members. The information is trackable and reportable, and the team uses the app as its system of record.

Internal Health Tracker

DBI also uses a version of its Client Health Tracker, as mentioned in a previous section, with internal processes and files. It has a team dedicated to reviewing and reporting on the health of internal processes, from beginning to end. If a process is marked yellow or red, the team reviews and tweaks the process until the issue is resolved. This is all within the CRM via case management.

Salesforce Integration

DBI also integrates its content and case management solutions with Salesforce. As soon as a salesperson closes a deal in Salesforce, client information is routed to the CRM and kicks off a case management process. The account is created, appropriate processes assigned, and cases are routed to the appropriate teams and employees. This is also when DBI first starts tracking the health of the client and reports are born.

Before that, though, Salesforce and DBI's content services platform are already working together. DBI built an application on the platform that pulls all the pending opportunities in Salesforce. It makes that information available to those with the appropriate rights and it kicks off case management processes when new information is presented. For example, if a prospective client reaches out to DBI and requests both an RFP and customer references, the app pulls that new information out of Salesforce, recognizes the request, and kicks off a case to fulfill those requests.

"We tie it all together," says Johnson. "And when that prospect becomes a customer, we flush out the prospect information and pull in the new sales information. Our case management solution creates the new account, populates it with pertinent information, and then returns that information to Salesforce. We're constantly feeding back and forth between the two systems."

Lookup Tables

DBI is moving away from Excel, replacing heavy spreadsheets with organized information views within the apps it is building. For its Client Services team, DBI built a view in its app that replaces a "gigantic spreadsheet" it used to track various things. The new view is fed by 20 core Ultipro fields updated in a data warehouse every day. It is a read-only view but allows DBI to track everything that was in the spreadsheet.

A simple benefit of this process is the ability for an employee covering for another employee to access case management capabilities, apply a couple of filters, and find all the pertinent information they may need. They no longer have to dig through a spreadsheet to find information. The employee can click a filter to find an employee with the skills he needs to complete a task. "They check the box, they go to find, they see six people trained to do what they need. It's just much more efficient on everything they do," says Johnson.

DBI also built an app called Lookup Tables. In the past, when a new supervisor started a job or someone moved from one department to another, the team would have to submit a ticket, edit a table, edit an electronic form, and republish the form – it could be a bit of a pain. The Lookup Tables app includes a number of classes that give teams the ability to input information and find what they need. They have built about 20 Lookup Tables for the company.

DocuSign

DBI started using DocuSign in 2016. In the past, DBI's onboarding team would create a contract and provide it to the client to sign. Once the client signed the contract, DBI expected the client to return it to the company. In most cases, that process flowed smoothly. Nevertheless, DBI found it difficult to track whether or not a client returned its contract. Moreover, if they did, it was just as hard to track whether they signed it properly. This was a challenge DBI needed to solve quickly.

DBI restructured the whole process, creating a legal tab in its case management application that tied every one of the fees it had to one of nine different agreements needed in a contract. For clients who arrived with FSA/HSA/Cobra, three different contracts, the solution would create a report to track those signatures.

Similarly, after a sale, based on fees, the solution would create a contract, using it's content services platform vendor's document packaging solution, and then send it out via DocuSign. Once signed and returned, all necessary fields are updated in the CRM. Employees now can go back and review the contract and, in many cases, past contracts.

For past contracts created before the DocuSign integration, DBI took on an enormous cleanup project to make sure those contracts weren't missing items. If so, DBI now has a process to recreate contracts for those older groups, which are pushed through DocuSign.

"We're incorporating all the doc packaging items with workflow and DocuSign and then, in the end, it's all updated on a nice legal tab in our CRM," says Johnson. "We know exactly where things end, where before it was probably one of the worst processes at DBI."

Client Notes and Call Tracking

Another process DBI built into its case management solution is its client notes and call tracking process. When DBI sets up an account and notices something unique about a client, DBI tracks it as a customization. Similarly, if something significant has occurred with the client or client group, such as a customer service issue, that interaction would be included in client notes and the issue tracker. Now, when a participant calls in, case management capabilities make all that information immediately available to the call center.

More than that, DBI's team built what it calls a "switchboard integration" to deliver information to the CSR. No need for the CSR to log in to the case management solution to see the information. It is there, through the integration, and ready to go.

"We're doing integrations like that that are constantly adding and removing those types of notes. This is huge for our phone team," says Johnson. "They don't have to take and escalate that info. It's all connected and right there."

4.2 Case Handling

Prior to implementing its case management solution, employees tracked and handled issues via email. After implementing its content services platform in 2009, DBI created "service request" functionality to streamline issue management with improved communication, tracking and visibility.

At the time, service requests were little more than an eForm that moved between team lifecycles, allowing staff to ask questions or assign a task. Over time, though, this process grew beyond the original scope and became an important part of DBI's growth.

In 2012, DBI leveraged the data management capabilities of its content services platform to build its CRM. The company then converted all of its information into the new application, which provides employees with the ability to create tracking events and notes for each customer. Today, this type of case management functionality helps DBI employees tie cases to each customer. The solutions also build specific and targeted filters, giving employees a way to find, track, sort and organize their work. They also maintain visibility into all pertinent open cases.

To develop the most effective case view, DBI began with the information already requested in each service request and then added items the employee team would typically input manually. Views change as needed, with variations based on team and role requirements.

DBI provides limited access to change items, giving employees only what they need to work thoroughly and effectively. This helps the company maintain efficiency and provides ease-of-use for staff. DBI does not lock down cases. Instead, the company organizes them into employee pods. Those pods work with specific case types, employers or by internal teams. DBI uses filters to organize work based on pods and teams.

4.3 Organization & Social

Prior to launching its case management solution, the DBI team presented the solution to its executive team to gather input and recommendations. Teams then reviewed it to see if anything was missing or if items could be removed. The solution was then released to a beta group of team analysts to test and work out any issues. Once everyone agreed was ready, DBI trained teams and the case management solution was officially launched.

DBI is a fast-paced environment that's constantly evolving. Employees must be agile and amicable to the non-stop changes. That would include changes in how work is completed. To help with the transition from its older eForm workflow process and encourage adoption, DBI provided employees time to work through all the old service requests before turning off that process.

At the same time, DBI took careful consideration with how it released its customer version, showcasing how they could now create cases from their online portal. Both employees and customers found adoption simple and straightforward and were encouraged by the implementation team's support through the transition.

5. HURDLES OVERCOME

Describe the challenges and the way in which the team addressed them, highlighting any human issues across the following sub-headings:

Management

The management at DBI knew there were difficulties with respect to getting a complete view of customers. However, they didn't realize how much they couldn't see. Once it was able to develop its overall case management solution and implement its Client Health Action Plan, DBI better understood the power of case management and what it could do with respect to building better client relationships. Now, with a simple glance, management knows where they stand with each customer and can build executable plans to better each relationship. That alone is attracting new customers and building brand champions.

Business

DBI knew it needed a better way of doing things early on. For example, prior to implementing both a workflow and case management solution, year-end customer renewal involved an all-paper process, with employees putting in 20-plus hours a week in overtime five months out of the year. Workflow automation completely cut out staff overtime – and frustration – and case management capabilities have allowed the company to grow without the need to add significant headcount.

Case management is giving time back to employees as well. Originally, the organization was processing 30 items out of Siebel and into its content management solution every day, a process that would take the average employee 30 minutes or more to complete. It now happens automatically, allowing the employee to focus on more strategic initiatives.

Organization Adoption

DBI enjoyed buy-in from the top down. "Our president, C-levels, executives and management all believe in what our solution can do for our company," says Johnson. "If there is a roadblock, our president will remove it and we move forward with what is best for DBI."

In an effort to improve business processes, the case management solution team comes up with ideas regularly. Employees are DBI's best resources when it comes to determining new challenges and opportunities. Most understand the solution and how it can better benefit the company.

"They come to us now with process improvement ideas, and a fair number of them have already worked out a great starting point for a new solution," says Johnson. "We then work with our stakeholders to produce their applications."

6. BENEFITS

1. While DBI hasn't measured specific hard ROI, it does know it's "a thousand times better off with what we have." But there is plenty of real-world evidence of the impact its case management solution has had, including the realization of ROI in less than eight months:

   - **Streamlined solutions and lower TCO:** DBI had strategic plans for its accounting software (Mas 500 or Sage), but it couldn't handle the data workload the company needed it to. The case management solution was able to handle the data, calculations and information storage. Eventually, DBI realized it was sending information back to its accounting software to have it essentially create an invoice. DBI was able to assist its accounting software with its case management solution, reducing its solution stack and lowering overall TCO with case management.

   - **Time savings for employees:** Originally, the organization was processing 30 items out of Siebel and into its content management solution every day. While that may not sound like much, it could take an employee a half hour or more to complete the work. This now happens automatically, freeing up time for the employee. Another time savings involves the reporting instance DBI created for accounting, which is then processed via its workflow tool and updated in its case management solution. Now, executives who would spend a significant amount of time to find information in Siebel can access that quickly and easily.

2. "We're doing a ton of little things like that," Johnson says. "Information our employees have either always wanted access to or struggle to find, now it's just there and they have it. I'm not sure how we quantify that, beyond saying it's huge."

7. BEST PRACTICES, LEARNING POINTS AND PITFALLS

7.1 Best Practices and Learning Points

   ✓ Research what the actual issue or need is before you begin a solution for anything
   ✓ Meet with the actual workers of the process to hear how it actually is done versus what management understands or feels it is done.
   ✓ Design with growth in mind and expect to hit a few limits that you may not believe will be a limit.
   ✓ Draw out the design for linking different class types needed before building.

✓ Build in "test" items to test steps or processes if an issue is brought up.

7.2 Pitfalls

× Start with a small test group; never decide it will work and release to every-one.

× Don't over-design. Nothing has to look perfect when you first release. Make sure functionality is correct, then make it look nice.

× Making changes soon after release. Set a timeline as to when you will apply the first updates (unless something is completely broken) because everyone will ask you to constantly make changes and you will never know what change affected what, if something goes wrong.

× Do not over "notify" employees. Too many emails in the beginning, and em-ployees will stop reading them.

× Do not automate everything because you need someone to check in on all the processes from time to time to verify everything is working.

8. COMPETITIVE ADVANTAGES

DBI receives accolades for its technology solutions, many of which, as outlined above, rely on the power of case management. It was recently named Partner of the Year at the annual WEX Health conference.

All the processes above contribute to DBI's competitive advantage. As DBI puts it, in terms of third-party administrators, DBI is in a class by itself.

"There isn't a third-party administrator in the country that can do what we've done," says Johnson. "There are third-party administrators that have the volume and staff that we do, and are bigger than us, but we've closed the ground so much with our use of content services and case management that other companies can't even touch what we're doing in our industry. It would take our nearest competitor a long time and a lot of work to catch up."

9. TECHNOLOGY

Hyland's case management platform – OnBase – is a low-code development plat-form focused on the creation of content-enabled, case-based solutions. The plat-form enables the configuration of case structures (case, milestone, task, processes, business rules, automated tasks, and so forth) via configuration (limited to no cod-ing), where the case models are designed as structures that abstract the re-trieval/storage of the case/entity data. The platform also provides rich case process handling (as process models or as rule/event-driven processes). Content is consid-ered first-class in any case solution because of its inherent integrations with a full range of content services. This depth of content-case interoperability is based on the platform's metadata-driven development model.

All solutions built atop the platform are implemented via menu- and wizard-driven administration modules where the admin will define the data models, user interface views (including mobile/responsive apps), searches, work baskets, reports, email notifications, process flows, process logic (rules/actions), interfaces, integrations, and so forth, without the need for any customization via coding/scripting. When an administrator defines the logical data model for their solution, the underlying database tables are created, indexed and linked appropriately for the solution to perform optimally.

Designing case-based solutions equip organizations to use a data model-first ap-proach (the process is secondary). You start by defining the logical data model, which consists of the entities, their metadata, and the relationships/associations

(1-1, 1-M, M-M) between them. The data store of the case data is typically the On-Base database (Hyland facilitates all storage/retrieval operations to abstract this from the solution developer).

To meet diverse pattern requirements, users can customize views of info, custom searches and reports. Access to personalized views (showing info relevant to their role) is comprised of widgets showing work queues, searches, case-folders, etc. A case's visual appearance may be altered as it flows through the process moving through different stages.

The OnBase platform architecture consists of all solution artifacts living in a single configuration database. One too many application servers allow for scaling to meet usage demands. Users access the system through a variety of user interfaces (installed desktop clients, web interfaces, APIs, mobile clients and so forth), as well as via robust integration with other applications and line-of-business systems. For DBI, these connected applications include DocuSign, Salesforce, UltiPro and Microsoft Outlook.

10. THE TECHNOLOGY AND SERVICE PROVIDERS
About OnBase

OnBase is a single enterprise information platform for managing content, processes and cases deployed on-premises or in the Hyland Cloud. Providing enterprise content management (ECM), case management, business process management (BPM), records management and capture all on a single platform, OnBase transforms organizations around the globe by empowering them to become more agile, efficient and effective. Enterprise cloud-based sharing capability for the OnBase platform is available with our complementary offering, ShareBase. To learn more about how more than 19,000 organizations are digitizing their workplaces to transform their business operations, visit OnBase.com.

About Hyland

Hyland is a leader in providing software solutions for managing content, processes and cases for organizations across the globe. For over 25 years, Hyland has enabled more than 19,000 organizations to digitalize their workplaces and fundamentally transform their operations. Named one of Fortune's Best Companies to Work For® since 2014, Hyland is widely known as both a great company to work for and a great company to do business with. For more information, please visit Hyland.com.

Home Health Care Management, USA
Nominated by i-Sight, Canada

1. EXECUTIVE SUMMARY / ABSTRACT

Case management software is used by Home Health Care Management's visiting caseworkers in eight counties. Users are nurses, physiotherapists, occupational therapists, speech therapists, social workers, dieticians and other mobile healthcare workers to report incidents, accidents, complaints and health and safety issues affecting themselves, their co-workers and their patients.

Implementation of a case management software solution improved customer service through the improved reporting of incidents, accidents, complaints and health and safety issues. It also improved operations by facilitating incident reporting from the field, saving hours of travel time and increasing the accuracy of reports. It also improved compliance with Department of Health reporting requirements and Joint Commission standards.

Since implementing case management software, Home Health Care Management has saved $50,000 per year in salaries and boosted their billable hours while increasing compliance and reducing the risk of fines.

Increased efficiency has resulted in faster turnaround for investigations and resolutions for clients and their families and quicker, more effective, reporting

- Incident resolution has decreased from two weeks or more to 72 hours.

- Ongoing reporting that used to take two people three hours is now done by one person in five minutes.

- Quarterly trend reporting that previously took eight hours now takes one hour.

- Submissions from the field have increased by four times providing the data HHCM needs to identify trends and address shortfalls.

2. OVERVIEW

HHCM's large staff of caregivers spend most of their time on the road, caring for their patients. The system they were using made reporting incidents, accidents, complaints and issues inefficient, inaccurate and time-consuming.

Their system couldn't be accessed by the field staff, so things were reported through the manager instead of directly from the field clinicians. Nurses and other clinicians would have to either return to the office to enter the information or call the office and leave the report on their manager's voicemail. The manager would then enter the report into the system. The information in the system was inconsistent and difficult to access for reporting to the Department of Health for surveys or complaint follow-up.

Another challenge was that HHCM was unable to use its data to identify trends because the system didn't have a mechanism to report by field, type, agency, etc. In fact, some parts of the business were still using spreadsheets to track incidents, so there wasn't one common source of data to analyze.

The company was at an increased risk of a citation by the Department of Health for missing reports. The inability of staff to report from the field resulted in reports not always being filed. HHCM was looking for a configurable system that made it easy for clinicians to enter data from the field.

They also needed to enforce a workflow that eliminated free-form input and incorporated drop-down menus to standardize the information being entered and make reporting and trend analysis easier.

The ability to build forms into the system was important to HHCM, to eliminate steps and paper. Some incidents required clinicians to fill out multiple forms, which was difficult to enforce. They wanted to combine the forms into one streamlined intake process to increase accurate reporting and ensure compliance with reporting requirements.

3. BUSINESS CONTEXT

Home Health Care Management (HHCM) serves eight counties with advanced nursing and physical, occupational and speech therapies as well as medical social work, dietitian service and hospice and palliative care.

With a total of 5028 patients visited in 2017, it's a busy operation with a lot of issues, which were being tracked and investigated using a home-grown system that was tethered to the office. This was causing delays and incomplete reports, resulting in incorrect and unavailable data. Case management was time consuming, innefficient and ineffective. There was no way to report on cases and look at trends and risks.

A reliance on paper forms made tasks time-consuming and inefficient. And the system was becoming obsolete and was prone to crashing. HHCM needed a new case management system that better matched the needs of a large public service organization with a mobile workforce.

The solution needed to include:

- A workflow that standardized input for reporting and trend analysis.
- Built-in forms to eliminate steps and paper.
- The ability to generate detailed reports for trend analysis.
- Compliance with Department of Health and the Joint Commission reporting requirements.
- A high level of configuration.

4. THE KEY INNOVATIONS

The organization is more efficient and effective and patients get better care since clinicians don't need to rush back to the office to update cases. The company savs about $50,000 per year in wages, due to increased efficiency.

4.1 Business

Increased efficiency has resulted in faster turnaround for investigations and resolutions for clients and their families and quicker, more effective, reporting: Incident resolution has decreased from two weeks or more to 72 hours.

HHCM is Joint Commission accredited and implementing a case manangement solution has helped them to comply with incident reporting standards of the Joint Commission. HHCM is able to provide thorough, organized, professional reports.

4.2 Case Handling

Before implementing case management software, cases were handled through a home-grown system that could only be accessed in the office. Clinicians would either travel back to the office to input case information, or telephone their managers and have them update case files.

Now managers don't have to get involved in updating cases, but have visibility into the case files if they need it. When a case file is modifided, the modification is date-stamped and time-stamped, providing a complete record of case activity, who completed it and when. Access roles can be set so that those collaborating on a case can access all or some information, depending on their level of access.

All case information resides in a centralized case file that is secure and organized, with each activity recorded in chronological order. Case reports can be generated from the case file, into a pre-formatted, professional document, with one click.

The technology is divided into three functions: intake, case management and reporting. Clinicians can open a case using a simple but detailed intake form that has pick lists and fields that guide the form completion in a logical and intuitive way. The level of detail required in the intake function ensures that all the relevant information is captured so that reporting is meaningful and detailed.

The next function, case management, is where the clinician gathers all the case information as they work. The technology allows users to upload images, video or audio files, add case notes from within the tool, send and receive emails related to a case and see all their cases in a case roll. Every activity is time and date stamped to provide a complete record of everything they have done related to a case. Clinicians can generate a complete, professional case report with one click, gathering all the case information from the case file and exporting it into a Word template that can be shared or saved.

And finally, the reporting function allows managers to drag and drop fields into any one of dozens of report templates (bar graphs, heat maps, line graphs, etc.) to get summary reports showing various views of the data. These are used for risk management, trend analysis and to spot areas where better oversight or targeted training may be required. This has helped HHCM to improve areas of the business by adding training for staff where they can see problems.

4.3 Organization & Social

Employees can now concentrate on conducting their patient visits in the field, rather than updating cases. Once they complete a visit, or even during a patient visit, they can log in to the case management tool on their mobile devices and add case notes, upload files and notify others of updates, if necessary. Manager can see case information and don't need verbal updates from clinicians.

5. HURDLES OVERCOME

The need to customize forms and combine them into one streamlined intake process required detailed analysis and discussion. Not all case management technology provides this. HHCM found a solution that would enable them to design their own dynamic forms with pick lists to minimize data entry and maximize the efficiency of form completion. This created an adaptive nature to the forms so that they would dynamically adjust to the entries of the user and the specific case type.

6. BENEFITS

HHCM has saved time and money by implementing case management software and employees work more efficiently. Managers have better oversight of cases, workers and productivity. With this oversight; improvements to patient care have been more quickly identified and acted upon by the HHCM organization. Repeated issues with treatments can be analysed through trend reporting in i-Sight and provided to senior management immediately to effect changes in the field. This one benefit alone has improved patient care, increased treatment success, and given trust in the organization's continuous improvement process.

6.1 Cost Savings / Time Reductions

HHCM saves about $50,000 per year in employee wages.

Incident resolution has decreased from two weeks or greater to 72 hours.

Ongoing reporting that used to take two people one hour is now done by one person in five minutes.

Quarterly trend reporting that previously took eight hours now takes one hour.

6.2 Increased Revenues

Clinicians spend less time on administration and more time in the field producing billable hours for the company.

6.3 Quality Improvements

Patients get better, more focused care and clinicians have more time to spend with them. Patient files are more detailed and accurate now that they are updated by the clinician, and not a third party, in a timely manner.

7. BEST PRACTICES, LEARNING POINTS AND PITFALLS

7.1 Best Practices and Learning Points

- ✓ Remote access to a case management system allows workers to update files either during a visit or immediately after, resulting in more accurate and timely information.
- ✓ Configurable access roles help to keep information secure and private. This is especially important with health information.
- ✓ Reporting for trend analysis is used to improve operations, reduce risk and monitor problem areas.
- ✓ The ability to configure forms to capture the information through pick lists helps to streamline information entry and reflect the language and workflow of the organization.
- ✓ The ability to configure fields in-house (without going back to the vendor each time) can save a company time and money.

8. COMPETITIVE ADVANTAGES

An efficient case management system allows HHCM to provide better care to patients because clinicians have more time to spend interacting with them, rather than taking notes and travelling to the office or making phone calls to update case files. Having complete data for reporting helps HHCM improve operations and tackle any issues as soon as a trend is spotted. They can target training for staff based on types of incidents or issues that are showing up in reports. This creates a safer, happier environment for staff and patients. Happier employees perform better.

9. TECHNOLOGY

The case management platform was utilized to enable HHCM to optimize their process. With the ability to use the platform on mobile devices as well as the strong reporting suite, these capabilities powered faster and more accurate data capture from the field and an ability for the management team to identify patient treatment improvements through identification of complaints or treatment side effects. This has resulted in a continuous improvement capability not viable with the previous manual process.

10. THE TECHNOLOGY AND SERVICE PROVIDERS

i-Sight Case Management (https://i-sight.com) was the vendor/product implemented by NYCHH. i-Sight is a global leader in web-based case management and reporting solutions for organizations of all sizes. i-Sight streamlines the investigative workflow, enabling users to create new cases, manage tasks and analyze the results with ease. i-Sight's logical workflow ensures that all steps are completed, deadlines are met and stakeholders are always in the loop.

i-Sight provides configurable fields so that organizations who implement the case management software can perform some customization as their needs change. This adaptive element of the software eliminates the need to spend time and money on small revisions to the product.

The project was overseen by Lynann DeCusatis, Interim CEO, Home Health Care Management.

IBM Global Sales Incentives

Nominated by IBM Corporation, US

1. EXECUTIVE SUMMARY / ABSTRACT

Using Robotics Process Automation (RPA) software, IBM has created an automated process to have a robot work as a delegate for sales managers. This robot, named Nano Second, can create Incentive Plan Letters (IPL) for sellers on a specific type of sales incentive plan known as a Pool Plan. The IPL is the formal agreement between IBM and each person who is eligible to be on an incentive plan.

By inventing a robot to follow a specific set of business rules and create the IPLs for 2H 2017 Pool Plans, sales managers are freed from manually entering data from other systems into the system where the IPLs are created and tracked. This has provided them with more time for other more productive engagements with their sellers and clients.

In the past, managers would typically spend about 10 minutes per IPL creation. With the creation of Nano, IPLs for thousands of sellers worldwide, are created in an average of 18 seconds per letter. In total, during each cycle, sales managers who have benefited from this new process, have saved on average, about 70 minutes each.

2. OVERVIEW

IBM is moving to Robotics Process Automation (RPA) in order to reduce manual tasks in processes, help things move faster, reduce errors, and deliver results by eliminating administrative or repetitive tasks. Using RPA frees employees up and enables them to focus on higher value work. IBM's Global Sales Incentives (GSI) organization has embraced RPA to lessen workloads of sales managers and sales incentives support personnel, freeing them up to spend more time engaging with their sellers and clients.

The concept of RPA is very similar to a flowcharter in a virtual environment. The software robot can be configured using rules-based logic to perform tasks such as cutting and pasting data from a spreadsheet into an application, in order to perform a particular task. The robot uses keyboard and mouse controls to take actions and execute automations. Business operations employees - people with process and subject matter expertise but no programing experience - can be trained to independently automate processes using RPA tools within a few weeks. The robot accesses end user computer systems - via the user interface with an established access control mechanism (e.g. logon ID and password) - so no underlying systems programming is required.

The first implementation was focused on the Incentive Plan Letter (IPL) for sellers on a particular type of incentive plan known as a Pool Plan. The IPL is the formal agreement between an eligible employee and IBM. This agreement allows eligible employees to be compensated for the sale of products and services directly to a specific set of customers, business partners and/or territories responsible for driving incremental revenue, profit and/or signings. The sales managers are ultimately responsible for creating, updating, and cancelling IPLs.

The Pool Plan sellers for 2H 2017 were identified by specific sales roles by having the robot run a query in the incentives database and extracting the data into a spreadsheet. The robot then logged in as a delegate for the sales managers in IBM's legacy system tool. This RPA process involved input into multiple screens following

IBM's business rules for the creation of Incentive Plan Letters. The robot then notified the sales managers about the draft IPLs that were created. The sales managers reviewed the draft IPLs and then offered them to the sellers for final acceptance.

3. BUSINESS CONTEXT

Prior to the use of the RPA process for IPL creation, managers had to manually compile information about their sellers such as job role, plan type and incentive element details. They would then need to log into IBM's legacy system tool and manually input data on multiple screens in order to create the IPLs for offering to their respective sellers.

With the creation of Nano, IPLs for thousands of sellers worldwide, are created in an average of 18 seconds per letter, saving sales managers on average, about 70 minutes each.

4. THE KEY INNOVATIONS

4.1 Business and Operational Impact
- Worldwide creation of more than 7,000 Incentive Plan Letters (IPLs)
- IPL creation improved from 10 minutes to 18 seconds per letter
- Average time savings of 70 minutes per sales manager
- Managers freed up to focus on higher value activities
  - Sales activities
  - Client engagements
  - Employee coaching/mentoring
- Accelerated 2H 2017 Start-up of new sales cycle
  - Incentive Plan Letters were able to be issued in a timely manner.
  - Met target of 98% of sellers on Plan 30 days sooner compared to prior year.
- Better data quality with automated inputs vs. manual inputs
- Much more cost-effective solution compared to development of a more expensive replacement of legacy systems.

4.2 Innovation
- Integration of RPA with existing tools and processes drives efficiency and productivity through automation.
- Using internal organization resources with business owner subject matter experts to develop and deploy RPA solutions is more effective and accelerated approach as compared to costly IT investments in reprogramming legacy systems.
- RPA can be used to access all kinds of applications from modern web solutions to legacy mainframe software which allows for flexibility to implement solutions to existing business rules across the organization.
- Changes in business processes can be easily updated using the RPA processes and tools.

4.3 Impact and Implementation
- The successful implementation of the Pool Plan IPL creation using robotics was met with great appreciation by the sales managers evidenced by this sampling of feedback:
  - "I must say, a great process improvement."
  - "Great progress for IPL deployment."
  - "Just to let you know that the enhancement made with pre/filled in information really has been helpful and speeded up the process."

- The RPA solution is easily scalable to all worldwide sale plan types (Individual Quota, Absolute and Pool Plans), evidenced by the creation of over 20,000 IPLs for 1H 2018 and the expectation of nearly 30,000 IPLs to be created for the 2H 2018 sales cycle.
- The organization is now identifying other business processes which involve manual and repetitive steps as candidates for future RPA solutions like:
  - Generation of specific and targeted automation e-mails
  - Query/Report processing
  - Automated refreshes of cognitive dashboards and presentations

5. HURDLES OVERCOME

5.1 Management

- The management challenge was to ensure that controls were in place to mitigate any business controls exposure
  - Robot was set with unique userid credentials.
  - All transactions processed by the robot were identifiable and trackable.

- **Business**
- The business challenge was to gain knowledge and build RPA skills with existing organizational resources
  - RPA workshops and boot camps assisted with training and development.
  - Acquisition of laptops with faster processors to handle speed/volumes.

- **Organization Adoption**
  - RPA solutions have freed up time spent on manual and repetitive tasks, redirecting the focus on higher value tasks (i.e. Customer engagements, deeper analysis, coaching/mentoring, acquiring/building skills).
  - Teams learned new skills at all stages of deployment.
  - Robotics has been made fun in the organization by "humanizing" the robot by giving it a name and face – Nano Second.

6. BENEFITS

6.1 Cost Savings / Time Reductions

- IPL creation improved from an average of 10 minutes to 18 seconds per letter.
- Average time savings of 70 minutes per sales manager.
- Met target of 98% of sellers on Plan 30 days sooner compared to prior year.

6.2 Increased Revenues

- When sellers and sales managers have more time to spend with clients and teams it supports revenue growth.

6.3 Quality Improvements

- Reducing keystrokes from trusted source data with automated input increases document accuracy and timeliness.

7. BEST PRACTICES, LEARNING POINTS AND PITFALLS

7.1 Best Practices and Learning Points

✓ *Ensure Subject Matter Experts are engaged in development of the RPA solutions*

✓ *RPA solutions are scalable and easily adaptable to other business processes using existing tools*

✓ *"Humanize" the robot to portray as a team member (i.e. name, picture, doll, etc.)*

✓ *Engage multiple worldwide resources across the organization for automation ideas to help build a backlog and gain buy-in from the teams*

✓ *Remove process inefficiencies to maximize automation*

✓ *Use video recording options to assist with process flow/requirements*

✓ *Celebrate successes*

7.2 Pitfalls

✗ *Don't start everything at once, start small and then scale*

✗ *Don't have too many projects to deliver on at the same time*

✗ *Don't automate from management directives, but rather from bottoms up*

8. COMPETITIVE ADVANTAGES

- There is tremendous upside in cost efficiency, savings, and productivity among other global organizations, both for our commissions support personnel and our salespeople. As noted in Section 4, our robot Nano Second can scale to heightened levels of workload volume (tens of thousands of Incentive Plan Letters across the globe) based on complex business rules. This generates significant impact on business operations and seller satisfaction.

- With an Incentive Plan Letter in place sooner than was historically done, the seller is more focused and motivated early on in the sales cycle, regarding what to sell based on their plan, with a clear line of sight as to how they will be compensated. This not only improves seller satisfaction, but ultimately drive revenue as well.

- The Nano Second project tightly aligns to our business strategy around workforce and cognition vis-à-vis robotic processing—specifically, transforming our employees to higher-skilled roles where they allow technology to execute processing while focusing their attention on review, analysis, and decision-making. This is about shifting the repetitive, rules-driven work onto our Nano Second robot with controls in place to ensure quality with less manual effort. IBM is very proud of creating and applying innovation like this to drive efficiency and productivity on such a huge scale.

9. TECHNOLOGY

- Simple automation using presentation integration (RPA software) can eliminate errors, reduce costs and perform high volume transactional work in a fraction of the time it takes humans.

- RPA software can be used to access all kinds of applications, from modern Web solutions to legacy mainframe software.

- A digital workforce is ideally suited to handle tasks that either happen too fast for humans to respond or too often to be worth human time to complete.

- The impetus is not necessarily to replace people, but to transform the work that humans do and create new ways of working.

- The human workforce recaptures time to do what it's best suited to do: think strategically, act creatively and interact humanely.

10. THE TECHNOLOGY AND SERVICE PROVIDERS

http://www.blueprism.com/

IIC Technologies, Canada/India/UK/US

Nominated by Bonitasoft, France

1. EXECUTIVE SUMMARY / ABSTRACT

Safer sailing in national waters with up-to-date information in Notices to Mariners

Government Hydrographic Offices are responsible for providing up to date information necessary for safe navigation in national waters, and they issue Notices to Mariners (NtMs) to advise mariners of matters affecting navigational safety at sea.

NtMs have to be released on time and ensure that the information is accurate, clearly described, and easy for the mariner to follow.

The previous nautical publications production process at one such national Hydrographic Office was a manual, Excel-spreadsheet based, desktop publishing exercise with a very complex workflow and many operational challenges.

After a lengthy, carefully-phased digital transformation implementation project with IIC Technologies, this Hydrographic Office is now using a fully integrated Workflow Management System (WfMS) on a BPM platform, integrated with the CARIS Publications Module (PM) software as their publication authoring platform.

Today, NtMs for this national water area, is more consistent and reliable. They are produced directly from the geospatial production system rather than from manual data entry. The information is processed and published much faster, and immediate notifications can be released in urgent cases. Data streams can replace static hard copy PDF publications.

Further, the Hydrographic Office now has the improved internal discipline to apply properly engineered business processes, which can be system driven and implemented with the appropriate checks to ensure that it is executed reliably and consistently every time. This is something normally very difficult to achieve but critical for safety to navigation.

When defining their overall improvement project in 2016, the Hydrographic Office recognized that good location information has the power to unlock the true potential behind geospatial information and making such information readily available to its user communities is critical.

Improving the existing operations and production processes contributed to realizing that vision.

2. OVERVIEW

Background

National Hydrographic Offices are responsible for providing reliable and up-to-date information necessary to facilitate safe navigation in their respective territorial waters as mandated by the International Hydrographic Organization (IHO). They achieve this objective by producing official nautical charts, safety alerts, and a variety of supporting nautical publications needed for safe navigation and making them readily available to the professional and recreational mariners.

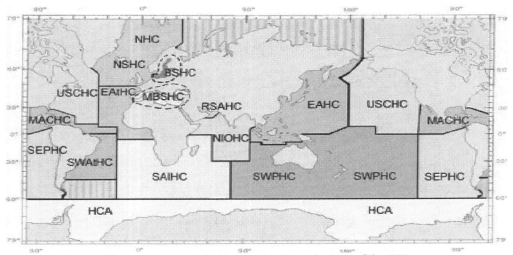

Figure 1. Regional Hydrographic Commissions of the IHO

The Hydrographic Office that called upon IIC Technologies expertise for their digital transformation project publishes a wide range of products, including portfolios of paper and electronic nautical charts along with the Annual and Fortnightly Notices to Mariners (NtMs), which advise mariners of matters affecting navigational safety and are used to correct nautical charts. NtMs play an important role as they aim to make the information required to keep nautical charts up to date available to the mariner as soon as possible due to direct safety at sea implications. For that reason, it is critical not only to release such notices timely but also to ensure that the information provided is accurate, clearly described, and easy for the mariner to follow.

Long-term vision: the potential of geospatial information

IIC Technologies has worked with this Hydrographic Office for over 10 years, providing a variety of geospatial data processing services. Both organizations recognized an opportunity for more strategic collaboration when the Hydrographic Office started executing their long-term vision, based on the recognition that location information has the power to unlock the true potential behind geospatial information, and making such information readily available to additional user communities would be very desirable.

Improving the Hydrographic Office's existing operations and production processes contributed to realizing that vision.

The nautical publications production process was selected as one of the primary candidates for across the board improvements, as it employed a traditional, largely manual, labour-intensive and difficult-to-manage process. It was largely a desktop publishing exercise which followed a very complex workflow and presented, especially in the case of NtMs' many operational challenges. This presented an opportunity to greatly optimize the related production process, and to deploy modern software tools capable of automating it. The related geospatial data was already available in the chart production system or could be easily entered there when needed, making it desirable to replace manual data entry with automated digital data harvesting.

In July 2016, the Hydrographic Office tasked IIC to conduct a feasibility study to explore the potential of using the CARIS Publications Module (PM) software as the new publication authoring platform and to optimize the existing production process around it. The study was successfully completed in November 2016 and confirmed, by way of producing several publication prototypes, that CARIS PM software could fulfil their requirements, and that its implementation would be a worthwhile initiative. The new production process was developed around CARIS PM and tested accordingly.

The feasibility study confirmed that deploying the CARIS PM toolset and the new production process would greatly streamline the production of the entire portfolio of nautical publications. It also highlighted that it would be a perfect opportunity to review the content of all publications and improve them to more effectively serve the current and future needs of all end users.

While conducting the study, IIC also observed that it could be equally worthwhile for this Hydrographic Office to use a modern workflow management system (WfMS) to manage all production related activities within one centralized system and that such a system could cover as many or as few production processes as needed. IIC Technologies then suggested a comprehensive geospatial data production automation and management system (WfMS) based on the Bonita platform, which would allow the Hydrographic Office to move away from its Excel-spreadsheet based system into a modern workflow management system to manage all production activities using tightly integrated systems. The proposed project was approved and successfully delivered about a year later and the resulting system is currently fully operational.

The Hydrographic Office is now using a fully integrated Workflow Management System (WfMS) solution that ensures transparency across teams and the organization of production activities, improves reliability; helps identify production inefficiencies, and fosters accountability. The system helps the entire team to monitor and execute all production in real time with tracking of production activities, task sequencing, and subtask handoffs, all happening automatically. The IIC Technologies team developed business intelligence and decision support tools that now help plan upcoming activities, analyze productivity and quality trends, and monitor key performance indicators.

Achieving this level of automation and functionality was not an easy task, as the entire production process consists of approximately 100 elements with complex interdependencies as is frequently found in the geospatial domain.

3. BUSINESS CONTEXT

The old nautical publications production process employed at the Hydrographic Office was largely a manual, Excel-spreadsheet based, desktop publishing exercise which followed a very complex workflow and presented many operational challenges. The execution and monitoring of all production activities also largely relied on direct supervision and team inter-communications. Task sequencing, task event notifications, and subtask handoffs were handled manually person-to-person resulting in unintended inefficiencies and occasional delays.

Similarly, while many production management documents were created and stored in the document management system, it was often difficult to extract comprehensive business reports from them. This has limited the possibilities to have meaningful business intelligence readily available and use it to plan upcoming production activities, analyze productivity and quality trends, and identify opportunities for process improvement and team training. It also limited the possibility of having timely key performance indicators at team or department level to take corrective actions when necessary or to ensure optimal production efficiency levels and delivery/service level targets. Overall, the transparency of production activities and their status across the organization was somewhat limited.

4. THE KEY INNOVATIONS

4.1 Business

The integrated nautical publication authoring, and workflow management system developed for the Hydrographic Office introduced multiple notable innovations and positively impacts several key stakeholders.

The first group directly affected were the end users of the nautical publications produced by the Hydrographic Office. The fundamental change is the ability to produce publications that make it easier for the users to find and use the information they contain by improving their organization and format.

There are, however, many other related benefits not immediately visible to the end users. By employing the system, the information provided is more consistent and reliable as it originates directly from the geospatial production system rather than manual data entry, which is considerably more error-prone. Similarly, the information can be processed and published much faster. Immediate notifications can be released in some urgent cases. Data streams can replace static hard copy PDF publications.

Ultimately, this allows the Hydrographic Office to provide better overall service to their customers with less production effort. In turn, this has begun to allow them to re-allocate some of the resources previously involved in production of nautical publications to produce products for new user communities. Overall, the system allows the agency to realize sizable product costs savings, reliability and consistency improvements, with the bonus of a wider range and additional products being produced by the same team.

While the above in itself would normally be sufficient justification and a great return on the investment, there are many other impacts as well. There is a sizable impact in the way the Hydrographic Office handles their internal operations that offers both tangible and intangible benefits related to structured process engineering practices. With the new system, we can see additional improvements as follows:

- using the new business intelligence and production management tools included with the system, the Hydrographic Office is now able to handle NtM production much more efficiently;
- they have much better insights into their operations in real time, with readily available key performance indicators along with the improved ability to manage quality trends, employee engagement, training needs etc.
- they have a way to produce reports easily with real-time data captured by the system;
- an improved internal discipline to apply a properly engineered business process, which can now be system-driven/implemented with the appropriate checks to ensure that it is executed reliably and consistently every time . This is something normally very difficult to achieve but critical for safety to navigation.

Although there are many business impacts that the resulting system allows the Hydrographic Office to benefit from, there is another layer which can be considered another key innovation in our opinion. Geospatial data production system are complex but usually closed ecosystems. They often provide some basic interfaces for integration. However, having been one of the leading companies providing geospatial data services, we have seen very little in the way of workflow or business intelligence integration in the geospatial domains. Most mainstream tool vendors provide no such tool and only some provide some very basic functionality. The system developed for this Hydrographic Office on the other hand provides full enterprise-level integration using two mainstream platforms, CARIS on the geospatial side and Bonita on the business process management side with custom set of extensions developed by IIC Technologies to closely integrate both system and deliver additional business intelligence tools, dashboards and reports. As far as we are aware, this type of integration and set of features is currently not available from any vendors in the geospatial domain.

Before the project, this Hydrographic Office was using the typical process applied by many Hydrographic Offices to capture and process NtM cases. This process was well-established and consisted of many manual steps, documented using written standard operating procedures and supported by multiple checklists, typically in the form of spreadsheets and reports. The process itself was very well-organized and all related documents were stored using documents management system. It was, however, very difficult to manage and execute the process in practice due to its complexities and large number of steps involved. The process was not captured using any modeling tools and partially relied on the key individuals within the organization to ensure its proper execution.

At the beginning of the project, the IIC team interviewed key specialists at the agency to establish the production process. The high-level data flow was modeled and reviewed. Subsequently, the high-level process flow for NtM products and publication of those products was established. This was followed by multiple rounds of interviews and refinements to arrive at the final detailed process model, which was turned into several BPMN 2.0 models for implementing on the BPM platform.

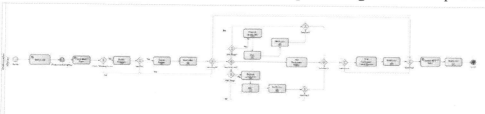

Figure 2. NtM Products high level process flow

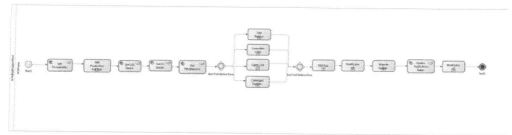

Figure 3. NtM Publication high level process flow

The resulting process models are now properly maintained and any changes to the process can be easily integrated into the system, making it easy not only to optimize the processes when needed but also to update the system accordingly without a big redevelopment effort.

4.2 Organization & Social

The new integrated solution ensures transparency across the teams and the organization of production activities, improves reliability, helps identify production inefficiencies and fosters accountability. There was a considerable shift in the employee and social perspective as the old process required a considerable amount of specialist-to-specialist interactions. It is worth noting that the NtM production task is one of many production tasks each of the Hydrographic Office's specialists handle each day. With approximately 100 steps in the process, this means a high number of interactions between a dozen or so specialists involved in the entire process end-to-end. This produced a significant number of manual status requests, which contributed to the overall perception of the tasks being a burden.

With the process improvements and dynamic notifications, the challenge of manually tracking each case fully disappeared. Each specialist gets an automated notification when any task is ready for them to work on. There is no need for reminders or follow up, and the tasks can be planned much easier around other production activities.

The team is happier and more concentrated on the production activities with less undesirable interruptions and less manual reporting.

The new system allows users to conduct activities in the same order each time, leading to improved product quality and more consistent results.

All activities are now traceable making team collaboration much simpler. Everyone can see real-time progress and status of cases within the notice production cycle, and this allows management to better plan and allocate resources.

5. Hurdles Overcome

5.1 Management

One of the key challenges with implementing workflow management systems in the geospatial domain is related to the fact that BPM platforms are relatively unknown in the geospatial community.

Although the management team was keen to make significant process improvements, it was a challenge to move past various workflow management options, possible solutions and expected benefits. Presentations and discussions explaining the benefits only go so far to establish the need, desirability and potential benefits of workflow automation. At the same time, the complexities of the geospatial domain lead to very complex production processes which are challenging and costly to implement.

This generally leads to some reservations that only the more progressive agencies and management teams are willing to take on.

In this case, IIC was able to work with a management team willing to explore the possibilities, keen to streamline and automate a complex production process that was causing significant challenges.

We focused on only one production stream to begin with, which helped constrain the effort and costs.

Once it was fully deployed, the Hydrographic Office's team was able to see the full potential and the actual benefits more readily, which we expect will lead to follow-on adoptions in other production areas.

BPM in the geospatial domain is currently very much an early adopter market. We expect to see wider adoption in this domain as its benefits prove out.

5.2 Business

The production team was equally cautious about the BPM system. However, their daily challenges were readily apparent to them and there was a high desire to overcome them and streamline the production processes. As this was an external implementation, both the management and the production team were involved in all initial project discussions, ultimately leading to a positive decision to implement a phased approach.

5.3 Organization Adoption

Organizational adoption of large integrated systems typically triggers the natural tendency for people to be apprehensive about change. Unfamiliar systems, such as BPM in the geospatial domain, amplify such feelings. Once the initial working release was available, the IIC team started on-site familiarization sessions, followed by training sessions to select team members. The initial resistance disappeared quickly when the system was presented from each user type perspective, highlighting the key benefits relevant to the particular user. For example, "as production manager, you will be able to see all NtMs in production, see their current progress and all other key indicators in real time." Similarly, the familiarization sessions for the production team focused on the task assignment, transition points, notifications, etc. Once virtually all of the Hydrographic Office's members were able to see and connect with their individual features and could clearly see the benefit they would be able to get in practice, they started to get excited about the system. From that point on, the adoption and the desire to have the system in place increased dramatically with the team looking forward to having the solution in place.

6. BENEFITS

6.1 Cost Savings / Time Reductions

For this government Hydrographic Office, being able to deliver the service levels expected is perhaps the most important benefit. The new integrated system already delivers timely and consistent NtMs and is expected to deliver wide improvements in nautical publication authoring and release, reduction of personnel needed; the ability to allocate these personnel to other tasks (improving the overall level of services provided by the Hydrographic Office); better production management, improved business insights and many others as described in previous sections.

The anticipated production cost reduction from the integrated system was about 30% and we expect the system to deliver this level of saving. Data is being captured now to confirm this initial assumption.

6.2 Increased Revenues

The Hydrographic Office provides NtM service free-of-charge, as this is part of the essential service any IHO member state needs to deliver to all mariners in their respective territorial waters. For that reason, there are no revenue implications for this service. The objective is to make the service accurate, timely, and easily accessible to all end users. This Hydrographic Office offers a good example of how some more developed national HOs help other nations with their charting activities, as they already help multiple other nations with adjacent national waters.

6.3 Quality Improvements

One of the quality improvements is that the Hydrographic Office is now using their geospatial data production system to generate *all* nautical publication. The geospatial data in that system is more accurate than what was/is present in some historical nautical publications authored manually in the past.

Similarly, manual data entry errors have been eliminated using automated data harvesting from the production system.

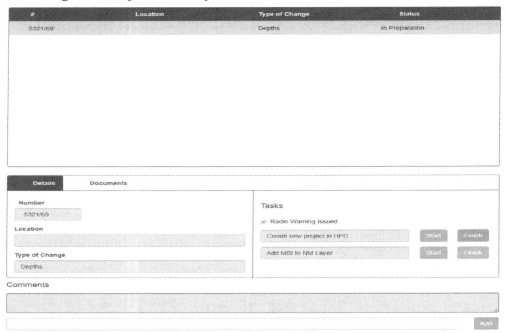

Figure 4. Handling basic metadata

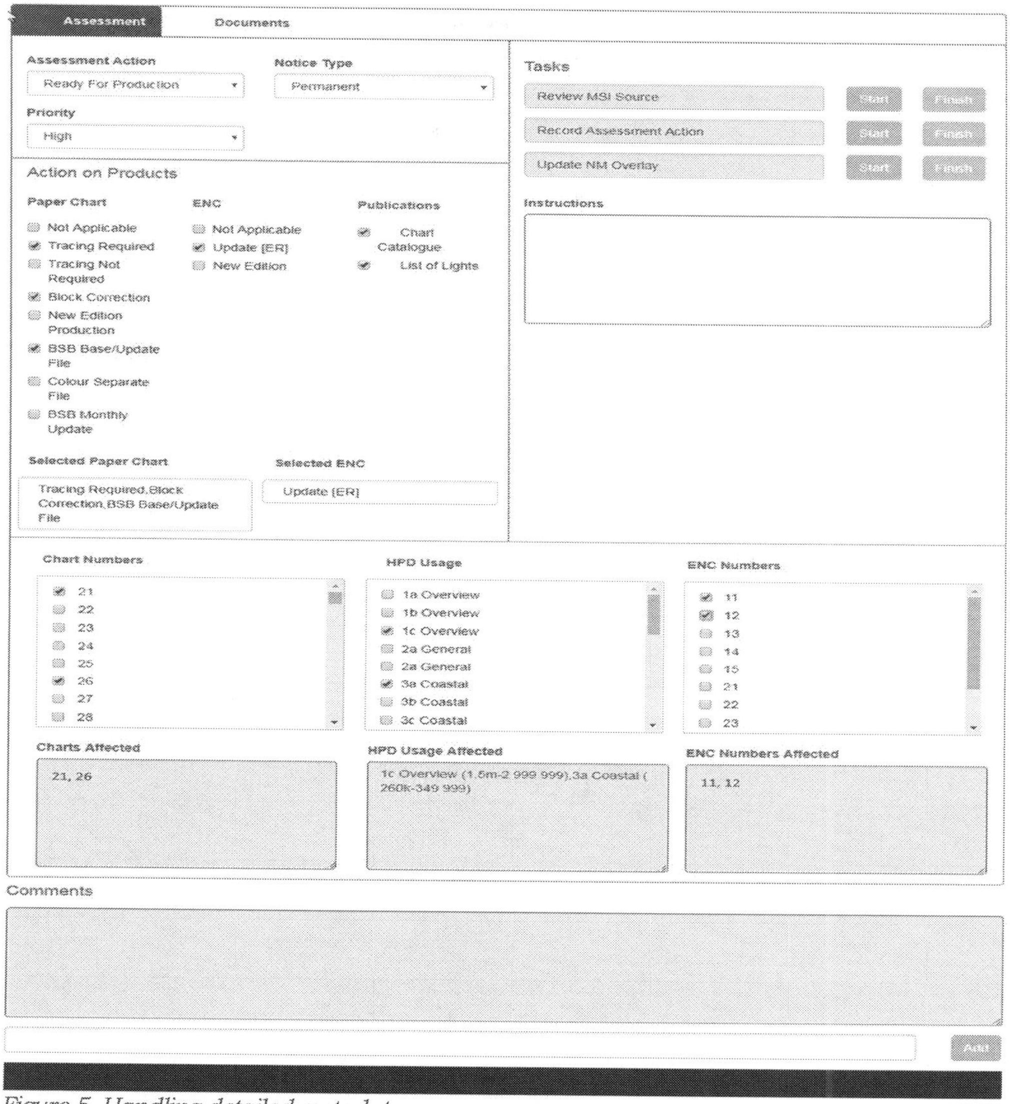

Figure 5. Handling detailed metadata

Using the workflow management system, the production process will be executed reliably and consistently.

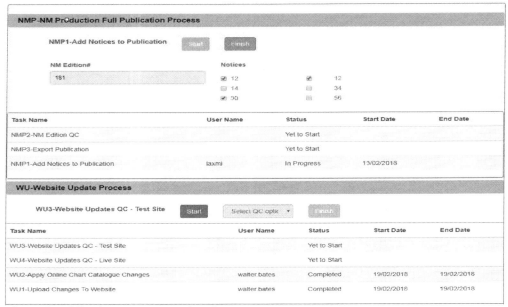

Figure 6. Publication process user interface

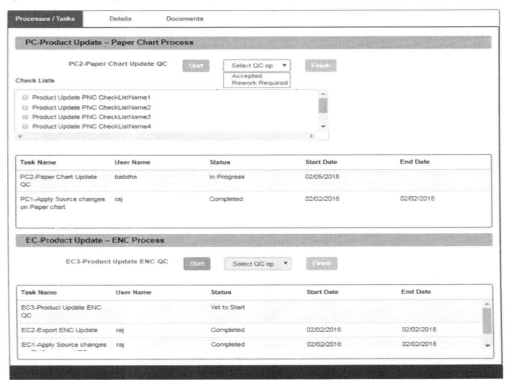

Figure 7. Product update process user interface

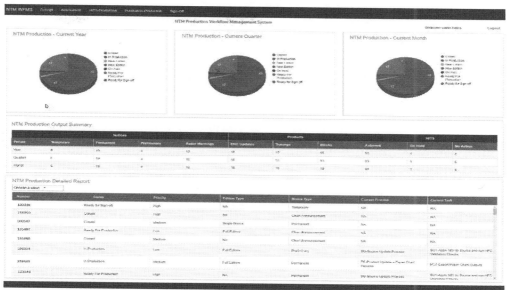

Figure 8. NtM dashboard

All in all, the resulting publication will enjoy quality improvements related to all individual improvements noted above.

7. BEST PRACTICES, LEARNING POINTS AND PITFALLS

7.1 Best Practices and Learning Points

✔ Use one of the Agile methodologies (IIC uses Disciplined Agile Delivery) to design and deliver BPM systems in new domains. Complex domains require deep understating of the underlying processes and close collaboration will help ultimately deliver the system that is needed.

✔ Use a phased approach. Again, in complex domains, it seems to be best to work with one sub-domain a time.

✔ Present the system from the perspective of the individual user's groups – i.e. production manager, team leads, specialists, etc. They are interested in finding out how the system will help them to execute their individual tasks and are not so much interested in the general overview benefits.

✔ Hold familiarization sessions before full user training.

7.2 Pitfalls

✗ Avoid trying to capture all requirements up front. It will not work with the users unfamiliar with BPM systems; they need to see multiple system iterations to get familiar with the possibilities.

✗ Avoid trying to design the entire system in one go. The requirements and design will likely change multiple times as users get familiar with the possibilities, so remaining flexible will allow to design and deliver the system the users would like to have rather than the one they thought they wanted initially.

✗ Do not limit training opportunities. More training than expected will likely be required for users new to BPM in complex domains.

8. COMPETITIVE ADVANTAGES

Geospatial agencies are largely not aware of the BPM domain in general. They focus on the more scientific aspects of data collection, capture and processing, and are often not structured or managed in the same way as corporate environments. They are just beginning to embrace some of the production process management ideas, often due to government budget reductions or requests for additional services within the same budget. Overall, there seems to be limited awareness of what benefits BPM systems can offer for them. Similarly, software providers focused on the BPM domain seem to have a good awareness of the mainstream corporate consumers but may not have the domain expertise needed to develop solutions for scientific domains such as geospatial.

For that reason, we believe companies like IIC Technologies, with some of the world's biggest geospatial agencies as customers, are uniquely positioned to bring advanced BPM solutions to the geospatial domain, and we expect to see this market expand worldwide, in the near future.

9. TECHNOLOGY

IIC used the Bonita platform, integrated with CARIS Publications Module (PM) software, to implement the NtM product and production processes.

10. THE TECHNOLOGY AND SERVICE PROVIDERS

Process modeling, optimization, application development, automation and integration, and deployment was provided by IIC Technologies: www.iictechnologies.com.

IIC Technologies is a CMMI level 3 rated, ISO 27001, ISO 20000-1 and ISO 9001 accredited global provider of geospatial solutions and services. It provides consultancy, training and specialist services to clients in government (national, state, and local), defense, Aeronautics, maritime, water resources, utilities, and transportation sectors. With decades of experience, in over thirty different countries, IIC Technologies specializes in developing and delivering geospatial solutions across all environments, be it air, land or marine in accordance with International quality standards.

Bonita application platform from Bonitasoft: www.bonitasoft.com

Bonita helps innovative companies worldwide deliver better digital user experiences for customers and employees. The extensible and open Bonita application platform offers multidisciplinary development teams the features, tooling, and frameworks to create applications that allow continuous and incremental improvement, connecting tailored user interfaces with reliable back-office operations. With more than 1000 customers in 75 countries and its ecosystem of more than 120,000 members, Bonitasoft is the largest provider of open-source Business Process Management, low-code and digital transformation software worldwide.

Palmas City Hall, Brazil
SINAX Integração e Gestão de Processos, Brazil

1. EXECUTIVE SUMMARY / ABSTRACT

Palmas is the capital and the largest city in the state of Tocantins. It is the newest state capital in Brazil, and it has the best quality of life among all municipalities in Northern Brazil. In 2017, a new project was initiated to modernize the city's public administration and citizen services with the objective of improving processes and reducing paper use. In the first year, the project has already shown several financial and productivity improvements. The Palmas City Hall initiative reflects a growing trend of Digital Transformation in the public sector in Brazil.

2. OVERVIEW

As the last thoroughly planned Brazilian city of the twentieth century, Palmas today has the highest population growth of all state capitals in Brazil. As of 2018, it now has 290,000 inhabitants according to IBGE (The Brazilian Institute of Geography and Statistics). Palmas also has the highest Human Development Index in the Northern Region of Brazil. Public administration is the most significant economic contributor, representing approximately 50% of the municipality's economy.

The 2017 Palmas municipal budget was approximately 1.3 billion reais, and one of the priorities of public management was to invest in the modernization and optimization of citizen services. As a result, it was necessary to search for new tools and ways of working with the following objectives:

(1) Reduce the bureaucracy in interactions with residents and optimize work routines;
(2) Minimize the use of the paper & images and the expenses associated with transporting and storing them;
(3) Promote a culture of efficiency, standardize processes and train public officials;
(4) Foster transparency and sustainability in the Public Service.

Because it involves substantial changes in the culture of the public service employees and the local population, the transformation started with pilot projects focusing on some of the leading municipal departments:

(1) "Resolve Palmas" Departments: The point of contact for citizen services and inquiries;
(2) State Secretary of Planning and Human Development: The agency responsible for the action plans developed by City Hall and for human resources management;
(3) Secretary of Urban Development, Landholding Regularization, and Regional Services: The agency responsible for the management of urban development, construction planning, land use, and use of public spaces, among others.

The strategy of starting the Digital Transformation in these agencies has led the initiative to achieve immediate visibility both for the public servants and residents. In the first week of implementation, the ombudsman of "Resolve Palmas" – the agency responsible for citizen complaints – already received the first compliment from a taxpayer who, before arriving at his destination, received an email informing him that his document is already available on the Internet so it would not be necessary to return to the service center.

Using the Sinax methodology, based on the best practices of CBOK – Guide to the Business Process Management Body of Knowledge with AS-IS & TO-BE analysis, process automation and assisted operation, the project implemented ad hoc processes, that is, process free and processes mapped according to the business rules using AO3 BPMS. By August 2018, 300 automated processes were already running, 26 of which were mapped. These processes represent the complaints logged by the citizens of Palmas and HR inquiries from public servants.

Activities that were irrelevant for the actual city businesses, like the transportation of paper documents, were ended and as a result, the time to issue real estate transmission tax guides (ITBI) was reduced from 1 week to 2 hours. Several other processes that previously depended on documentation transport have also become faster.

3. BUSINESS CONTEXT

In general, there is a systemic management problem in Brazilian public administration. Excessive bureaucracy and a lack of efficiency mean that everyday work is not taking into consideration its primary purpose: citizen satisfaction.

In Palmas City Hall, it was no different, especially in departments assigned to the pilot project. Excess bureaucracy, an absence of clear responsibility and a large volume of physical documents were causing the loss of or difficulties in retrieving relevant information.

The citizen cases which were opened in the "Resolve Palmas" units, and the departments responsible for direct citizen services, generated folders of paper documents which needed to be sent through mailbags to the other municipal departments which are responsible for its analysis. These shipments significantly slowed the entire process, since department buildings are not close to each other and the transportation depended heavily on the availability of cars and drivers to make the deliveries.

Another major difficulty for the public administration was the dissemination/processing of internal official announcements. When it was necessary to issue an urgent announcement to all the 30 departments that make up the municipal government, the procedure was to print and personally deliver official letters to all 30 areas. It was common for managers to learn about announcements long after they were made.

All public agencies are liable to requests for data by the control bodies. Frequently, finding the requested reports/documents and sending them was an extremely complex errand. It required searches in several spots to find the paper record and then send it to the control body. Depending on the lifetime of the archive, page misfortune and even wear and tear could be perceived due to inappropriate storage.

4. THE KEY INNOVATIONS

The project has brought several benefits to the public administration of the city of Palmas in a few aspects.

Business

The Digital Transformation applied in Palmas City Hall was made a priority in the units of "Resolve Palmas", Secretariat of Planning and Human Resources and the Department of Urban Development, Land Regularization, and Regional Services, so that the results appear faster and more efficient. In this way, citizens have been served with greater agility in their demands, and the City Hall teams involved in this service would enhance their performance and management.

In parallel, the virtualization of the processes of 8 secretariats took place, so that they were inputs for the digital transformation of processes with direct impacts on the citizen. More than 33,500 ad hoc processes have been opened by September 2018. Out of the 274 types of ad hoc, the most opened processes registered are:

1. Traffic Fine Appeal
2. Transfer Traffic Infraction to Another License Holder
3. Installment payment of municipal debts
4. Renewal of Sanitary Permit
5. Real Estate Title Transfer
6. Tax Restitution
7. Parking Credentials
8. Donation of Plant Seedlings
9. Exemption from IPTU (Property Tax) and Garbage Collection Fee
10. Taxation Complaints

For the processes mapped out in the Department of Urban Development, Land Regularization, and Regional Services, more than 2,600 of the following kinds were opened:

1. Issuance of Securities
2. Issuance of Work Completion Certificate
3. Land Use Certificate
4. Issuance of Habite-se (Property Occupation License granted by the Municipal Authority)
5. Land Regularization
6. Issuance of Infraction Notice
7. Issuance of Embargo Notification
8. Building Permit
9. Migration and Storage of the paper boxes
10. Requests for a carton for paper boxes
11. Requests for archived documents
12. Emergency Document Scanning Request

As for the mapped processes of the Secretariat of Planning and Human Resources, there were more than 3,900 processes opened of the following kinds:

1. Request for a functional dossier
2. Function Reassignment (concession)
3. Function Reassignment (extension)
4. Special Treatment License – LIP (License without remuneration granted to the server, at the discretion of the administration, for the dealing of private matters)
5. Extension or Revocation of LIP (License without remuneration granted to the server, at the discretion of the administration, for the dealing of private matters)
6. Information for PREVIPALMAS
7. Contribution Timing Requirement
8. Budget Amendment
9. Workload Reduction – children with disabilities
10. A Special Work Schedule for the Student Server
11. Maternity/Adoption Leave
12. Server Relocation

13. Medical leave for Health Treatment
14. Document Insertion

Process, Platform and Automation

For the continuity of the project, the mobile app "Conecta Cidadão" (Connect Citizen) is expected to be made available in order to provide better service to citizens. With it, it will be possible to perform the opening of requests from anywhere, avoiding unnecessary commutes to the agencies, reducing lines, bureaucracy and waiting time.

Furthermore, it will be possible to check process statuses and validate the authenticity of electronically signed documents by the agency with the use of a tag with the QR Code. Documents issued by Palmas City Hall employees which demanded a notarized signature will, therefore, be authenticated only with the consultation of the original online version of the document on the City Hall website.

Organization & Social

During this first year of the project, it was possible to start engaging the City Hall staff about the benefits of the mapping of processes and Digital Transformation using AO3 BPMS. The resistance that still exists falls under the matter of changes in the law.

In a national context, Brazil has been seeking to modernize its laws with the goal of simplifying and optimizing the work performed in Citizen Service. This movement will assist municipalities such as Palmas to recognize the need to follow this trend.

The initiative to implement management by processes in the Palmas City Hall was born from the Information Technology sector, which used to answer hierarchically to the Finance Department. With a strategic view about management improvement with the support of IT, the management has implemented important changes to the organizational structure.

The first big change was the creation of a specific agency to deal with the matters of technological modernization of the City Hall, the Technology Agency of the Municipality of Palmas – AGTEC in the Portuguese acronym. The second great change was to place this new agency directly connected to the Mayor's Office, signalling in this way a more corporate understanding of the actions of modernization of municipal public governance.

5. HURDLES OVERCOME

5.1 Management

The 'Term of Reference' is the official document to be followed by public administration managers in the execution of contracts. This document describes details of the project such as scope, deadline, restrictions, basic premises, among others. For the project, the staff in the Palmas City Hall demanded that the best project management practices and market processes were met.

This kind of demand becomes a facilitator of transparency since it requires many formalizations and approvals. However, it generates problems caused by the culture of sluggishness present in some public employees. To reduce the impact of this issue, close management to contractual managers, technical managers and process actors has been applied, allowing for the validations and alignments to occur in an agile and efficient manner.

The constant management changes in the staff of the City Hall, a reality in all agencies of Brazil, have generated some impacts in the project management. Each new associate who entered the project presented a different vision. This obstacle was overcome with project frequent presentations/meetings and the use of formalization of the decisions and approvals. The outcome achieved was the new associate integrated into the project and transformed, most times, into a positive influencer.

5.2 Business

The great challenge faced in Digital Transformation have been and still, are legal issues related to applicable laws in the municipality. In many cases, the business processes are tied to laws and decrees that limit the form of entry and flow conduct. Initially, it was necessary to publish a normative decree for the implementation of paperless ad hoc processes (free transaction).

Every digital transformation entails a change in the ecosystem it is being implemented on. In the case of the Palmas project, it has been well-accepted by the majority of the population, which started to be efficiently serviced. For elderly citizens and/or citizens in need, there have been difficulties which have been overcome with the service structure applied by municipal management with priority service. The service in the "Resolve Palmas" units is still being carried out by apprentice minors participating in a first job program, which means by enthusiastic youths with the opportunity to learn a new market skill.

The processes associated with building constructions represented a significant advance in the form of request and process flow inside the Palmas City Hall. These processes, filed by engineers and architects, started to have their documents, mostly blueprints in A0 size, digitally signed. To explain the beginning of the change, rounds of meetings were held with agencies and class entities of these professionals which, in their majority, understood that the cost x benefit relation of the token acquisition was more advantageous than to continue printing projects in specialized stores.

5.3 Organization Adoption

It is no easy task to implement management by processes in any organization, especially in public institutions. The structure of these organizations guarantees job stability for public employees, which means, performance-based layoffs rarely happen. This generates another characteristic that consists in the creation of comfort zones in which people work for years in the same function without the application of improvements in job execution.

To make a change in culture and mindset possible, it was necessary to get the people involved, through meetings, from the beginning of the project. These meetings had the goal of jointly proposing a new and more efficient, safe and modern form of working. It was verified that presenting the functioning of the work was very helpful for the public employees to realize its benefits and thus improve service provision for society.

There has been a sensitive moment to the project at the end of the year 2017, in which the management decided to implement the Digital Transformation in a short time frame and without involving all the people. This obstacle was overcome through numerous trainings to promote the benefit of the transformation for all.

6. BENEFITS

Cost Savings / Time Reductions

The transformation executed by the project resulted in expressive gains when it came to the reduction of deadlines for the conclusion of projects. This analysis shows the delivery of value to the citizens of the city of Palmas, as well as to the internal communication in the City Hall. Listed below are the processes with the most expressive gains.

Processes	Previous average time	Current average time	Reduction
Issuing of ITBI	5 days	1 day	80%
Medical leave for health treatment	30 days	12 days	60%
Relocation of function	60 days	40 days	33%
Certificate of land use	15 days	10 days	33%
Contribution Timing Requirement	30 days	15 days	50%
Special Treatment License – LIP	45 days	22 days	51%
Building permit	30 days	15 days	50%
Internal memos	3 days	8 hours	89%

The reduction in the amount of paper used in the City Hall until the present moment has contributed to the reduction of the box storage. The data below represents the months of January to September 2018.

Process group	Average pages per process	Total of open processes in the period	Total pages per process group	Amount of boxes necessary
Secretariat of Finance	67	11,474	768,758	1.538
Secretariat of Transit and Transport	10	12,627	126,270	253
Secretariat of Urban Development	90	4,625	416,250	833
Environmental Foundation	95	1,392	132,240	264
Secretariat of Health	42	2,678	112,476	225
Secretariat of Planning	30	3,927	117,810	236
Other agencies	25	1,852	46,300	93
Internal memos	7	20,336	142,352	285
Total		58,911	1862,456	3,725

The purchase cost of paper, prints, boxes and storage that stopped being generated for the City Hall is demonstrated below. Considering boxes of approximately 5 kilograms each, that adds up to more than 18 tons of paper saved.

Unit	Total pages per process group	Unit cost (R$)	Total cost (R$)
Sheet of paper	1862,456	0.051	94,985.26
A4 print		0.075	139,684.20
Box and storage	3,725	5	18,625
		Total	253,294.46

Increased Revenues

The data analysis of the period between January to September of 2017 and January to September of 2018 allows for the perception of increase in the amount of processes that generate fees to be paid by the citizen, and with that an increase in revenue is to be expected. For the next year of the project, the City Hall management expects to analyze this aspect more carefully, since the arrival of the transformation project has caused great impact in the culture of the city and for public employees.

Processes	Documented amount 2017	Documented amount 2018	Increase
Issuing of ITBI	1,907	2,191	15%
Certificate of land use	1,838	2,056	12%
Other processes that generate revenue	9,136	9,554	5%

Quality Improvements

The most impacted by the Digital Transformation generated by the project was the citizen. As results achieved in the implementation of agile attendance requests and online documents, transparency, in short, is a better provision of services to all.

Furthermore, the quality of public employees' work in addressing requests has increased, since the necessary and mandatory information became a criterion for the process flow. With that, each day sees an increase in the maturing of internal working routines.

With the AO3 BPMS, the area managers started to have control over where the process is, which employee it is with and information on the performance of civil servants. With that, the public employees themselves became more attentive and agile in the execution of their working routines.

7. BEST PRACTICES, LEARNING POINTS AND PITFALLS

7.1 Best Practices and Learning Points

✓ Utilize the best practices approached by PMBOk - Project Management Body of Knowledge e BPM CBOK - Business Process Management Common Book of Knowledge;

✓ Formalize all decisions and communications about the work;

✓ Guarantee alignment about the progress of activities among all involved;

✓ Engage the process actors and demonstrate that a group effort will bring benefits to their daily routine and especially for the citizens;

✓ Involve the legal team and high management from the beginning of the project;

✓ Guarantee that contract and technical managers for the client are engaged and contributing to the better progress of the project;

✓ Speed up the automation of the process as much as possible so that the actors see their expected outcome.

7.2 Pitfalls

✗ Exaggerating the number of documents generated for processes;

✗ Not documenting some decisions, meetings, interviews and approvals;

✗ Not involving process actors and their hierarchical superiors in the automation;

✗ Not keeping track of some strategic client decisions;

✗ Not generating expectations which will not be executed by the project, be it for technical unfeasibility or for contractual issues;

    ×   *Not identifying, monitoring and managing the negative influencers.*

8. COMPETITIVE ADVANTAGES

Soon after the first phase of implementation of the Digital Transformation, the case of the Palmas City Hall became a reference for other City Halls in the North, Northeast and South regions of Brazil. Countless presentations have been made by the technical staff to advertise the benefits already achieved.

When the time reduction results are presented, it becomes evident that they contribute in a positive way to improve the citizens' perception of public service provided, contributing to an increase in revenue.

Sustainability is another positive factor which accompanies this transformation. It is ever more evident that corporations, public or private, must align with the practices of Lean Manufacturing and Sustainability. The amount of paper saved in one year may easily surpass 5 tons.

9. TECHNOLOGY

The project utilizes AO3 BPMS as a tool of Digital Transformation. The facility of use of the solution has enabled the absorption and change of culture to happen more easily. Its main characteristics are:

- Web solution which may be accessed from all devices (desktop computers, tablets, smartphones, etc);
- Organizational chart management embedded the solution which means automatically two-way sync between pools, rows and organization chart;
- Utilization of electronic signature technologies through a login and password, and also digital signature through token compliant to ICP-Brazil;
- Digital governance of managers through real-time monitoring of processes;
- Generation of management performance reports.
- Low code for automation of processes by the process analyst, independent from the IT team;
- Automatic generating of documents from process data;
- Fast and intuitive implementation of ad hoc processes;
- ECM module for document management;
- Easy integration with legacy system using web services

10. THE TECHNOLOGY AND SERVICE PROVIDERS

The AO3 BPMS is a BPMS and ECM platform with a focus on security, efficiency, agility and accessibility of information management. It allows for the monitoring and supervision of the flow for all the processes, identifying gaps and facilitating the decision making of managers. It also contributes to financial savings through the elimination of paper normally used daily in an organization.

The AO3 BPMS is part of the set of solutions developed by AO3 and licensed as service integrator by SINAX Integration and process management (www.sinax.com.br) which also provides a team of experienced BPM consultants for the development of the best solution for each client.

PowerHealth, Australia
Nominated by IDIOM Limited, New Zealand

1. EXECUTIVE SUMMARY / ABSTRACT

PowerHealth (Australia) [PHS] provides its PowerPerformance Manager [PPM] and PowerBilling and Revenue Collection [PBRC] applications to healthcare organizations worldwide as Commercial Off the Shelf [COTS] applications.

PHS started a rules initiative that is the subject of this case study, with the objective of making costing/revenue and billing rules a plug-n-play feature within their applications. The separation of rules from the underlying applications was required to allow PHS to support bespoke customer rules within their otherwise standard applications.

A national client, with over 40 hospitals and more than 100 clinics, tendered for a new enterprise-wide billing application to span their 27,000 bed and 65,000 staff organisation, with an annual budget of USD 10B. The client had previously developed an in-house billing system that provided excellent functionality. However, ten years later, this system was proving difficult to maintain due to the billing logic being hard-coded within the software program code; meaning that changes had to be implemented by programmers. In addition, the technology platform used to develop the software was fast becoming obsolete.

The current PowerBilling and Revenue Collection (PBRC) application was built in response to the tender and extended the scale and complexity of the rules then under management by PHS. When complete, PBRC provided a new rules-driven billing capability on the global market for enterprise health billing solutions, which was at the time dominated by heavily siloed, departmental scale solutions.

Since the adoption of the rules initiative as described by this case study, PHS has expanded its footprint in its Australasian home market and expanded into overseas markets to include customers in the UK/Europe, the Middle East, South East Asia, and North America.

This submission uses the development of PBRC for this tender as a reference project for the initiative, to highlight the benefits of using rules as a formal architectural component within COTS applications.

2. OVERVIEW

The subject of this case study is the PowerHealth (Australia) [PHS] rules initiative, which separated and promoted the use of rules within their COTS applications, supported by the additional specific discussion around a single reference project that demonstrates key elements of the initiative.

The initiative is a key pillar of PHS's go-to-market strategy – it offers PHS's customers' autonomy in the management of their business rules while also claiming the benefits of a COTS application. To achieve this, the COTS application is fundamentally refactored to include an interface to the rules' engine, but no rules. The rules are then supplied on demand independently of the application itself.

The primary focus of the PHS rules is to convert raw patient encounter data into cost/revenue and billing data for the PPM and PBRC applications.

While the explicit focus of each of these applications is slightly different, the rules approach is consistent across the two applications. The separation of rules from the underlying applications allows PHS to provide bespoke costing/revenue and billing calculations from the otherwise standard applications.

Rules autonomy for the customer is flexible, with technology included within the rules toolset that provides an option for the customer to use PHS's rules, or to use the customer's own rules, either alone or in combination at any level of complexity. Both sets of rules, that is, PHS-supplied rules and the customer's own rules, can be updated independently, so that rule sharing is complete and ongoing.

Using this technology, PHS can provide a baseline, pre-configured rules that can be modified or added to by the customer (generally a hospital), who owns and manages the rules ongoing. Autonomous sets of rules can also be delegated to specialist departments throughout the enterprise, which is then dynamically re-acquired by the application and executed via the interface within the PHS defined rules topology, to achieve enterprise-wide coordination of discrete sets of rules within a single enterprise-wide process.

This approach required initial development and understanding of a rules topology, which was a critical outcome of the Project

The customer benefits and cost advantages of plug-n-play rules have helped PHS to become one of the world's largest suppliers of health costing/revenue and billing software, with expansion in its scope of operations since the rules initiative to the UK/Europe, the Middle East, South East Asia, and North America.

The reference Project for this submission is a national client with a requirement for enterprise scale billing system encompassing 40+ hospitals and 100+ clinics, and over 60,000 staff. This project exemplifies the advantages of the approach. Since the implementation of the new billing system, the client has claimed improvements in business agility, managing enterprise-wide variations in business practice, and managing complexity and performance, while processing 1,650,000 invoice items in real-time to generate 4,000 invoices per day at the point of care.

3. BUSINESS CONTEXT

PHS was established in 1995 with an innovative mission to build horizontal customer-centric applications rather than the vertical service or departmental centric applications that were then typical of the health market. The difference is significant – one billing platform instead of many; one bill instead of many; and enterprise-wide access to unified costing/revenue and billing data, rather than discrete siloed viewpoints on an application by application basis.

With customers in Australia and New Zealand, PHS recognized the advantages of using a rules approach: to manage the wide variety of cost input systems; to build a neutral middle-tier cost and revenue concept model; and ultimately to output unified costs, revenues, and invoices to service the wide variety of destination viewpoints required.

When a national tender for a new billing system was issued, PHS found that the client vision matched closely with PHS's vision for enterprise-wide billing. At that time, PHS was the only vendor able to represent this concept and was uncontested within the client's prime vendor shortlist.

The proposed new PBRC rules-centric billing application was selected. This required PHS to scale its rules approach to a new level, to span 40+ hospitals and 100+ clinics within a single billing system for consolidated enterprise-wide, real-time billing.

The requirements sought by the client at this time included the following:

- ***Business agility***

The hardcoded business logic of the incumbent in-house developed system proved extremely difficult to change in response to new business requirements. As the client's business practice is driven by external demand and government policy, it is imperative that new policies and policy changes can be actioned quickly.

- ***Enterprise-wide***

The old system was hospital- and episode-based and deployed as separate standalone systems at each hospital/clinic. Where a patient presented at more than one hospital or was transferred between hospitals, they were recorded under different IDs with no data sharing among locations. As the client wanted to move to an enterprise-wide patient-based system, the only practical option was to replace the old system.

- ***Variations in business practice***

Although the same core software was deployed across the organization, each instance operated independently and according to individual facilities' preferred billing processes. Invoices were branded with hospital identities and not the organization brand. Each system maintained separate patient records, and service codes were also interpreted inconsistently.

- ***Complexity***

The client's billing policy requires complex decision making based on many factors. The in-house development was struggling to meet these requirements. It was therefore a top priority that the replacement software could handle both the complexity and need for regular change without constant enhancements to the underlying program code.

- ***Performance***

To operate effectively, the client's billing model required a patient facing system that provides fast turnaround in order to issue invoices and collect payment at time of service. Time taken by the billing system to generate an invoice while the patient is waiting is therefore vitally important, particularly during peak periods.

From a rules' perspective, both PBRC and PPM have the need to transform large numbers of raw cost events for each patient encounter into intermediate forms before generation of invoice line items or service delivery costs/revenues, respectively.

An encounter refers to a period of treatment, more or less from admission to discharge. For the sake of clarity, the encounter refers to the period rather than the treatment, so that one encounter may include many treatments. This subtle distinction is important because the various treatments may require multiple sets of discrete funding rules from a variety of funding parties that may overlap. Partially for this reason, the rules need to transform the inbound cost factors into more or less neutral concepts before re-collating them by funder/funding agreement. At this point, cost sharing and allocation rules may add significant complexity.

For instance, consider a patient having a private knee operation who has heart failure during anaesthesia; which funding agreement pays what in these circumstances? Until discharged, this constitutes one encounter, and for in-patients, this can be an extended period (usually days, but extending to years in some cases).

The input costs span many medical and support disciplines, while the revenue is likely to be derived from multiple funding agreements, both public and private.

In each case, raw medical and administrative 'factors' that describe the consumption of the health provider's resources are acquired by electronically receiving messages from a wide variety of clinical and administrative systems. The totality of these messages includes all data required to calculate correct costs and charges according to defined rules, and may include service codes, ward transfer details to calculate time spent in wards and other locations, and/or data coded using industry coding systems such as DRG & ICD.

These raw message items need to be transformed into a neutral, schema defined format. Some of these costs are attributed directly (e.g. a service is provided) or they may be apportioned indirectly (e.g. overhead for a particular ward stay based on presence in the ward), often on an hour-by-hour basis.

These items then need to be transformed into cost, revenue, and/or billing values in accordance with the contract rules in multiple funding agreements. Meta rules regarding shared funding capped funding, and other cross-contract aggregation or apportioning also need to be applied, which can add significant complexity.

These rules come from different sources, including PHS themselves, the hospital organization, and the multitude of public and private funding agencies. Often, the funding contracts are the same or similar across hospital organizations, providing an additional opportunity for sharing of rules.

Coding each hospital's rules from scratch is expensive and time-consuming. PHS, therefore, seeks to provide rule supersets that provide an estimated complete set of rules for adjustment and tailoring during the implementation process. By using a rules engine to achieve this, the application is relieved of responsibility for managing these rules. In fact, the PHS applications are not aware of the rules they contain – they are only aware of the specific outputs that are generated at the conclusion of each rules cycle. This means that one COTS application image can manage the cost/revenue and/or billing rules respectively for any and all hospitals across multiple jurisdictions.

In summary, the rules engine must manage a complex set of transformations at scale, to ultimately apply a complex set of rules representing multiple parties while maximizing the reuse of rules on a global basis.

4. THE KEY INNOVATIONS

4.1 Business and Operational Impact

The PHS Initiative

Using a rules engine that accepts rules from multiple sources (both internal and external) and which executes them as a contiguous set has allowed PHS to offer an agile and cost-effective solution to its customers worldwide. By normalizing and reusing rules at many levels, including global rules, jurisdictional rules, rules per funding contract, and rules for each and every cost center in the hospital, PHS has been able to reduce the investment required to convert cost items into cost/revenue and/or invoice line items in accordance with funding contracts and the hospitals own cost accounting procedures.

This has led to increased sales, and ultimately, global expansion.

The Project

This project exemplifies the benefits of the initiative described above. In the first year of operation, the metrics included more than 20 million encounters, with nearly two million inbound cost messages per day resulting in several thousand invoices being presented in real-time at the point of discharge per day.

The validation and transformation of these cost elements required unique algorithms for each specialist department. There are 26 distinct decision models operating in concert to achieve unified, enterprise-wide billing.

The result is fine-grained variation in rules while maximizing reuse on a large scale.

In achieving this business objective and throughput, substantial complexity was addressed. In business terms, some examples include:

Radiology weighting rules

Using PBRC's business rules engine, the client can group radiology charges by order number and modality and apply a discount where the patient only pays for the four most expensive items on a sliding scale. The business rules use the minimum allowed price in the official gazette to control the level of discount.

Invoice bundling

The client has complex cycle requirements for determining when to create invoices for different situations and how to group the charges on the invoices. These are configured into workflows which automatically generate invoices at the appropriate times.

Teaching hospitals

Complexities due to local variations in charging models were easily configured into PBRC's enterprise billing logic. For example, PBRC calculates charges and splits revenue differently for teaching hospitals where the university shares the cost of delivering services and receives a revenue share as payment for university doctors working at the hospital.

NEP Obstetric Services

The client requested a non-standard NEP Obstetrics module to manage the growing demand for obstetric services from mainland China by non-eligible persons (NEP). PHS delivered the functionality to handle registration, printing and issuing of certificates, as well as booking antenatal appointments, tracking attendance, and receipting payments. The flexibility of PBRC's configurable logic allows the client to maintain this module in compliance with future policy changes.

Increased business agility was demonstrated by a Radiology charging policy change. Shortly after the go-live, the client needed to change the radiology bundling logic, which had the most complicated business rules. PHS consultants worked with the client to rework the business rules and deployed this mid-production. The transition went smoothly and the new charges took effect without impacting the previous charges or affecting the go-live schedules. This was an excellent demonstration of the system's business agility.

4.2 Innovation

In the case of health cost/revenue and billing management, there is a series of distinct transformations that are required to deliver value to the organization by managing the inherently complex many-to-many relationship between input raw cost factors and output revenue line items.

There are three major transformations required to resolve these many-to-many relationships:

- Transform unqualified raw data as supplied by external systems, into validated and standardized data that appropriately describes the required input costs;
- Transform validated, standardized input costs into the neutral idiom of the rules metaphor;
- Transform the costs now described by the idiom into the value-added outcomes required by each user of the application – new values, new reports, new workflows.

These three transformational phases form a standard design pattern for solutions that need to manage complex many-to-many rules matrices between inputs and outputs.

Firstly, raw data is input to the rules. Raw data describes the external reality. In most cases, the raw data is approximately equally available to all organizations because it is inherent to the domain – it is commodity-like, which allows the COTS application interfaces to be standardized. The rules that were involved in on-boarding this data into the domain of the rules are tactical in nature, essentially designed to ensure that the quality and quantity of data is sufficient enough to be able to achieve the ultimate purpose of the rules (e.g. billing values). These are the validation and acquisition rules.

Once the raw data has been acquired and validated, it starts its transformation journey towards the idiom of the organization that is seeking to harvest value from the data. It is normal for this intermediate step to generate a completely new state that is described in quite different terms to that of the raw data, but which is nonetheless internally consistent with it.

For instance, ward arrival and departure times for both patients and staff in the raw data might be transformed into an apportioned cost per hour per patient in the intermediate format, before the final transformation into actual billing items as defined by contracts, which might then include per diem payments, co-pays, lump sum payments etc. Note the distinct transformations – preparation and input of raw data into the idiom that is aligned with the purpose, then into the outputs, namely new state values, reports and workflows.

The three basic steps described above can be further complicated by internal domain and organizational variations.

It usually requires a range of subject matter expertise to validate and transform each of the domain-specific elements into the billing or costing idiom. Consequently, there is a rules topology that has multiple dimensions, starting with the basic three steps – validation, transformation into the idiom, derivation of outcomes.

This is then compounded by areas of domain expertise on the input side (see the 26 models of the client's billing repository below), and by the management disciplines that require the outcomes (billing, accounting, audit/compliance, operations/workflow, personnel management, etc.).

Decision Models

- PayorDeterminationRules
- s10PPMI
- s12IPAdmissionFee
- s13IPMaintenanceFeePatient
- s14IPMaintenanceFeeAccompany
- s15IPDoctorFee
- s16InpatientDiet
- s21OPAttendenceFee
- s22FCSActualCharges
- s236AandE
- s2ActualCharges
- s31DayHospitalServices
- s32DayHospitalDiet
- s4CommunityServices
- s61PathologyServices
- s62RadiologyBundling
- s62RadiologyServices
- s63DiagnosticTherapeutic
- s64Operations
- s65Rehabilitation
- s71ObstetricPackage
- s81CertificateAndMedicalReports
- s82HearingAidsEarMoulds
- s83DentalTreatment
- s84MiscellaneousServices
- s9AdministrativeCharge

The above is a screenshot taken directly from the rules' development tool.

The rules topology might involve dozens of substantial algorithms (which we call decision models) that all need to be orchestrated in a single process to onboard the reality as described by the raw data and to ultimately produce the variety of outcomes that are desired by the various internal and external consumers.

In order to manage the navigation of various use cases through this topology, we have developed the concept of a control model. A control model is another algorithm whose purpose is to orchestrate the flow of each transactional use case (in this case, a patient encounter) through the topology.

The control model also allows us to add another dimension to the rules topology – that is time. Over time, we need to add and change the models that comprise the topology. If we run our use case from last year through the rules topography, it should obey the rules that applied last year. This requires an 'effective date' concept that is universal across commercial rules use cases. With a control model, we can orchestrate the application of complete decision models through time.

Providing each specialty with a unique decision model gives the business the ability to fine-tune hospital cost and revenue management without impacting other rules or the application itself. These changes can be made and deployed locally at any time. The conversion of unique cost structures into a standard idiom provides a value-added bridge, a 'safe-harbour' that allows the business to resolve the complex many-to-many relationship between input costs and revenue received, at the individual item level.

Dealing with the cost aggregation separately from the revenue item generation significantly reduces complexity – no one person or algorithm have to deal with the end-to-end complexity. In fact, the complexity 'emerges' from the integration of multiple simpler sets of rules, each of which is of manageable complexity by individual subject matter experts (SMEs) – dealing with the cost complexity alone and separate from the revenue complexity gives us complexity times two; trying to resolve the many-to many relationships in a single algorithm gives us complexity squared.

The major innovation is to reduce the complexity of the whole by addressing it via many individually simpler models and to then reassemble those models into an end-to-end solution on a just-in-time basis inside the rules engine, using a rules topology with a control decision model to orchestrate the multiple parts. The concept of a control model to orchestrate the topology is novel and reduces the complexity as it is seen by individual rules authors – no individual or group needs to see or address the full scope of complexity.

4.3 Impact and Implementation

The approach taken for this Project, and repeated throughout the PHS Initiative, is to allow the customer to use any preferred strategy for the internal management of their rules. An initial roadmap for the required rules topology is provided by PHS. It is the customer's responsibility to provide the rules within the constraints of the topology, regardless of whether they use default rules supplied by PHS, their own rules, or a combination thereof.

This approach allowed the project to quickly develop the original topology, which includes the 26 decision models in the preceding screenshot that cross 26 areas of expertise and are supported by 155 reference tables to provide a complete, correct, and consistent enterprise-wide set of rules.

The 26 decision models shown above generate ~300,000 lines of Java code when deployed, which demonstrates the scale of logic involved. This volume of code makes the rules a substantial component of the overall solution.

The complete set of rules was developed in approximately ten weeks of rules development effort, including seven weeks consultancy support from the rules vendor, within the nearly two-year development and implementation effort for the entire PBRC.

The rules have been fully supported by the client without vendor support since go-live ago.

This project demonstrated improved development and operational efficiency while addressing enterprise-wide complexity for a substantial organization.

5. HURDLES OVERCOME

Some specific hurdles itemized by the PBRC Project team include:

- Managing User and Regional Executive expectations – where there was a very high level of expectation that the new PBRC would deliver complete flexibility for the foreseeable future, satisfy all of the functional deficiencies inherent in the old home-grown application, and provide significant additional functionality to cater for requirements not previously covered by a software solution. Requests for functional enhancements were further driven by the knowledge that the software was under development when the implementation started, and the cultural change from implementing commercial off the shelf software (COTS) rather than an in-house developed application.
- Occasional significant variations in business practice and interpretation of Government policy and billing rules between management regions,

prompting the need to obtain consensus between regional management and users to define a common set of rules that were acceptable across all entities.

- Highly complex integration requirements arising from the number of feeder systems that needed to automatically provide essential data to the new PBRC to enable automation of the billing process, compounded by the need to retrofit a message-based integration architecture to existing client applications – 18 separate systems required 58 distinct interfaces. In addition, a significant number of data gaps in the essential data required from feeder systems needed to be closed by the integration solution, along with data mapping to resolve variations in service codes used by the various regions.

- To eliminate the need to have a very long transition from old to new systems with both running in parallel for a significant period of time, very large amounts of data needed to be migrated from the legacy to the new PBRC. The migration process was in itself a complex project as it was not a simple one to one transfer of data but involved a considerable amount of data enrichment on the way through.

- The Pilot site status of the implementation arising from the selection of a new generation software product that had not previously been implemented as an Enterprise-wide solution for such a large and complex organization. The testing strategy, therefore, needed to be very detailed and extremely thorough to ensure all potential business scenarios were covered as well as meeting demanding performance goals.

- Ongoing scope change caused by the addition of new functionality to solve previously out of scope business problems, and enhancement of current product functionality i.e. over the life of the implementation project, PBRC moved several years forward in a normal COTS software development lifecycle.

5.1 Management

Belief in the outcome is a key issue when developing at this scale because the elapsed development time becomes a critical factor in its own right.

The rules technology has its own on-board execution and testing environment so that rules can be developed and tested in parallel with the development of the underlying applications.

This provides 'quick wins' by making key business outcomes visible early in the process, helping to sustain belief and giving breathing room to the more traditional SDLC elements in the Project.

5.2 Business

A critical objective of the Project was to enable customer ownership and management of the rules. This was achieved by working closely with the SMEs, who were customer staff, to empower them in managing their own rules. Previously, these rules were codified in system code in multiple systems and were not visible or directly available to the SMEs.

In this Project, the transfer of active rule management was fully supported by the rules tool vendor, so that during the development of each and every set of rules, there was an active process to handover rules understanding and ownership. When each set of rules was finished, the new SME custodians assumed ownership going forward. As a result, handover was almost simultaneous with go-live.

5.3 Organization Adoption

Testing was a major issue for an enterprise system of this scale with nearly 1,000 active users at a dozen different locations.

The client developed some 14,000 test cases in preparation for meticulous and rigorous user acceptance testing. These test cases were developed by the the client implementation team in consultation with users. Over the course of the user acceptance testing process, the project team invited selected users to the head office for week-long sessions to test the scripted scenarios and to undertake freehand testing.

During the implementation process, the client implementation team logged some 2,000 support logs covering functional, as well as performance issues. Majority of the issues were resolved and closed prior to the first Go-live, with a few deferred for incorporation as subsequent enhancements to the core software.

Some of the logged issues related to requirements that had never been delivered before by a COTS billing package and resulted in the addition of new functionality into the core product in order to deliver a robust and fit for purpose solution.

For example, social services can issue waiver certificates which apply discounts to charges in a logical but complex fashion. Where a patient has multiple certificates with overlapping periods, there is a set priority which is used to determine which certificate gets applied to the charges. But there are other receipting systems upstream of PBRC, and a patient may have presented to them a different waiver certificate. It is important that PBRC retains the integrity of the receipting which occurs upstream. New functionality was therefore added to enable exceptions to the waiver priority, with specific charges being reserved, so as to allow waiving by one specific waiver certificate and no other. By necessity, this has been designed to work even if the certificate and the charge have not yet been created in PBRC. There were many such significant enhancements to the core system.

Go-Live

The first phase was rolled out to 318 users in seven participating hospitals.

Radiology format change

Two months prior to the go-live, there was a change in the Radiology message format. This had a major impact on the automated interface linking the Radiology system to PBRC. The interface was modified and deployed within a month, without affecting the go-live deadline.

Rehearsals

The first go-live underwent three cut-over rehearsals, where selected participating users used the new system for one week, concentrating on one thing at a time:
- The 1st rehearsal focused on product readiness
- The 2nd focused on staff and hospital readiness
- The 3rd focused on readiness for handling the transaction volumes.

Go-Live Sequence

On day one of the Go-live process, the old system for the relevant hospitals was switched off, and the new system switched on.

Billing operations continued by using manual processing for one week, while data from the legacy system for each separate go-live site was migrated into the new enterprise system.

At the start of the next week, all billing and receipting activities commenced using the new system.

Performance

The go-live went smoothly with most attention being focused on data volumes and performance tuning. Application issues that showed up were minor edge cases and workarounds were used while the issues were being resolved.

Radiology charging policy change

Shortly after this go-live, the client needed to change the radiology bundling logic, which had the most complicated business rules. PHS consultants worked with the client to rework the business rules and deployed this mid production. The transition went smooth and the new charges took effect without impacting the previous charges or affecting the go-live schedules. This was an excellent demonstration of system's business agility.

Remaining Users

All other users were converted in two tranches on schedule and without incident.

6. BENEFITS

6.1 Cost Savings / Time Reductions

PBRC design philosophy separates business logic and high-level workflow processing logic from the core software processing functions, to allow for customization by configuration rather than changing core software program code. This met the client's top priority of business agility.

Business logic

PBRC uses a rules engine which has a graphical interface for modelling business rules. Client staff can modify these rules in response to changes in business policies and government regulations and deploy these changes swiftly. For example:

- "Income splitting" rules to calculate the division of revenue between public and private practitioners, based on individual agreements.
- "Radiology bundling" rules to generate individual charges for all services, calculate several possible packaged permutations and select the cheapest package and individual charges for the patient.

Processing logic

PBRC uses a workflow engine for controlling billing processing. client staff can configure the workflows to customize the billing processes. For example:

- Eligibility checking — perform web service callouts to the public sector (for employee rates) and the immigration department (for citizen rates) to verify financial class.
- Administration fees – where an additional charge (late payment fee) is automatically created once a patient's invoice becomes overdue.

Consolidated invoices

PBRC servers are located at the client's data centers, serving users in hospitals and clinics. PBRC bills for services from all locations in a consolidated patient invoice, thus simplifying invoicing and payment for both patients and HKHA, resulting in a reduced number of transactions and improved efficiency.

Reduced labor costs

Increased automation reduces the amount of manual input and labor cost, as fewer clerks are needed to perform manual procedures.

Reduced operational costs

By consolidating previously separate systems into one new enterprise billing system, the client experienced cost savings (e.g. computer servers, office space).

Reduced maintenance & support effort

With a centralized system, the client's IT can more easily resource maintenance and support. For example, upgrades are now performed once instead of multiple times as is required by a distributed architecture. System administrators find it much easier to monitor and tune one system instead of many. Additionally, the clients' PCs require minimal maintenance and support with PBRC launching from a web browser, where relevant software upgrades are performed automatically.

6.2 Increased Revenues

Invoicing and receipting at Point-of-Service

In some circumstances, the client's policy requires payment prior to treatment with the generation of invoices on patient arrival at the point-of-service. This time-sensitivity places significant performance demands on billing processing speed, especially at peak times. PBRC's scalable architecture allows real-time addition of software agents and hardware servers to meet fluctuations in processing demand.

Monthly statements:

Patients with outstanding accounts are sent itemized monthly statements, with amounts paid & owed and an optional reminder of when payment is due. This makes it easier for patients to settle their accounts and results in improved cash flow and reduced outstanding debts.

6.3 Quality Improvements

Reliability

With their complicated business logic configured into the system, the client can be confident that charges are being applied correctly, consistently and reliably. Discrepancies due to human error are eliminated by this automation.

Centralized revenue collection

With the new enterprise-wide system, invoices can now be paid at any of the client's facilities regardless of where treatment is received.

Standardized procedures

The patient-based system has centralized billing services and introduced consistency to the client's billing as all hospitals are now using the same system and procedures.

Enterprise reporting

With a single enterprise-wide repository, prompt and accurate reporting across hospitals, patients, and services is now possible.

Organizational management

PBRC supports central administration by the client's head office and distributed management by the client's regions.

Corporate branding

All PBRC documents such as invoices and statements are custom formatted, and the client's IT staff can easily deploy changes by simply updating the document templates.

Efficient revenue collection across all locations

Previously, payments could only be collected by hospitals and clinics for services provided at that location. PBRC now detects outstanding amounts for all locations and the client can therefore request payment for outstanding amounts when a patient presents for treatment at any location.

7. BEST PRACTICES, LEARNING POINTS AND PITFALLS

7.1 Best Practices and Learning Points

✓ *Developing a rules topography to guide rules development is an important precursor step to take in any rules development and is essential for effective normalization of rules.*

✓ *Rules should be fully normalized – this means the fewest number of rules to implement the required algorithms, means that the algorithm is in its simplest form.*

✓ *Normalized rules allow greater agility (less to change), fewer errors, more re-use, and less development effort.*

✓ *When rules are normalized, it follows that patterns for reuse of rules must be achieved at many levels, with special emphasis on the decision model itself. This is the driver for a rules topology.*

✓ *Identify and develop the core rules first. These are the rules that define the* **purpose of the system**. *Then follow through with development of transformation rules, validation rules, and finally workflow and reporting rules. That is, build from the inside out, starting with the core, and working back to the inputs (via transformations and validations), and then working forward to the outputs (new state values, reports, workflows).*

✓ *Use the best subject matter experts to develop the reusable rules in order to codify and then leverage their expertise.*

7.2 Pitfalls

✗ *In general, avoid the antithesis of the above.*

✗ *Don't build monolithic rules structures that mix purpose and expertise.*

✗ *Don't mix rules by type in the same algorithm (e.g. core calculation, transformation, validation, workflow, etc.).*

8. COMPETITIVE ADVANTAGES

PHS takes on what no other organization seeks to do. For example, with PBRC, PHS recognized that public hospital billing was fragmented and inefficient and no vendor actually specialized in patient billing. Existing systems were all linked to a clinical application, albeit large multinationals, but if you wanted a Pharmacy, Radiology or Pathology system, then you bought that system, and each came with their own billing module. This implied separate staff, training, accounts receivables, etc., for each system. It also meant that at times, the decision on what clinical system to buy was greatly influenced by the appropriateness of the billing module that came with it.

What PHS has done is to say, 'don't worry about the billing module that comes with any clinical application. PHS has developed a fit-for-purpose enterprise-wide billing application that integrates to all clinical systems and is dedicated to automating and simplifying the billing process across all customer clinical application'.

What's more, billing rules were typically coded into the application but because a billing system is in essence an accounting package, while billing rules change all the time, it was disastrous to have a system that should remain consistent in its behavior while the code was changing all the time. PHS realized very early on in the development of PBRC that an appropriate logic/rules engine would be ideal to code billing rules. This decision was made in 2004, fully 18 months before Gartner published an article extolling the benefits of adopting a rules engine as part of any software development project.

PHS has a four-step commercial strategy to encourage customers to stay committed to the substantial advantages described above:

- PHS doesn't license as a SaaS model. We license with an upfront license fee and implementation and then a 20% annual support fee. The sale is harder to get but this ensures that as new tech is introduced, which is cheaper and would likely undercut an existing SaaS model pricing, that new price will still be much higher than what our clients are paying for at 20%.
- Maintain a very high Net Promoter Score (hovers between 65 and 75. (Apple has a 70) by providing great support to all our clients
- Invest significantly in R&D to keep the product continually fresh and relevant.
- Following the initial 3- to 5-year Term, offer our clients new modules (developed under R&D) free of charge with a three-year renewal.

Given clients are satisfied, have access to new functionality every three years, free of charge and would have to pay more for an alternative solution, PHS is able to keep clients long-term. In 16 years, only one client has ever stopped using a PHS system. That is how PHS sustains completive advantage.

9. TECHNOLOGY

The use of a rules product fosters a fundamental redesign of the traditional SDLC by fully separating the development and automation of business policy (deciding) from the development of the system's activities that support it (doing). This is effective in spawning a 'Business Policy Development Life Cycle' that is managed independently of and alongside the traditional System Development Life Cycle. The rules technology used offers a number of compelling features to support this

Scale and Complexity: The rules development paradigm, and its supporting decision engine was required to deal with substantial complexity across the entire scope of the enterprise. That is, the scope of rules, and their interrelationships, extended across all aspects of the enterprise. With 42 hospitals and 121 clinics supporting 20 million patient encounters per year in our reference Project, the scale was substantial. In this case, the rules technology was able to address many distinct subdomains (e.g. each specialist area) in a clear, consistent, and coordinated manner without introducing additional complexity.

Performance: Millions of items per day are being processed, with outcomes required in real-time at the point of discharge for the patient, and sometimes before. The rules technology generates compiled code that can run 'in-process', so that minimal processing overhead is incurred. Rules processing per output item is in the single millisecond range and it means that the overall application is able to achieve the customer's desired performance benchmarks. The rules process is stateless and thread-safe, so as many instances of the rules can be used as required to achieve unlimited throughput while maintaining fast response times.

Ease of Use: The initial rules approach and rules development was performed by PHS with the assistance of the rules vendor. Seven weeks of assistance from the rules vendor delivered approximately 70% of the rules development, with the balance delivered by PHS and the client's domain experts. Rules training for the client occurred as an intended by-product of the rules development process, so that after a few days additional training, the rules were handed over to the customer as part of the go-live transition. This specific customer has managed the rules independently (a period of seven years) without a single service call to the rules vendor.

Versatility: In addition to the 'business end' of business rules (calculations, et al.), the rules can be used for more traditional IT functions that also rely on standard, user-defined logic including validation and transformation (the heart of EVTL) at the entry point; and reporting and workflow (what do we need to do now) at the exit point. This demonstrates versatility in how the rules can be used.

Data Agility: A simple change to an XML schema is all that is required to introduce new facts into the scope of the rules by the application. Data can be added at will on an ongoing basis and are immediately available to subsequent rules processing.

Time Sensitive: All rules are effective dated at every level and are always executable as at any effective date – past, present, or future. This means that long-lived use cases can span changes in business policy and always be evaluated according to the applicable policy at the time, which is itself a policy issue to be controlled by rules (do you charge as at the time of admission, time of discharge, re-price on annual boundaries, etc.).

Version Consistency: The technical format of the rules has been backwards compatible since the inception of the product (2001), so that version upgrades in the rules are never mandated by technology requirements. Of course, new product features can only be accessed with new versions. However, the rules themselves will always execute without a change in all future versions of the rules product.

On Board Execution: The rules tool has an onboard execution engine and extensive support for both on-board step-by-step and full regression/simulation testing. This allows an independent rules development cycle that can start early in the project to provide morale-boosting optics and important requirements feedback for the more traditional SDLC developments, as well as significantly speeding up development and reducing testing overheads across the project. The complete independence of the rules development cycle provides many advantages, including multi-party rules development; rules production prior to, during, and after applications development; and smaller and more durable applications.

As a consequence, PHS achieves the following key Value Propositions:
- 100% alignment of systems-based decision making with business policy, because the business owners have hands-on custody and control of the policy definitions being used by the system.
- Increased agility with reduced business risk through business modeling and empirical testing of policy definitions prior to automated generation and implementation.
- Significant reduction in the business cost of developing and implementing automated business policy.
- Further reduction in software development cost, time, & risk through reduced system complexity, fewer moving parts, and clear separation of concerns.

10. THE TECHNOLOGY AND SERVICE PROVIDERS

PowerHealth Solutions (Australia) powerhealthsolutions.com

PowerHealth Solutions is an international healthcare software company specializing in Costing & Revenue, Enterprise Billing and Safety & Quality software for hospitals and other healthcare organizations.

PowerHealth Solutions supplies the PowerBilling and Revenue Collection™ and PowerPerformance Manager™ applications.

IDIOM Limited (New Zealand) www.idiomsoftware.com

IDIOM Limited supplies the IDIOM Decision Manager™, which was used to construct all decision models referenced in this case study. IDIOM Decision Manager™ is a graphical modelling tool that is used by subject matter experts to build, test, and deploy very large and complex decision models for any domain.

Sicoob Coopercredi, Brazil
Nominated by Lecom Technology, Brazil

1. Executive Summary / Abstract

Founded in 1995, Sicoob Coopercredi is a Cooperative of Economy and Mutual Credit of Municipal Servers, with participation by public servants, entrepreneurs and professionals of the Western Metropolitan Region of the Capital of São Paulo State. It is duly registered and supervised by the Central Bank of Brazil. Its purpose is to unite the savings of its members, accumulating the capital of the cooperative, which becomes a fund to be loaned among the participants of this society, offered at lower interest rates. It operates within the concept of shared economy, with many exchanges and mutual gains. By becoming an associate, the server is encouraged to save by depositing a monthly capital share. Currently, there are more than eight thousand members participating in the decisions and enjoying the results, which have personalized services as Credit, Current Account; Debit and Credit Card; Special Check; Private Pension; Savings; Application in DRC; Consortiums; and Insurance, among others.

In 2012, the cooperative made a leap of growth, where with an administration attentive to the changes, it was highlighted in the cooperative system. By 2016, they incorporated two other cooperatives resulting in even greater growth. To accommodate the changes and growth, they began to structure new organizational, structural and business strategies. In this period, all the existing processes in the cooperative were mapped, starting with a troubled team integration process.

2. Overview

In 2016, the cooperative began mapping processes, with the purpose of better understanding its operation, in order to optimize its financial scenario and the way its employees work. At first, they noticed that each team member had a different way of performing the same activity. They managed to achieve good results with the billing, but the need for structuring processes still persisted. The BPM culture was brought by a new manager with experience with this discipline in the market. The suggestion was very well-accepted by the board, so they started the search for tools that would be more appropriate to the reality of the cooperative. At that time, about 50 employees directly connected to the Business area were involved in this search for effective and supporting tools.

Currently, the cooperative has a member dedicated specially to take care of the processes, to optimize them and to develop new models according to the demands of the areas. Of the 40 processes prioritized by the company, 16 were automated through a BPMS.

Processes such as credit card application, salary portability and overdraft, had lost their complete traceability, both physical and digital, within the existing system. Today, with the wide use of a BPMS, such processes are orchestrated quickly and efficiently among areas, with effective gains in time. Previously the analysis period, which is up to three days, could take longer because the request was often incomplete, as well as delays due to the lack of SLA (Service Level Agreement) warnings of the process. Today, all processes are reviewed within the regulatory SLA, about 95 monthly credit card applications and 90 overdraft requests.

Sicoob (Coopercredi) is the largest cooperative financial system in the country, with more than 3.7 million members and 2,600 service points distributed throughout Brazil. According to UN data, in the world; one in seven people is associated with one of the existing cooperatives, generating more than 250 million direct jobs. In Brazil, there are almost seven thousand cooperatives, in the most different sectors of the economy, with 13 million cooperatives and 350 thousand employees.

% de fichas de adesão cadastradas dentro do prazo (↑)

Scenario of union forms registered within the deadline before BPMS

3. BUSINESS CONTEXT

With the processes in the BPMS tool, the cooperative started to guarantee the quality in the data input. Previously, in Excel, typos were common. Currently with information tracked, it is no longer possible to enter data incorrectly in the system, and the resulting reliability of the processes is guaranteed.

Another important example is the expense control project. There was a need for greater control of existing prints and every end of the month, a survey is made on how impressions were consumed. In just two months, the cooperative managed to reduce around 30,000 impressions to 15,000, achieving a 50 percent reduction, estimated on average R$ 3,000/month.

It is important to highlight the engagement of the team that worked for seven months, discussing the best and most adherent alternatives. Therefore, it is very positive for the management of Coopercredi to see all these suggestions implemented in a collaborative way.

An additional example of ample improvement was the credit card application process, where the cooperative requested a new card, filled out a paper form, and there was no standard SLA for attendance due to lack of organization and traceability, from attendance to completion. In this example, it is also possible to check the impressive reduction and process execution time after BPMS deployment. It is important to mention that because Central Bank which is an institution that grants credit and maximum financial and regulatory authority in Brazil, it requires that some documentation be kept on a physical medium. Today, such requests are re-solved in up to two days. Previously, it took up to seven days, depending on the area, that is, which is a reduction of up to 72 percent of the time spent with this request.

In the process of requesting the detachment of members, there was also a reduction of impressions. Previously, about 60 closure interviews were printed per month and, after automating the process, there was a 100 percent reduction of these im-pressions.

The number of disconnection requests has also been reduced, on average of 60 requests/month. The conversion rate, reversing the disconnection request, has gone up. Currently, the cooperative manages to withhold from 25 percent to 35 percent of its members who have requested stoppage.

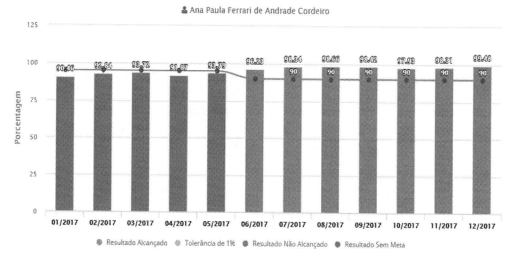

Percentage of passwords called within the goal in minutes

4. THE KEY INNOVATIONS

4.1 Business

The cooperative has already implemented a significant improvement in processes that directly involve the cooperative. For some requests such as credit card for example, the cooperative can place their orders directly on the website of the coop-erative. The BPMS tool will be integrated with the requests generated on the site. Soon after the opening of the process, the request goes directly to the area of credit analysis and behavior of the cooperative, giving agility to the process.

The IT area, as a great supporter of the project, managed with the cooperative's central office, an unprecedented integration of the entity's internal system, integrating it with the BPMS.

Sicoob Coopercredi website

5. HURDLES OVERCOME

At the end of the process mapping work, employees had standards to follow.

However, we realized that in a few months, the previous disorder, where each employee does the work in his own way, had reoccurred. The work of months was lost. It was very clear that all theoretical work would have to become concrete.

The BPMS tool was ideal for consolidating flows and standards into something real. The BPMS for the cooperative was the continuance of a work of process improvements that is still in the development phase. However, each day it gains maturity, elimination of waste, costs and time. The Agile concept, allied to the implementation of digital processes, allows us to start projects in a simpler way, showing the results in a faster way. The implementation of processes requires an improvement not only of processes, but of people's perception of the jobs they perform and their responsibility to follow the standards. It is a chain of improvements that goes from systems, interaction with associates and leaderships.

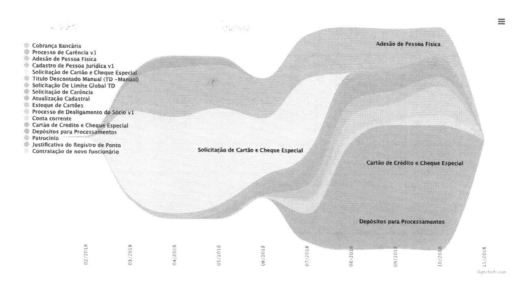

Cobrança Bancária
Processo de Carência v1
Adesão de Pessoa Física
Cadastro de Pessoa Jurídica v1
Solicitação de Cartão e Cheque Especial
Título Descontado Manual (TD –Manual)
Solicitação De Limite Global TD
Solicitação de Carência
Atualização Cadastral
Estoque de Cartões
Processo de Desligamento do Sócio v1
Conta corrente
Cartão de Crédito e Cheque Especial
Depósitos para Processamentos
Patrocínio
Justificativa do Registro de Ponto
Contratação de novo funcionário

Adesão de Pessoa Física

Solicitação de Cartão e Cheque Especial

Cartão de Crédito e Cheque Especial

Depósitos para Processamentos

Map of the main processes currently developed in Coopercredi

Currently, BPMS permeates the entire organization, involving areas such as Customer Service, Financial; Registration, and specially the end customer. Today, 14 processes are essentially executed, such as: Request for Card and Special Check, Grace Process; Bank Collection; Adhesion of Individuals; Registration of Legal Entity; Cadastral Update; Stock of Cards, among others. Since its first installation in December 2017, Coopercredi has executed 5,272 instances of processes, of which 3,688 are the average cycles of the last year.

Like any growing business, the cooperative is concerned about what the members expect from a cooperative credit institution. System portability, more credit in account; excellence in service, are examples of the need of the members and the cooperative is seeking improvements in these points. Another interesting challenge is that the cooperative is preparing to work with the young members, which is not yet a reality today, given the profile of the public servant. It will be a watershed in business.

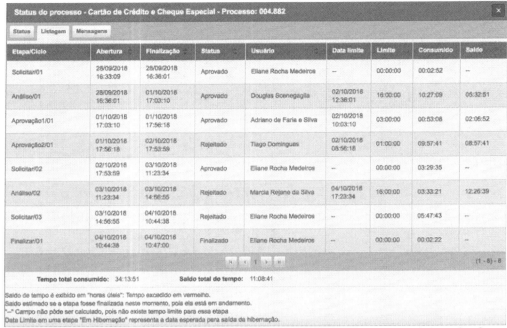

Status do processo - Cartão de Crédito e Cheque Especial - Processo: 004.882									

Status | Listagem | Mensagens

Etapa/Ciclo	Abertura	Finalização	Status	Usuário	Data limite	Limite	Consumido	Saldo
Solicitar/01	28/09/2018 16:33:09	28/09/2018 16:36:01	Aprovado	Eliane Rocha Medeiros	--	00:00:00	00:02:52	--
Análise/01	28/09/2018 16:36:01	01/10/2018 17:03:10	Aprovado	Douglas Scenegaglia	02/10/2018 12:36:01	16:00:00	10:27:09	05:32:51
Aprovação1/01	01/10/2018 17:03:10	01/10/2018 17:56:18	Aprovado	Adriano de Faria e Silva	02/10/2018 10:03:10	03:00:00	00:53:08	02:06:52
Aprovação2/01	01/10/2018 17:56:18	02/10/2018 17:53:59	Rejeitado	Tiago Domingues	02/10/2018 08:56:18	01:00:00	09:57:41	08:57:41
Solicitar/02	02/10/2018 17:53:59	03/10/2018 11:23:34	Aprovado	Eliane Rocha Medeiros	--	00:00:00	03:29:35	--
Análise/02	03/10/2018 11:23:34	03/10/2018 14:56:55	Rejeitado	Marcia Rejane da Silva	04/10/2018 17:23:34	16:00:00	03:33:21	12:26:39
Solicitar/03	03/10/2018 14:56:55	04/10/2018 10:44:38	Rejeitado	Eliane Rocha Medeiros	--	00:00:00	05:47:43	--
Finalizar/01	04/10/2018 10:44:38	04/10/2018 10:47:00	Finalizado	Eliane Rocha Medeiros	--	00:00:00	00:02:22	--

(1 - 8) - 8

Tempo total consumido: 34:13:51   Saldo total do tempo: 11:08:41

Saldo de tempo é exibido em "horas úteis": Tempo excedido em vermelho.
Saldo estimado se a etapa fosse finalizada neste momento, pois ela está em andamento.
"--" Campo não pôde ser calculado, pois não existe tempo limite para essa etapa
Data Limite em uma etapa "Em Hibernação" representa a data esperada para saída da hibernação.

Sample BPMS screen for checking credit card requests and overdraft

6. BENEFITS

The major gain realized by partners today is the saving in time. There is greater agility in the performance and execution of all the processes that are in BPMS. It is important to mention the traceability generated through the BPMS tool. The effective control of information, the areas contained in the flows no longer waste time searching documents (reduction of time and rework), less impressions in most processes (cost reduction and environmental impact), focus on more important and less operational tasks and development of metrics to measure productivity.

With the BPMS tool, the managers of the cooperative had easy access to the production controls of the team. The main processes that are already used are request for membership, request for membership withdrawal; credit card application; overdraft; salary portability; deposit procedures; bank payment; checking account, and request for installment deficiency.

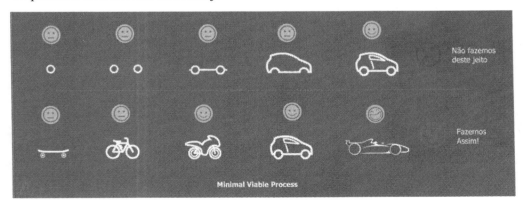

7. BEST PRACTICES, LEARNING POINTS AND PITFALLS

An interesting learning point is the issue of employee development for process culture and BPM. It is very important for the whole cooperative to accept, understand and use BPMS in their favor, generating improvements for the cooperative. The cooperative understands that the focus should be on learning whether its employees see the overall cooperative and not just the department. With that in mind, employees work to make the processes more mature, contributing not only to their specific area, but to the entire cooperative.

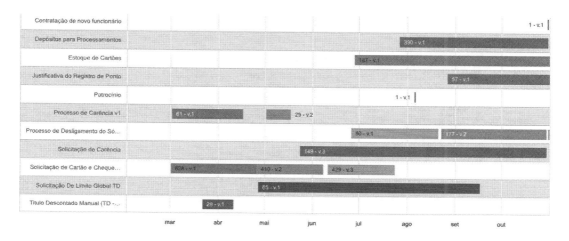

Agile Method and Lecom BPM

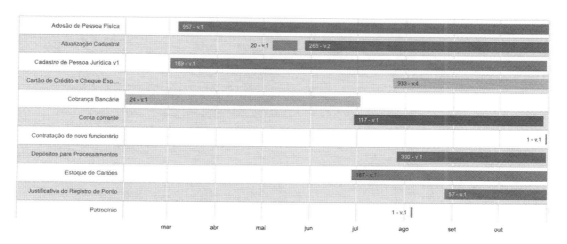

Timetable of processes running on Coopercredi per month

7.1 Best Practices and Learning Points

In the implementation of the BPMS tool presented by Lecom, the Agile methodology was used. This method consists of making small but continuous deliveries, with an emphasis on delivering value and according to business objectives. Thus, at the beginning of the project, it was already possible to collect results and check for improvements with little project time.

7.2 Pitfalls
- Enable the involvement of all to improve processes;
- Develop the process culture in the areas

8. COMPETITIVE ADVANTAGES

The cooperative understands that as next steps, it will seek to improve its forms of control, verify what is being produced in a more strategic way; identifying what can be improved through the generation of KPIs, and in appropriating the information that can be generated through digital processes. With the analysis of the input data, it can act in a preventive way and work on the needs of immediate mode and make planning solutions more appropriate to the daily problems. It also can read the "trends" of business flows.

"The BPMS is the materialization of a process mapping project that I participated in the front line. It allows us to consolidate all the theory and flowcharts we have created in countless team meetings. Implanting at Sicoob Coopercredi-SP allowed us to see our activities beyond the rhetoric of the constructive debates we carry out. The clarity in the tasks of each employee is evident and the flows became more agile, allowing us to track, measure and improve processes", says Tiago Domingues, Planning and Control Management at Sicoob Coopercredi -SP.

9. TECHNOLOGY

The solution is available in the cloud, a flexibility that the company offers. Internal collaborators' access is via a VPN between the cooperative and the LECOM environment. The use of the solution's resources enables high customization, performance and control of the cooperative's operational processes.

It is a great facility for tracking processes. The solution enabled better management of operational workflows, automation and productivity through an integrative and easy-to-use solution, allowing the organization of process management with excellence in monitoring and follow-up.

The tool allows us to analyze indicators maximizing technological and process countermeasures.

10. THE TECHNOLOGY AND SERVICE PROVIDERS

Lecom: Provider of the Lecom BPM Platform: www.lecom.com.br

Tiago Domingues of Planning and Control Management of SICOOB COOPERCREDI-SP participated in the development process of this case.

From the team of Lecom Tecnologia, the case was supported by Germano Canela, Project Manager, who works with clients from several segments such as Automotive, Energy, Shopping Administration, among others. He has also worked in multinational companies such as HP and EDS in several national and international projects (Vale, Braskem, BankBoston, General Motors, NET, etc.)

Vinnitsa EMD Center (VEMC)
Nominated by Eccentex

1. Executive Summary / Abstract

Vinnitsa EMD Center (VEMC) is the full-service emergency service and major public safety agency in Vinnitsa region, Ukraine. There are 1,763 people in the emergency medical care system, including 248 doctors, 803 paramedics and other employees. Ambulance fleet is up to 210 cars. Agency services for more than 1,460,000 citizens.

The ERIM (Emergency Response Incident Management) Solution reduces response time to incident and treatment by half. The time of arrival was reduced to less than 10 minutes in the city, where the majority of incidents occur, and 20 minutes in rural areas. The true benefit is saving lives, with survival rates for out-of-hospital critical care treatments improved by over 22 percent.

In 2017, the agency:
- Processed more than 1,000,000 calls
- Registered up to 420,505 emergency incidents were processed
- Performed up to than 270,755 out-of-hospital treatments
- Over 750 lives saved in 2017, expect to double in 2018 to 1500 lives saved

Solution provides two major case types - incidents and service requests (transportation, blood delivery and non-emergency care). Solution provides ability to configure and implement changes in case procedures, business rules and forms on the fly as soon as possible.

An example in September 2017 was when one of Ukraine's largest ammunition depots was blasted after a terrorist attack. It was the country's second largest stock of artillery storing 82,000 tons of ammunition. Airway and railroad connections in the area were closed. For one hour, our organization implemented new case types, changes in rules and procedures to handle crisis situation. Incidents and tasks were routed to personnel from other PSAPs. The emergency evacuation of 40,000 residents from neighboring villages and towns was successfully performed during the night. More than 500 people with disabilities from their homes and more than 30 severely-injured persons were successfully evacuated.

2. Overview

VEMC is the full-service emergency service and major public safety agency in Vinnitsa region Ukraine (26513 square kilometers). VEMC is providing 24-hour-a-day, 365-day-a-year emergency ambulance and coronary rescue services ready to respond to calls whenever medical emergencies, mass casualty incidents, terrorist attacks, disasters or crisis strikes. As well as providing a rapid, life-saving response in the 'golden hour' of a medical incident, it also cares for patients by treating them in their own homes or public settings, providing telephone advice and referring them to other health services. VEMC is supporting the whole patient journey from the initial call to treatment in order to ensure the best patient outcomes and reduce wasted time, making use of resources effectively, whether this is achieved by treating the patient at home or taking them to the hospital.

Agency services for more than 1,600,000 residents. The VEMC employs around 1,760 staff, including 248 doctors, 803 paramedics and other employees, operating out of 71 ambulance stations across the region with an ambulance fleet of up to 210 cars.

3. BUSINESS CONTEXT

Ambulance services in Ukraine have been traditionally seen as services intended merely to transport patients from one place to another, usually the nearest hospital. People in Ukraine were encouraged to telephone 103 in both medical emergency and in non-emergency situations.

Typically, EMD used an outdated system with an absence of business continuity and backup systems. Before the project, the region had several independent EMD agencies one per each of 18 districts in the region. Each of them operated separately using their own information system or worked manually.

The semi-manual systems to be replaced included:
- Dispatch systems could not distinguish between emergency and non-emergency incidents;
- Dispatch systems could not distinguish between duplicate calls for the same incident;
- Previously logged calls could be lost;
- There were no automated tracking devices, "lost" ambulances. Without accurate knowledge of vehicle locations and status, the system could not allocate optimum resources;
- It was not possible to tell if the ambulance had been dispatched;
- Frustration by operators resulted in slow inaccurate information being passed back to dispatch, mistakes in ambulance meant call signs were mixed up, dispatches further delayed, the public repeating their calls and in turn a further increased load on the system;
- The response to emergency calls could be several hours;
- People were waiting half an hour to be answered by emergency services;
- Survival rate for out-of-hospital critical care treatments was up to 0.8 percent,
- Field personal were wasting large amounts of time organizing documents by hand.

4. THE KEY INNOVATIONS
- There are no other ambulance services working in the region. Right now, only VEMC is responsible for the whole service.
- VEMC established one emergency operations center that supervises all processes
  - 25 staff on duty 24/7
  - Up to 10 call handlers
  - Serving over 1700 emergency medical care people
- Deployed a real-time command & control (C&C) system to maintain a high quality of service to all citizens designed on top of case management platform for all EMD services in the region.
- The ambulance fleet was equipped by with GPS positioning devices and tablet computers.
- Deployed in on-premise, private cloud and designed around web, with availability of service up to 99 percent.

- Designed for IP networks where calls are routed by IP / SIP.
- EU and EENA NG 112 compliant.

Business

A new system was designed to automate end-to-end incident process, including delivering patients to the nearest hospital and creation of electronic medical record. The implementation started in 2013. The system has been operational since 2016. No paper backup system since this moment.

In 2017, the agency:

- Processed more than 1,000,000 calls
- Registered up to 420,505 emergency incidents that were processed
- Performed up to than 270,755 out-of-hospital treatments
- Over 750 lives saved in 2017, expect to double in 2018 to 1500 lives saved

New system provides:

- Integrated call handling and case management
- Standardized emergency medical protocols with clear emergency response checklists
- Dispatchers receive critical information about the location of an incident in real time
- Helps identify duplicated and non-emergency calls
- Gives ability to dispatch the most appropriate vehicles and personnel faster
- Broadcasts incident information to vehicle and field personnel
- Helps field personnel reach the scene of an emergency quickly
- Allows seamless cooperation on the same incident for multiple teams
- Provides interoperability between emergency services
- Comprehensive view of the information
- Supports whole process from call intake to hospital
- Provides accurate statistic and quality indicators

Case Handling

Solution provides integrated case management, call handling, and helps identify duplicated and non-emergency calls.

Solution provides two major case types - incidents and service requests (door-to-door services provide pre-booked transportation for people with mobility problems, blood delivery and non-emergency care, diagnostic cardio center, psychological help, and etc.).

The solution separates allocators and call-takers. VEMC call-takers receives up to one million and 103 calls every year and dispatches a response to 420,000 emergency incidents. This level of demand is higher than the demand for other ambulance services in Ukraine.

From the moment of call intake incidents cases are processed based on configurable emergency protocols through clear emergency response checklists. During intake process incidents attended by the VEMC were divided into three separate categories based on their urgency and life-threatening:

- **Category C** – immediately life-threatening incidents. In 2016/17 up to 15 of incidents attended by the VEMC were in this category. Dispatchers make the decision to activate protocols on their own including multi-casualty protocols, they don't need to call anybody first.

- **Category E** – serious but not immediately life-threatening incidents. In 2016/17, up to 43 of incidents were in this category

- **Category N** – not serious or immediately life-threatening incidents. In 2016/17, up to 42 of incidents were in this category

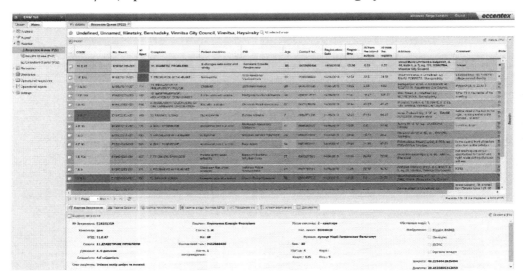

For Category «C» and «E», all ambulance services must meet a national target: to have a response at the scene of the incident within ten minutes, on 80 percent per cent of occasions.

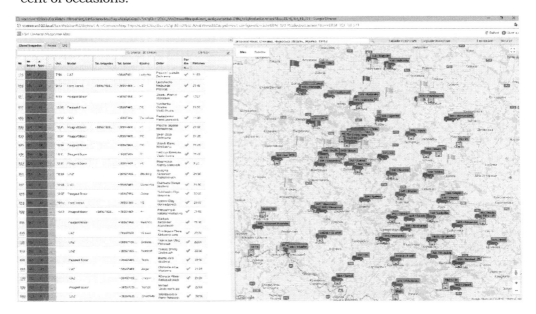

All incident resolution process is digital. The vehicles and centers are connected via a cellular network.

Dispatchers could see ambulances racing to respond to calls in territory, as well as the reported nature of each emergency.

The ambulances send location and status information to the control centers to build a real-time situation awareness picture on an electronic map utilizing the system. The center broadcasts incident information to vehicle and field personnel.

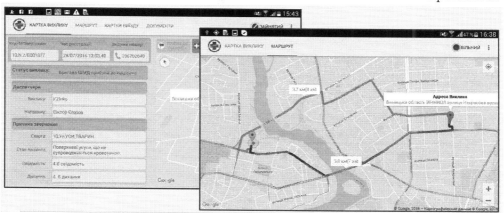

Solution gives VEMC dispatchers (allocators) flexibility in resource allocation and ability to exploit any available EMS resource when responding to incident and help them reach the scene of an emergency quickly.

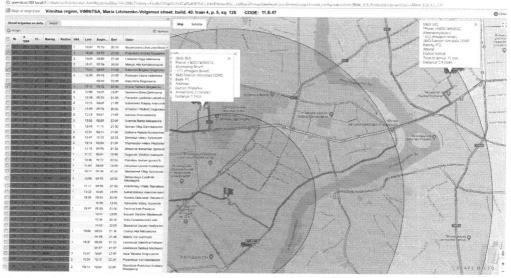

During the examination, the physician records data on what he does, in the online form 110 - a medical help team call card. This information is about examination, diagnosis, treatment, which will be needed in the future. Solution is configured to link all information, digital assets, messages and notes related to incident into the case in real-time providing 360-degree view, visualization of flows and connections between the different steps of the process in the flow, ability for online collaboration not only for VEMC personnel but also for the regional hospitals connected to the system.

5. HURDLES OVERCOME

Management

- Project was started and developed as national program in cooperation with AVAYA and Hewlett Packard. Each company was responsible for own part of the project. Luck Lead contractor responsible for the whole project made Eccentex became more responsible for the whole success.
- Customer project manager was career healthcare man, not an IT professional or professional project manager.

Business

- Limited budget raised concerns over the project timetable
- Project delays caused by Ukrainian revolution in 2014 and Russian military intervention in Ukraine since 2014 and raised concerns over the project feasibility at all.

Organization Adoption

VEMC personnel have shown a positive attitude to the introduction of new technology despite some initial technical problems in the systems integration. The significant effort and involvement of VEMC personnel – paramedics, dispatchers and others in the requirements and specification stages of the project – greatly contributed to the success of the project resulting in massive day-to-day use and meeting of objectives.

6. BENEFITS

Cost Savings / Time Reductions

VEMC become more efficient by reducing the number of occasions on which it dispatchers send a vehicle, especially than one vehicle. Previously, services often dispatch multiple vehicles to an incident to ensure there is a response on scene as quickly as possible.

Average response time and time-to-treatment after implementation of new solution have been reduced by 2.5 times.

Increased Revenues

VEMC is nonprofit organization. As a nonprofit organization, the high cost of providing solution support can be prohibitive. VEMC is required by the region government to make total savings. One of the key project requirements was regarding design cost-effective of solutions in order to satisfy the available budget and support a customer to be able to make individual configuration changes. Changes to VEMC operation were required to be extremely simple for staff to intervene and correct the system on the fly.

This became especially important during latest terror attacks. In September 2017, one of Ukraine's largest ammunition depots was blasted after terrorist attack. Stocks of weapons and ammunition in Vinnitsa region have caught fire with the subsequent detonation of the ammunition. It was the country's second largest stock of artillery and rocket storing 82,000 tons of ammunition. Airways and railroad connections in the area were closed. For one hour, our organization implemented new case types, changes in rules and procedures to handle crisis situation. Incidents and tasks were routed to personal from other PSAPs. The emergency evacuation of 40,000 residents from neighboring villages and towns was successfully performed during the night. More than 500 people with disabilities from their homes and over 30 severely injured persons were successfully evacuated.

Quality Improvements

- Calls answered in 5 seconds (95 percent of occasions)
- Dispatched within 45 seconds (85 percent of occasions)
- Average call handling time 180 seconds
- The time of arrival in the city - up to 10 minutes - 89.7 percent, in the countryside to 20 minutes - 88.6 percent.
- Survival rates for out-of-hospital critical care treatments now more than 23 percent (comparing with 0,8 percent before).

7. BEST PRACTICES, LEARNING POINTS AND PITFALLS

Best Practices and Learning Points

- ✓ *Predictability - minimize risk of the project with a predictable scope, predictable timeline, and predictable outcome*
- ✓ *Rapid Deployment standardize implementation project with pre-configured software to quickly address major business needs*
- ✓ *Agility - provide flexibility of making changes with minimal costs*
- ✓ *Productivity - facilitate the automation as much as possible of repetitive elements*
- ✓ *Efficiency - focus on efficiency and explore any opportunity to save resources*
- ✓ *Technology Integration - focus is not on "applications" but rather on "processes", along with the applications that support them*
- ✓ *Trust - a cornerstone for successful project, supplier should use the budget wisely and responsibly to forward the common mission in the best way possible*

Pitfalls

- ✗ *Initially, we relied on senior vendors (AVAYA, HPE) to drive the project, but it became clearer that the project would be more effective if it was driven by the Eccentex themselves.*

8. COMPETITIVE ADVANTAGES

The last two years, VEMC performs better against national response time targets for serious, life-threatening incidents. The VEMC is already ahead of other ambulance services in identifying the patients that are frequent users of its service. The VEMC has put in place an individual 'frequent caller procedure', these patients account for about three per cent of all calls to the VEMC.

For the future year, the focus of the VEMC performance target is shifting onto patient outcomes rather than just response times.

9. TECHNOLOGY

Eccentex provided VEMC with a complete turnkey Command & Control solution named ERIM (Emergency Response Incident Management), providing requirements analysis, system specification & design, applications - design and development, design of installation, system integration and testing, pilot system in ambulances and centers, teaching, training and system assimilation in vehicles and centers, region wide deployment.

EMERGENCY INCIDENT MANAGEMENT SOLUTION

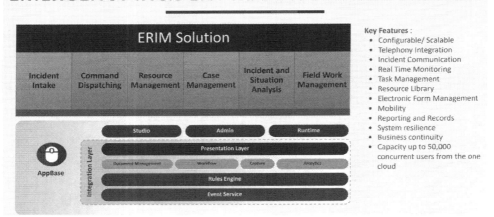

Eccentex developed the ERIM on top of its AppBase Dynamic Case Management platform and integrated the hardware, communications and software components for the operational solution. Eccentex also provides VEMC with maintenance and support including a helpdesk and remote login.

The AppBase DCM has been designed from the ground up as a dynamic case management platform and includes all the necessary functionalities to perform this objective. Business Process Management (BPM) is one of the key components of the platform.

The BPM module controls case-related workflows. Individual cases may take different path, based on the use of business rules that take into account case-specific parameters.

Furthermore, AppBase DCM is a dynamic case management system. This implies that knowledge workers can change the flow of individual case handling by adding (ad hoc) tasks and procedures to the standard workflow, as may be required.

The platform supports a virtually unlimited number of case types, each of which has its own workflow (predetermined pattern). Case types may be selected automatically, using a set of business rules, based on certain criteria, obtained during case initiation and data capture.

Key to the AppBase DCM platform is the ability to configure and utilize solution- and case-specific data objects (database tables that maintain case-related information), workflows (processes), rules and user interface to support these activities.

The platform comes with a powerful integration layer, Business Intelligence (BI) module, comprehensive content (document) management module, Single Sign-On (SSO) and Multi-Factor Authentication.

10. The Technology and Service Providers

Eccentex Corporation is a leading provider of Enterprise-Grade Dynamic Case Management Platform as a Service/Software as a Service (PaaS/SaaS) solutions, with a focus in both private and public sectors around the globe. Based in Los Angeles, California, Eccentex was founded by pioneers in the workflow and case management industry. Eccentex proudly maintains a 100 percent success rate in customer implementations over an almost 20-year history in this industry. Eccentex has a very successful record of accomplishment in delivering complex, enterprise-grade solutions around the globe.

Section 3
Appendices

WfMC Structure and Standards

What is the Workflow Management Coalition?

The Workflow Management Coalition (WfMC), founded in August 1993, is a non-profit, international organization of BPM and workflow vendors, users, analysts and university/research groups.

The WfMC creates and contributes to process-related standards, educates the market on related issues, and is the only standards organization that concentrates purely on process.

The Coalition's mission has been to promote and develop the use of collaborative technologies such as workflow, BPM and case management through the establishment of standards for software terminology, interoperability and connectivity among products and to publicize successful use cases.

Disbanded August 2019

In August 2019, the Coalition's Executive Steering Committee declared "Successful Conclusion" with respect to the frameworks, standards and languages that the members produced. The WfMC acknowledges deep appreciation to the members worldwide who generously devoted their time, knowledge and expertise in developing these critical standards. Its pioneering work complete, the Coalition has accordingly been disbanded.

Workflow Standards Framework

The Coalition developed the framework for the establishment of workflow standards. This framework includes five categories of interoperability and communication standards that allow multiple collaboration products to coexist and interoperate within a user's environment. Technical details are included in the white paper entitled, "The Work of the Coalition," available at www.wfmc.org.

The WfMC created Wf-XML and XPDL, the leading process definition language used today in over 80 known solutions to store and exchange process models. XPDL is a process design format for storing the visual diagram and all design-time attributes.

Achievements

The initial work of the Coalition focused on publishing the Reference Model and Glossary, defining a common architecture and terminology for the industry. A major milestone was achieved with the publication of the first versions of the Workflow API (WAPI) specification, covering the Workflow Client Application Interface, and the Workflow Interoperability specification.

Publications

The first workflow publication produced under the auspices of the Coalition was *WfMC Workflow Handbook* [1] in 1997 edited by Peter Lawrence. *The Workflow Handbook 2001* [2], was released in October 2000 by Future Strategies Inc., edited by Layna Fischer.

---

[1] The WfMC Workflow Handbook (P. Lawrence, ed) ISBN 0471969478

[2] Workflow Handbook 2001 (L. Fischer, ed) ISBN 978-0970350909 © Future Strategies Inc.

Future Strategies, Inc., has published over 50 titles in print and digital editions in collaboration with WfMC including the annual *Workflow Handbook* series, a number of special editions and the annual *Excellence in Practice* series, profiling industry case studies and outstanding workflow and BPM implementations.

In addition to a series of successful industry-wide tutorials, the WfMC members invested considerable effort over the past 25 years helping to drive awareness, understanding and adoption of XPDL, now the standard means for business process definition in over 80 BPM products. As a result, it has been cited as the most deployed BPM standard by a number of industry analysts, and continues to receive a growing amount of media attention.

Workflow Reference Model

The Workflow Reference Model was published in 1995 and still forms the basis of most BPM and workflow software systems in use today. It was developed from the generic workflow application structure by identifying the interfaces which enable products to interoperate at a variety of levels.

All workflow systems contain a number of generic components which interact in a defined set of ways; different products will typically exhibit different levels of capability within each of these generic components. To achieve interoperability between workflow products a standardized set of interfaces and data interchange formats between such components is necessary.

A number of distinct interoperability scenarios can then be constructed by reference to such interfaces, identifying different levels of functional conformance as appropriate to the range of products in the market.

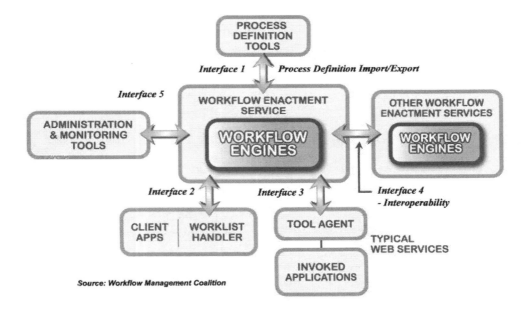

WORKFLOW REFERENCE MODEL DIAGRAM

XPDL (XML Process Definition Language)

An XML based language for describing a process definition, developed by the WfMC. Version 1.0 was released in 2002. Version 2.0 was released in Oct 2005. The goal of XPDL is to store and exchange the process diagram, to allow one tool to model a process diagram, and another to read the diagram and edit, another to "run" the process model on an XPDL-compliant BPM engine, and so on.

For this reason, XPDL is not an executable programming language like BPEL, but specifically a process design format that literally represents the "drawing" of the process definition. Thus it has 'XY' or vector coordinates, including lines and points that define process flows. This allows an XPDL to store a one-to-one representation of a BPMN process diagram.

For this reason, XPDL is effectively the file format or "serialization" of BPMN, as well as any non-BPMN design method or process model which use in their underlying definition the XPDL meta-model (there are presently about 60 tools which use XPDL for storing process models.)

In spring 2012, the WfMC completed XPDL 2.2 as the *fifth* revision of this specification. XPDL 2.2 builds on version 2.1 by introducing support for the process modeling extensions added to BPMN 2.0.

BPSim

The Business Process Simulation (BPSim) framework is a standardized specification that allows business process models captured in either BPMN or XPDL to be augmented with information in support of rigorous methods of analysis. It defines the parameterization and interchange of process analysis data allowing structural and capacity analysis of process models.

BPSim is meant to support both pre-execution and post-execution optimization of said process models. The BPSim specification consists of an underlying computer-interpretable representation (meta-model) and an accompanying electronic file format to ease the safeguard and transfer of this data between different tools (interchange format).

Wf-XML

Wf-XML is designed and implemented as an extension to the OASIS Asynchronous Service Access Protocol (ASAP). ASAP provides a standardized way that a program can start and monitor a program that might take a long time to complete. It provides the capability to monitor the running service, and be informed of changes in its status.

Wf-XML extends this by providing additional standard web service operations that allow sending and retrieving the "program" or definition of the service which is provided. A process engine has this behavior of providing a service that lasts a long time, and also being programmable by being able to install process definitions.

AWARDS

The Workflow Management Coalition sponsors several annual award programs.

Business Transformation Awards.

These prestigious Global Awards for Excellence in Business Transformation recognize user organizations that have demonstrably excelled in implementing innovative business solutions to meet strategic business objectives.

Business Transformation (BT) aligns people, organizational processes and technology initiatives of a company with its business strategy and vision with the aim of achieving significant competitive advantages.

The awards programs comprise three main categories:

1. The **Global Awards for Excellence in BPM & Workflow**[3] recognizes organizations that have implemented particularly innovative workflow solutions. Every year between 10 and 15 BPM and workflow solutions are recognized in this manner. Winning case studies are published in the annual Excellence in Practice[4] series.

2. **Excellence in Case Management** to recognize and focus upon successful use cases for coordinating unpredictable work patterns. Awards are given in the category of Production Case Management and in Adaptive Case Management which are both new technological approaches to supporting knowledge work in today's leading edge organizations. These awards are designed to highlight the best examples of technology to support knowledge workers.

3. The **Marvin L. Manheim Award For Significant Contributions** in the Field of Workflow is given to one person every year in recognition of individual contributions to workflow and BPM standards. This award commemorates Marvin Manheim who played a key motivational role in the founding of the WfMC.

Recipients:

- 2019: Layna Fischer, USA
- 2018: Nathaniel Palmer, USA
- 2017: Derek Miers, United Kingdom
- 2016: Sandy Kemsley, Canada
- 2015: Jim Sinur, United States
- 2014: Connie W Moore, United States
- 2006: David Hollingsworth, United Kingdom
- 2005: Robert Shapiro, United States
- 2003: Keith Swenson, United States
- 2002: Jon Pyke, United Kingdom
- 2001: Haruo Hayami, Japan

The Workflow Management Coalition created the opportunity for a large number of dedicated participants to create a set of standards for the workflow industry.

Their contribution ensured that significant progress was made in development and adoption of royalty-free workflow and process standards.

THE SECRETARIAT

Workflow Management Coalition (WfMC)

www.WfMC.org

---

[3] http://BTAwards.org

Author Appendix

Roy Altman

Founder and CEO at PeopleServ

Roy Altman is founder/CEO of Peopleserv, a software/services company. Over a multifaceted career, Roy has a history of delivering ROI to well-known companies in several industry sectors. He is the creator of multiple commercial software products. Roy has contributed to five books in the Future Strategies BPM series and has also published articles in IHRIM Workforce Solutions Review and The Saturday Evening Post. Altman has presented at several HR and BPM industry and academic conferences. He is on the faculty of NYU's MS in Human Capital Analytics and Technology program.

Layna Fischer

Publisher and CEO, Future Strategies Inc., USA

Ms Fischer is Editor-in-Chief and Publisher at Future Strategies Inc., the official publishers to WfMC.org. She previously also served concurrently as Executive Director of the Workflow Management Coalition (WfMC) and director of the Business Process Business Process Modeling Initiative (BPMI, now merged with OMG). She continues to work closely with these organizations to promote industry awareness of emerging technologies, explaining the how and why they impact enterprises of all sizes.

The publications produced by Future Strategies Inc., have made a significant contribution to the worldwide understanding and uptake of process-related standards, educating the market on related issues. In 1997, in collaboration with WfMC, Ms Fischer inaugurated the renowned annual awards for *Excellence in BPM and Workflow* and the *Adaptive Case Management* which later evolved to *WfMC Awards for Excellence in Business Transformation.*

Future Strategies, Inc., has published over 50 titles in print and digital editions in collaboration with WfMC including the annual *Workflow Handbook* series, a number of special editions and the annual *Excellence in Practice* series, profiling industry case studies and outstanding workflow and BPM implementations.

Ms. Fischer has been involved in technology-related journalism and publishing for over 25 years. In 2019, she received the coveted *Marvin L. Manheim Award for Significant Contributions in the Field of Workflow and BPM.*

Karl Walter Keirstead

Process Control Engineer, Management Consultant

Karl Walter Keirstead, M.Sc. (EE), P.Eng. is a process control engineer and management consultant with international experience in healthcare, law enforcement and manufacturing industry mission-critical applications. He is Managing Director of Civerex Systems, Creative Director of CvX Productions and Chairman of Jay-Kell Technologies Inc., a Montreal-based holding company. His area of expertise is bridging the gap between strategy and operations.

Setrag Khoshafian

Chief Evangelist and VP of BPM Technology, Pegasystems Inc., USA

Dr. Setrag Khoshafian is one of the industry´s pioneers and recognized experts in Digital Enterprises, especially Digital Transformation through IoT, Evolved CRM and intelligent BPM. He has been a senior executive in the software industry for the past 25 years, where he has invented, architected, and steered the production of several enterprise software products and solutions. Currently, he is Pega's Chief Evangelist and strategic IoT & BPM technology thought leader involved in numerous technology, thought leadership, marketing, alliance, and customer initiatives. The majority of his time is spent with Fortune 500 companies, specifically on their transformational journeys leveraging digital technologies (especially digital transformation, IoT, agility & process improvement through Pega). Previously he was the Senior VP of Technology at Savvion where he invented and led the development of the world's first web centric BPM platform. He was a senior architect at Ashton-Tate where he invented Intelligent SQL, and previously an OODBMS researcher at MCC, where he invented several object databases technologies. Dr. Khoshafian is a frequent speaker and presenter at international workshops and conferences. He is the lead author of more than 10 books and more than 50 publications in various industry and academic journals.

Dr. Khoshafian holds a PhD in Computer Science from the University of Wisconsin-Madison. He also holds an MSc in Mathematics.

FRANK KOWALKOWSKI

President, Knowledge Consultants, Inc., USA

Frank Kowalkowski is President of Knowledge Consultants, Inc., a firm focusing on business performance, business/IT architecture and business analytical techniques. He has over 30 years of management and consulting experience in a wide variety of industries. He has been involved with many projects including business analysis, process management, business performance measurement, business and competitive intelligence and knowledge management. In addition to being a keynote speaker at international conferences as well as a conference chair, he has written numerous papers and spoken at conferences on a variety of subjects. He is the author of a 1996 book on Enterprise Analysis (Prentice – Hall, ISBN 0-13-282-3365) and numerous papers. Frank is currently working on a both a BPM book for managers and a new edition of the enterprise analysis book. He conducts frequent seminars nationally and internationally on a variety of business management and information technology topics. He is co-author of a quarterly column on architecture for the website TDAN.

ALBERTO MANUEL

Global Digital Advisor at Microsoft

Alberto Manuel has over 15 years of Business Process Management hands-on experience, Alberto helps companies to improve, redesign and implement business process. Working as a mentor, coach and consultant, driving companies to reach successful outcomes on disciplines like: Enterprise Engineering, Business Process Management and Change Management. He is involved in BPM communities where he plays a critical role in developing international standards and new methods for business process management. Alberto is also the chair of the BPM Conference Portugal and Post-Graduate on BPM.
He has seven years of experience on R&D of consumer goods products and improving manufacturing operations.
He blogs about BPM on http://ultrabpm.wordpress.com

GERRY McCOOL

Director, Industry Principal – Manufacturing & High Tech
Pegasystems Inc.

Gerry McCool is an Industry Principal at Pegasystems, the leader in software for customer engagement and operational excellence. He has over 20 years of experience leading complex process and technology change initiatives through his work with Jabil, MITRE, Department of Defense, Accenture, and companies in diversified manufacturing, oil and gas, chemicals, and consumer products industries. Gerry has led cross-functional teams to achieve significant financial and productivity improvements in enterprise procure-to-pay, order-to-cash, and customer care processes. Gerry also has a passion for connecting strategic goals and execution through business architecture and change management.

Gerry received his MS from Florida Institute of Technology and BS from Auburn University. He holds numerous professional certifications, including, Master Black Belt, APICS Certified Supply Chain Professional, and Prosci Change Management.

NATHANIEL PALMER

Executive Director, Executive Director WfMC, USA; Editor-in-Chief of BPM.com

Rated as the #1 Most Influential Thought Leader in Business Process Management (BPM) by independent research, Nathaniel is recognized as one of the early originators of BPM, and has the led the design for some of the industry's largest-scale and most complex projects involving investments of $200 Million or more. Today he is the Editor-in-Chief of BPM.com, as well as the Executive Director of the Workflow Management Coalition.

Previously he had been the BPM Practice Director of SRA International, and prior to that Director, Business Consulting for Perot Systems Corp, as well as spent over a decade with Delphi Group serving as VP and CTO. He frequently tops the lists of the most recognized names in his field, and was the first individual named as *Laureate in Workflow*. Nathaniel has authored or co-authored over a dozen books on process innovation and business transformation, including "Digital Transformation" (2017) "The Art of BPM" (2016),"Thriving on Adaptability" (2016) "BPM Everywhere" (2015) "Intelligent BPM" (2013), "How Knowledge Workers Get Things Done" (2012), "Social BPM" (2011), "Mastering the Unpredictable" (2008) which reached #2 on the Amazon.com Best Seller's List, "Excellence in Practice" (2007), "Encyclopedia of Database Systems" (2007) and "The X-Economy" (2001).

In 2018 he received the *Marvin L. Manheim Award for Significant Contributions To Workflow and BPM*. He has been featured in numerous media ranging from Fortune and The New York Times to National Public Radio. Nathaniel holds a DISCO Secret Clearance as well as a Position of Trust with in the U.S. federal government.

CAROLYN ROSTETTER

Senior Director, Industry Principal – Manufacturing & High Tech
Pegasystems Inc.

Carolyn Rostetter is a Business Optimization Leader with over 20 years of experience in some of the world's leading organizations. She provides vision and expertise in areas such as Strategic Planning, Productivity, Quality, Change Management and Organizational Transformation. She has led global Lean Six Sigma deployments in industries including Financial Services, Media & Entertainment, and Manufacturing. Carolyn has successfully led enterprise scale programs such as Client Services, Revenue Management & Treasury Services, Application Portfolio Optimization, Master Data Management, Digital Process Automation, Compliance & Regulatory Services, Shared Services Consolidation, and Supplier/Vendor Management. Carolyn has an MBA in Finance, and she is a GE-certified Lean Six Sigma Master Black Belt and a Pega-certified System Architect.

KEITH SWENSON

Senior Vice President of R&D, Fujitsu America Inc.

Keith Swenson is Vice President of Research and Development at Fujitsu North America and also the Chairman of the Workflow Management Coalition. As a speaker, author, and contributor to many workflow and BPM standards, he is known for having been a pioneer in collaboration software and web services. He has led agile software development teams at MS2, Netscape, Ashton Tate & Fujitsu. He received the 2014 *Marvin L. Manheim Award for Outstanding Contributions in the Field of Workflow*. Co-author on more than 10 books, his latest book, "When Thinking Matters in the Workplace," explains how to avoid stifling creativity and enhance innovation through the appropriate use of process technology. His 2010 book "Mastering the Unpredictable" introduced and defined the field of adaptive case management and established him as a Top Influencer in the field of case management. He blogs at https://social-biz.org/.

KAY WINKLER

Director and Partner at NSI Soluciones; Founder & President of the ABPMP Panama
Chapter, NSI Soluciones, Panama

Kay Winkler earned his PhD in economics and business administration at the Universidad Latina de Panama. His investigation focused on establishing measurement frameworks for BPM benefit determination with "time" as a main variable. At NSI he is responsible for the distribution and implementation of BPM and ECM solutions in Latin America. Having been responsible for the automation and optimization of mission-critical processes for hundreds of international companies, he had the opportunity of accumulating proven and applied practices related to BPM and IT business solutions. He is sharing this knowledge together with insights from other recognized experts in his role of president at the local ABPMP chapter. He can be reached through LinkedIn at: https://pa.linkedin.com/in/kaywinkler

Case Studies

Winner:
Company: Alquería, Colombia

Nominated by:
Company: AuraPortal
Website: www.auraportal.com

Winner:
Company: California Resources Corporation, USA

Nominated by:
Company: ProcessMaker
Website: www.processmaker.com

Winner:
Company: City of Fort Worth, Texas, USA

Nominated by:
Company: BP Logix
Website: www.bplogix.com

Winner:
Company: Discovery Benefits Inc., USA

Nominated by:
Company: Hyland Software
Website: www.hyland.com/en

Winner:
Company: Home Health Care Management, USA

Nominated by:
Company: i-Sight
Website: i-sight.com

Winner:
Company: IBM Global Sales Incentives, USA

Nominated by:
Company: IBM, USA
Website: www.ibm.com/us-en

Winner:
Company: IIC Technologies, Canada/India/UK/US

Nominated by:
Company: Bonitasoft
Website: www.bonitasoft.com

Winner:
Company: Palmas City Hall, Brazil

Nominated by:
Company: AO3 BPMS / SINAX
Website: Error! Hyperlink reference not valid.

Winner:
Company: PowerHealth (Australia) [PHS]

Nominated by:
Company: IDIOM Limited, New Zealand
Website: www.idiomsoftware.com

Winner:
Company: Sicoob Coopercredi, Brazil

Nominated by:
Company: Lecom Tecnologia
Website: www.lecom.com.br

Winner:
Company: Vinnitsa EMD Center (VEMC), Ukraine

Nominated by:
Company: Eccentex
Website: www.eccentex.com

Index

ABPMP CBOK, 55

Adaptive Case Management (ACM), 17, 26, 49, 116

adaptive collaborative environment, 101

agile approach, 37

Agile Creation of Management Applications, 109

Agile Management of Documents and Content, 109

Agile Manifesto, 38

agile organization, 37, 39, 41, 45, 48, 49

Agility Quotient (AQ), 37

AI Assisted Work, 88

Alquería, Colombia, 107

Amazon Kiva robots, 19

analytic algorithms, 69

Analytics-Based Approach, 42

AO3 BPMS, 170, 176

artificial Intelligence (AI), 68, 85, 99, 102

assisted reasoning, 102

augmenting human intelligence, 99

AuraPortal iBPMS, 111

automation of operational processes, 67

Bain & Company, 51

Bersin by Deloitte., 37

Bonitasoft application platform, 168

BP Logix, 130

BPM task automation, examples of, 27

business automation initiatives, 19

business intelligence (BI), 68

Business Process Management (BPM), 17, 25, 51

Business Process Simulation (BPSim) framework, 215

Business Rules Engine (BRE), 21

Business Rules Management, 109

California Resources Corporation (CRC), 113

CARIS Publications Module (PM), 157

cartography of human interaction, 98

case management software, 145-149

case management solution, 133-142

cellular platform, 108

Citizen Developers, 86, 90

Citizens Portal, 122

commercial off the shelf software (COTS), 186

Competency Center for Digital Transformation, 91

complex workflow; diagrammed, 113

continuous improvement, 85, 92

control theory, 69

data mining, 51, 63

data science, 51, 53, 54, 61

data-driven machine intelligence, 20

data-driven processes, 20

Decision Automation, 21, 23

Design Thinking, 90, 92

Digital Business Platform, 107

digital disruption, 17

Digital Innovation Speed, 90

Digital Process Automation (DPA), 85

Digital Process Automation capabilities, 85

Digital Process Automation, 85, 86, 87, 89, 93, 95

Digital Technologies, 86

Digital Transformation (DX), 85, 170

digital transformation; engine, 17

Discovery Benefits Inc. (DBI),, 133

DPA-enabled continuous improvement approach, 85

Dynamic Case Management (DCM), 86, 87, 210

Eccentex Corporation, 210

Ecosystem of Organizations, 42

ERIM (Emergency Response Incident Management) Solution, 203, 209

Excellence in Case Management, 216

FOMM. (Figure of Merit Matrices [Rand Corporation]), 26-32, 36

Forms Portal, 119

future of work, 97, 98, 99, 100, 101, 103

gatekeeper process, 31

gig economy, 40

Global Awards for Excellence in BPM, 216

Global Sales Incentives (GSI), 151

Government Hydrographic Offices, 157

hierarchical method, 39, 40

hierarchical structures, 37, 38, 48

Hodrick-Prescott filter, 63

Home Health Care Management, 145

Human augmentation, 101

human redundancy, 99

human-led approach, 103

Hyland OnBase, 143

IDIOM Limited, 192

IIC Technologies, 157

Incentive Plan Letters (IPL), 151

Industrial Internet of Things (IIoT), 88

Intelligence Automation; promise of, 24

Intelligence/Empathy Grid, 45

intelligent analytics, 67-84

Intelligent Automation Platform, 21

Intelligent Automation; value proposition, 24

intelligent BPM (iBPM), 51

Intelligent Business Processes, 51

Intelligent Virtual Assistants, 89

Internet of Things (IoT), 47, 68

Internet of Things; Industrial (IIoT), 88

i-Sight Case Management, 149

key pain points, 72

knowledge worker, 21

Landscape analytics, 73

lean initiatives, 95

Lean Manufacturing and Sustainability, 176

Lecom BPM Platform, 202

long-life dairy products, 107

Machine Learning algorithms (ML), 47

Machine Learning, 65

machine-assisted reasoning, 102

man-machine, 98, 102, 103

Marvin L. Manheim Award, 216

multi-level hierarchical structure, 37

Nano Second; robot, 151

Natural Language processing (NLP), 47

network of teams, 37, 40, 41

Notices to Mariners (NtMs), 157

Objectives and Key Results (OKR), 45

Operational Data Store (ODS), 21

operational effectiveness, 25, 26

operational efficiency, 25-28, 36

operational excellence approach, 85

Operational Excellence, 85, 87, 89, 91, 92

Operational Technology (OT), 88

operations improvements, 85

Organizational Culture; impact on, 86

Organizational Network Analysis (ONA), 48

Palmas City Hall, Brazil, 169

parts procurement workflow, 113

performance management, 67

PESTLE data gathering, 73

PowerHealth (Australia) [PHS], 177

predictive analytics, 68

process analytics, 83

process cost measurement., 55

process mapping project, 202

process mining, 51, 58, 64

process performances measuring (PPM), 57

ProcessMaker BPMN workflow solution, 116

Protocol; transition to IA, 25

Quality Assurance; surveillance-based, 24

RALB. (Resource Allocation, Leveling and Balancing), 26-36

RBV (Resource-Based View), 35

robotic automation, 85, 87, 89, 92

Robotic Process Automation (RPA), 20, 25, 46, 51, 68, 88, 101, 151

rule-based algorithmic automation, 47

rules initiative, 179

Rules, Robots and Relationships, 22

"Search Before You Buy!" protocol, 114

Sicoob Coopercredi, 195

SINAX Integration, 176

singularity, 97

singularity; achievement of 97

Smart Manufacturing, 88

Strategic analytics, 76

transition to IA; checklist, 36

Turing Test, 18

ubiquitous computing, 97

Viable System Model (VSM), 98

Vinnitsa EMD Center (VEMC), 203

Wf-XML, 215

workflow automation, 20

Workflow Management Coalition (WfMC), 213

workflow management methods, 25

workflow measurement, 69

Workflow Reference Model, 214

Workforce upskilling, 101

XPDL (XML Process Definition Language), 214

Reading and Resources

Get special 45% Discount on ALL these Books (see below)

INTELLIGENT AUTOMATION

Rules, Relationships and Robots. Designing Strategies and Practical Implementation

Intelligent automation is about real business change and long-term value. If you're serious about transforming the nature of work in your organization through automation, you need to think beyond robotic process automation (RPA) and point solutions. A true intelligent automation strategy utilizes a combination of powerful technologies like AI, RPA, and data access alongside established processes to work holistically, resulting in smarter systems and actionable data insight.

https://bpm-books.com/products/intelligent-automation

DIGITAL TRANSFORMATION WITH BPM

"Today's BPM platforms deliver the ability to manage work while dynamically adapting the steps of a process according to an awareness and understanding of content, data, and business events that unfold," says Nathaniel Palmer. "This is the basis of intelligent automation, making BPM the ideal platform for digital transformation."

https://bpm-books.com/products/digital-transformation-with-bpm

INTELLIGENT ADAPTABILITY

As adaptive case management (ACM) systems mature, we are moving beyond simple systems that allow knowledge workers to define ad hoc processes, to creating more intelligent systems that support and guide them. Knowledge workers still need to dynamically add information, define activities and collaborate with others in order to get their work done, but those are now just the table stakes in a world of big data and intelligent agents. To drive innovation and maintain operational efficiencies, we need to augment case work—typically seen as relying primarily on human intelligence—with machine intelligence.

https://bpm-books.com/products/intelligent-adaptability

THRIVING ON ADAPTABILITY: BEST PRACTICES FOR KNOWLEDGE WORKERS

ACM helps organizations focus on improving or optimizing the line of interaction where our people and systems come into direct contact with customers. It's a whole different thing; a new way of doing business that enables organizations to literally become one living-breathing entity via collaboration and adaptive data-driven biological-like operating systems. --*Surendra Reddy*.

https://bpm-books.com/products/thriving-on-adaptability-digital

BUSINESS AND DYNAMIC CHANGE

The Arrival of Business Architecture

http://bpm-books.com/products/business-and-dynamic-change

These visionaries see the need for *business* leaders to define their organizations to be agile and robust in the face of external changes.

This book will stimulate thinking about a more complete approach to *business* architecture. As such, it is imperative reading for executives, managers, business analysts, and IT professionals that require an understanding of the structural relationships of the components of an enterprise.

BPM EVERYWHERE

Internet of Things, Process of Everything

http://bpm-books.com/products/bpm-everywhere-print

Critical issues currently face BPM adopters and practitioners, such as the key roles played by process mining uncovering engagement patterns and the need for process management platforms to coordinate interaction and control of smart devices.

BPME represents the strategy for leveraging, not simply surviving but fully exploiting the wave of disruption facing every business over the next 5 years and beyond.

PASSPORTS TO SUCCESS IN BPM:

Real-World Theory and Applications

https://bpm-books.com/products/passports-to-success-in-bpm

Is your BPM project set up for success or failure?
Knowing what BPM success will look like before you even begin will help you achieve it. So will knowing what are the most common causes of failure.
BPM projects fail more often as a result of missed expectations than inadequate technology.

EMPOWERING KNOWLEDGE WORKERS: NEW WAYS TO LEVERAGE CASE MANAGEMENT

https://bpm-books.com/products/empowering-knowledge-workers-print-edition

ACM allows work to follow the worker, providing cohesiveness of a single point of access. Case Management provides the long-term record of how work is done, as well as the guidance, rules, visibility and input that allow knowledge workers to be more productive. ACM is ultimately about allowing knowledge workers to work the way that they want to work and to provide them with the tools and information they need to do so effectively.

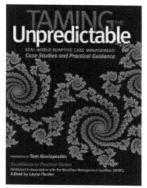

TAMING THE UNPREDICTABLE

https://bpm-books.com/products/taming-the-unpredictable-print-edition

The core element of Adaptive Case Management (ACM) is the support for real-time decision-making by knowledge workers.

Taming the Unpredictable presents the logical starting point for understanding how to take advantage of ACM. This book goes beyond talking about concepts, and delivers actionable advice for embarking on your own journey of ACM-driven transformation.

HOW KNOWLEDGE WORKERS GET THINGS DONE

https://bpm-books.com/products/how-knowledge-workers-get-things-done-print

How Knowledge Workers Get Things Done describes the work of managers, decision makers, executives, doctors, lawyers, campaign managers, emergency responders, strategist, and many others who have to think for a living.

These are people who figure out what needs to be done, at the same time that they do it, and there is a new approach to support this presents the logical starting point for understanding how to take advantage of ACM.

BPMN 2.0 Handbook SECOND EDITION

(see two-BPM book bundle offer on website: get BPMN Reference Guide Free)

http://futstrat.com/books/bpmnhandbook2.php

Updated and expanded with exciting new content!

Authored by members of WfMC, OMG and other key participants in the development of BPMN 2.0, the BPMN 2.0 Handbook brings together worldwide thought-leaders and experts in this space. Exclusive and unique contributions examine a variety of aspects that start with an introduction of what's new in BPMN 2.0, and look closely at interchange, analytics, conformance, optimization, simulation and more.

BPMN MODELING AND REFERENCE GUIDE

(see two-BPM book bundle offer on website: get BPMN Reference Guide Free)

http://www.futstrat.com/books/BPMN-Guide.php

Understanding and Using BPMN

How to develop rigorous yet understandable graphical representations of business processes.

Business Process Modeling Notation (BPMN) is a standard, graphical modeling representation for business processes. It provides an easy to use, flow-charting notation that is independent of the implementation environment.

See special 2-book offer online

iBPMS - INTELLIGENT BPM SYSTEMS

https://bpm-books.com/products/ibpms-intelligent-bpm-systems-print

"The need for Intelligent Business Operations (IBO) supported by intelligent processes is driving the need for a new convergence of process technologies lead by the iBPMS. The iBPMS changes the way processes help organizations keep up with business change," notes Gartner Emeritus Jim Sinur in his Foreword.

The co-authors of this important book describe various aspects and approaches of iBPMS with regard to impact and opportunity.

Social BPM

https://bpm-books.com/products/social-bpm-print-edition

Work, Planning, and Collaboration Under the Impact of Social Technology

Today we see the transformation of both the look and feel of BPM technologies along the lines of social media, as well as the increasing adoption of social tools and techniques democratizing process development and design. It is along these two trend lines; the evolution of system interfaces and the increased engagement of stakeholders in process improvement, that Social BPM has taken shape.

Get **special** 45% Discount on ALL Books

Use the discount code **BOOK45** to get **45% discount** on ALL books in the store; both Print and Digital Editions. Limit two copies per title. This applies to already-discounted prices.

Use this link to get 45% discount automatically applied at checkout:

https://bpm-books.com/discount/BOOK45

Digital Edition Benefits:

Enjoy immediate download, live URLs, searchable text, graphics and charts in color. No shipping charges. Download from our website now.

Published by Future Strategies Inc.

BPM-BOOKS.COM